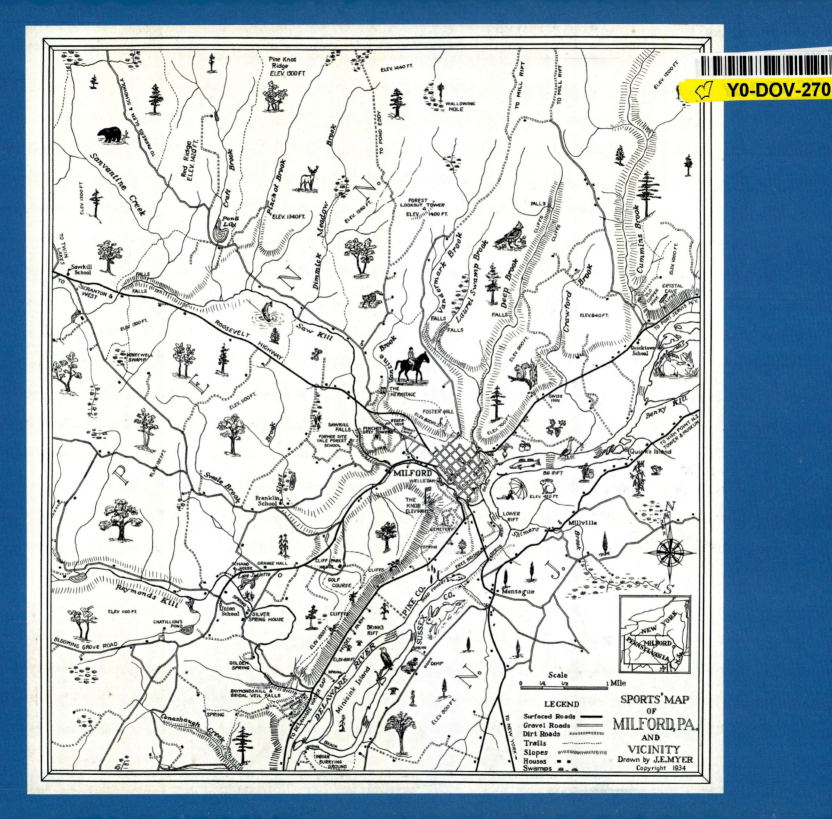

SPORTS' MAP
OF
MILFORD, PA.
AND
VICINITY

Drawn by J.E. MYER
Copyright 1934

LEGEND
Surfaced Roads
Gravel Roads
Dirt Roads
Trails
Slopes
Houses
Swamps

Scale
0   ¼   ½   1 Mile

All Roads Lead To
Milford, Pennsylvania

Featuring

Postcards from the Past

Selected and Arranged
by
Skip Gregory

Text by
Sandy Leiser

Published by
Randolph A. Gregory
P.O. Box 308 • Milford, PA 18337
Copyright 2007

*To Aggie
Enjoy "The Book" in Good Health
Skip Gregory
11/12/08*

❈ PREFACE ❈

Dear Reader,

As the title of this book <u>All Roads Lead to Milford, Pennsylvania</u> suggests, we would like within these pages to take you on a journey to some of the areas in and around Milford, Pennsylvania. Skip Gregory has chosen the images to share with you from his collection of postcards. In April 2005 he asked me to write the captions for the cards. I eagerly agreed. I love history and considered it a privilege to be involved in this project and gather information to tell you about each picture. However, I soon realized I was doing more than writing captions for each individual card. My research, and that of Lorraine Gregory, often led to stories about the subject matter depicted in the postcard that went beyond an actual description of the picture. Thus it evolved that in many cases I have not written captions but rather have provided information that enhances the pictures you will be seeing. Also, I am often privileged to be able to present information, as yet unpublished, from newly discovered sources that we have woven together to provide the reader with a new perspective regarding historical and present-day subjects. I am frequently using other people's words to tell these stories. We have included a bibliography and acknowledgments and we have tried at all times to thank and name those people from whom we gathered the information you will be reading.

All of us involved in this project hope you enjoy this book, Skip's postcards, and my stories as we travel these roads together. And if you learn a little local history along the way, I will have done my job.

Thank you,

Sandy Leiser

Sandy Leiser

❧ INTRODUCTION ❧

My hobby of collecting postcards started in 1958 when I found a trunk in the attic of a house I had purchased in Milford. The trunk contained an assortment of old postcards. I was fascinated by them as some depicted street scenes of Milford before I was born and buildings that no longer existed. These cards became the nucleus of my collection and over the years I have acquired thousands of cards relating to Milford and the surrounding area, some dating to the 1900s. I have often thought about sharing some of these images and decided in April 2005 to publish a book featuring part of my collection.

Sandy Leiser was my choice to write the text. In 1983, during my term as Milford's Mayor, Sandy helped Norman Lehde and me publish Heritage: 250, a book about the history of Milford. Again in 1989, when I was Pike County Commissioner, we worked together with Norman to publish the Pike County History Book. Special thanks to Sandy for writing the book's text and to Jim Levell for his computer skills in coordinating cards with the text. I'd also like to thank Bruce Frank who shared ideas for the cover, and my wife, Lorraine for her extensive research. Others who contributed to the completion of this book include Dee Dee Backus, Geri Fanelli, Miral Hauber, Marie Hoffman, and Lee Helms. From the beginning these people have helped me bring to fruition my vision of taking the reader on a journey in and around Milford through the use of my postcards. Thank you all.

All Roads Lead to Milford, Pennsylvania depicts what was then and what is now. The 1934 J. Edson Myer's map and the 1915 topographic map on the endpapers of this book help show where the old roads were in comparison to today's roads. All cards are placed in the geographical order in which you will see the sights on our pictorial journey.

Our journey begins as we cross the bridge over the Delaware River from Montague, NJ to Milford, PA, where you'll drive past Metz's Ice House. As we travel west on Harford Street, you'll see the Dimmick Inn, Milford High School, and Grey Towers. Drive past Apple Valley and up Route 6 to visit Camp Sagamore and the bridge where a truck accident provided Lucy Brooks and others with free Maxwell House Coffee. I'll take you along Broad Street, over the three-lane and onto the back road to the Half Way House and Evergreen Lodge. We will continue our journey to Matamoras where Sandy will tell you about the elephants that swam across the Delaware from Port Jervis, NY to Matamoras, PA. Come with me in your horse and buggy along Milford's shady streets, Ann, Catharine, and High, to see the Bluff House, Milford Inn, and Milford's churches. Then journey up Foster Hill to Malibu Ranch and down into Moon Valley. Here I pay tribute to the memory of my life long friend Richard Canouse, who, with his wife Viola, ran Moon Valley Amusement Park. We'll motor along Route 2001 past the Upper Mill and Cliff Park Inn to Log Tavern Road, past Mt. Haven to Gold Key Lake. Finally, we will take a bittersweet journey over the Mott Street Bridge down Route 209, the Old River Road, to Dingmans Ferry. You will see the Raymondskill Falls, Indian Point House, and the Conashaugh Spring House. In the village of Dingmans Ferry you can take a drink of water from an old oaken bucket and become acquainted with Chief Thundercloud. Finally, you can select an entree from the menu at the Bellevue Hotel, courtesy of Fred and Helen Cron, and dance with the bears at the Delaware House.

It is my sincere wish that you enjoy your journey into history as much as I have enjoyed taking you there.

Skip Gregory

Randolph "Skip" Gregory

This book is in tribute to and
in fond remembrance of
Norman and Elise Lehde
for their contributions toward
preserving Milford's history.

This book is also in tribute to
Frances I. Hankins
a dedicated Milford High School teacher
who helped me appreciate local history.

Skip

DEDICATION

This book is dedicated to my wife
Lorraine Helms Gregory
in honor of her support of
my hobby of collecting postcards
over the last forty years.

❦ ACKNOWLEDGMENTS ❦

Skip, Lorraine and I have spoken to many people throughout the years it has taken to complete this book. We are indebted to all of you, as each person has contributed pieces of information that have enhanced the stories you will read in this book. Much of the information you will read is derived from written history. We have given credit to the authors in the bibliography. But the fun, funny, sad, interesting, personal tidbits are from the people who have "remembered" things for us and to them we say "thank you."

They include: Jim Alborano, Marion Almquist, Fred and Sharon Assmus, DeeDee Backus, Daniel Banks, Shirley Basham, Alicia Batko, Sandy Beecher, Michele Ricciardi Bensley, Joe Biondo, Janice Strippel Black, Bob Blackman, Ed Brannon, Charles C. Bridge, Dennis and Diane Brink, Donald and Joan Brink, Lucy Brooks, Harry Buchanan, Sheriff Phil Bueki, Jack Callenberg, Viola Canouse, Mim Carpenter, Bob Carr, Lois Castle, Ernie and Mary Chamberlin, Davis Chant, Victorine Spotts Ciesielski, Bill Clark, Jr., Andrea Cobb, Nick Coffman, Mrs. Alteo Colaiaco, Tom Coleman, Jr., Ray Commins, Harriet Cotterill, Paula Coughlin, Craig Cox, Teresa Crerand, Fred and Helen Cron, Leroy and Roberta Cron, Scott B. Dane, Carla Daniel, Kathy Donahoe, Godfrey Drake, Jr., Jane Drake, Patricia Dudzinski, Matthew Elson, Shirley Estok, Brenda Evans, Scott Fean, Judy Miller Feller, Geri Fanelli, Tina Filone, Robert Fish, Denise Fitzpatrick, Bill and Bertha Fleming, George Fluhr, Gloria Foss, Diana Francisco, Bruce Frank, Allen and Sonia Gatzke, Harry Geiger, Jerry Goldberg, Elaine (Bunny) Gorewitz, Allen Greening, Ronald Gregory, Krista Gromalski, Kathleen Gross, Nancy Gumble, Gerry Hansen, Bill Harkness, Miral Haubner, Doug Hay, Mary Veronica Hazen, Red and Joyce Helms, Betty Hendrian, Kate Herring, Judy Hess, Tom Hoff, Leith and Jeanne Hoffman, Marie Hoffman, Frances Hotalen, Harvey Hotalen, Rhonda Hotalen, Marilynne Hunt, Carol Husson, Leon "Mickey" Husson, Judge Joseph Kameen, Aurelia Kaposci, Maurie Caitlin Kelly, Sharon Kelly, Bernadette Knapp, Dolores Kolvenbach, Isabel Kramer, John Kurz, Isabel Lang, Bette Lieberman, James Leiser, John and Amy Leiser, Steve and Sandra Leiser, Rhonda Leister, John and Mary Lenz, Eddie and Mae Lloyd, Beth Lovett, Alice Jane Loewrigkeit, Jim and Wendy Luhrs, Dick and Pamela Lutfy, Donna Machuca, Jackie Cole Mackey, David Malhame, Gary Martin, Helen Martin, Jim May, Judy Brink McCarty, Phil and Thelma McCarty, Willard McCullough, Lori McKean, Tom and Joan A. McKean, August Metz III, Susan Metz, Ed and Gretel Metzger, Valerie Meyer, Donald Minasian, John Misenhelder, Emil and Arlene Moglia, Helen Monisera, Rosalyn Moon, Herb Moore, Carl Mulhauser, Carolyn Purdue Mundhenk, Kristen Olson Murtaugh, Danny and Colleen Musselwhite, Ethel (Mrs. Glen) Musselwhite, Terry Musselwhite, Donald Myer, Greg and Kitty Myer, Walter Myer, Eddie Nikles, Dora O'Dea, Sherelyn Bosler Odgen, Bill Oeklers, Ellen Lloyd Orben, Gary Orben, John Orben, Matthew and Carol Osterberg, Jack Padalino, Tom Parkinson, Richie Paul, Bob Phillips, Jr., Rebecca Philpot, Peter Pinchot, Allen and April Quinn, Centa Quinn, Jim Quinn, Merritt Quinn, Ed Raarup, Honey Raider, Carol Ramagosa, Robert Ramagosa, William Ramagosa, Arthur and Jane Ridley, John Ridley, Peter Rigas, Pastor Rodney Ryle, Gladys Roberts, Leonard Robinson, Tony Russo, Mr. and Mrs. Julio S. Santos, Pastor Glenn Scheyhing, Lee Schields, Linda Schmalzle, Robert Schorr, Mary Jane Seidenstricker, Martha Shadler, Jeff and Bobbi Sidle, Evelyn Smith, Richard L. Snyder, Rick and Nancy Staffieri, Bruce and Marion Steele, June Steele, Leanna Steele, Jeanne Steuhl, Lori Strelecki, Tim and Patty Stroyan, Sean Strub, Lou and Mary Ellen Theodore, Judge Harold Thomson, Jr., Nancy Vocci, Tim Walter, Jospeh Paul Weidner, Darryl and Michelle Wood, Olive Wright, Pamela Zeigler, and Charlotte Zulick.

Thanks also to Jim Levell who has patiently and repeatedly formatted and proof-printed these pages for publication.

I would especially like to thank my husband Bill Leiser and our children James, John, Amy, Steve, and Sandra who have provided help, reassurance, and support during this entire project.

If we have inadvertently omitted your name from our list, please accept our apology. We believe it was the people who made our communities what they were and the people who make our communities what they are today. We remember and honor them and you in this publication.

Skip Gregory and Sandy Leiser

❦ TABLE OF CONTENTS ❦

BIRD'S-EYE VIEW OF MILFORD

Birdseye View of Milford, Pa. from New Jersey.

The journey in <u>All Roads Lead to Milford</u> begins with a bird's-eye view of Milford from the hill on the now closed Bridge Road near Montague, New Jersey. In 1825 John Clark, James Stoll, Daniel Brodhead and James Wallace formed the Milford Delaware Bridge Company. They built the first bridge connecting Montague, NJ and Milford, PA in 1826 for $16,000. It was a toll bridge and the first toll collector was John Brink, Jr. who earned an annual salary of $100. In the same year the congregation of the Methodist Episcopal Church began building their first church on property near the bridge. By 1835 the persistent spring floods caused the congregation to dismantle and move their church but the bridge survived until 1856 when it was destroyed by an ice jam in the river. Two more wooden bridges were subsequently constructed. The last was in use until destroyed by the great flood of March 22, 1888. The buildings pictured south of the bridge on the Pennsylvania side of the Delaware River are part of the former Edward Blood Homestead.

THE OLD TOLL BRIDGE

In 1889 the Milford Delaware Bridge Company, now managed by John H. Wallace, John C. Mott and Henry B. Wells, decided to build an iron bridge. This well-built bridge was open to traffic until 1953 when the new bridge was built. Earlier, in 1922 the Federal Government bought the bridge for $31,500 and made it toll free. Thus, while it was no longer necessary to have a toll collector, a caretaker was needed. The caretaker, three of whom in recent memory were Ben Cole, Mike Gatzke and Bill Fleming, was responsible for controlling the traffic on the bridge. While two cars could successfully cross side by side on the bridge, a large truck and a car could not. It was the responsibility of the caretaker to redirect the trucks to an alternate route.

Toll Bridge over the Delaware River and Road leading to New Jersey, Milford, Pa.

BOB'S BEACH

Bob Carr tells us his grandparents Edward and Katherine Klein Blood lived in the Blood Homestead pictured on the opposite page at the turn of the century. Bob's mother Edna was born in the home in 1903 and his uncle Robert "Bob" was born there in 1905. After World War II Bob Blood returned home and established "Bob's Beach." He built a beach house on the foundation abandoned by the Methodist Church. He created a sandy beach on the river and provided picnic tables and outdoor fireplaces on a large lawn surrounding the beach. Bob offered a stay at his Tourist Home for $5 per night. Tourists and locals could rent a canoe from him for $5 per day and could reserve a room or canoe by phoning Bob at Milford 5055. Bob's Beach was a popular attraction that served the public until the government bought it in 1972. Today the property is called Milford Beach and is maintained by the National Park Service.

LOOKING UP THE RIVER AT OLD BRIDGE

John Kurz, Skip's longtime friend, told us he was delivering ice for Gus Metz in July of 1948. He had his Model A Ford truck loaded with 25 blocks of ice, each weighing 325 pounds. He was on a run to New Jersey and had no problem crossing the bridge until he reached the steep hill on the NJ side. His truck went up the hill but the ice blocks did not! He had forgotten to put up the tailgate! Bridge Caretaker Ben Cole helped him throw the blocks of ice into the river. Later that day, John took a load of ice to Dingmans Ferry. He was filling the ice box in the bar of the Delaware House when Fred Hotalen, an avid fisherman, came in with his day's catch and ordered a drink. Fred took his first sip and remarked, "Must be awful cold up-country. There's ice chunks in the river."

NEW BRIDGE OVER THE DELAWARE

The new bridge over the Delaware was opened to traffic on December 30, 1953. It replaced the 64-year-old iron bridge which, some people said, had become "rickety!" The bridge is a four-span continuous steel deck structure 1,150 feet in length. The two-lane bridge has a roadway width of 27 feet 6 inches, with a four-foot pedestrian sidewalk located on the outside of the north truss.

DELAWARE RIVER JOINT TOLL BRIDGE

The new bridge cost $3,000,000 to build and is the northern most bridge crossing the Delaware River under the Delaware River Joint Toll Bridge Commission. It is located seven miles south of the New York state line and connects US Route 206 at Montague, New Jersey to US Route 209 at Milford, Pennsylvania.

The Delaware River Joint Toll Bridge Commission announced on Wednesday, July 27, 2005 that it would go forward with a $10,000,000 to $15,000,000 project to rehabilitate the bridge. The bridge was once honored as America's most beautiful steel bridge.

SNAKE PIPELINE TO THE OLD MILL

One key word on this postcard is "mill." According to William Henn in his <u>Mills of Milford</u>, our area was successfully developed because streams were able to provide the water power necessary for early pioneers to grind their grain and cut lumber to build their homes. Mr. Henn tells us: "They were pioneers who ventured across the Delaware into what was then the new frontier and built a saw mill and grist mill."

The other key word is "old" as the site of the mill on the Sawkill to which this card is referring was first used by three Wells brothers, Jesse, James, and Israel circa 1750.

Eventually the brothers built a ferry so farmers on the Jersey side, where there was no mill stream, could cross the river and bring their grain for grinding. The area became known as Wells' Ferry and later, because of a ford near the mill, mill-on-the-ford. In 1793-1796 when Judge John Biddis bought the land that is now the town, mill-on-the-ford had become Milford.

FLUME LINE

Pipe lines, or flumes, augment the power of a mill stream. The process begins when the dam gate is opened and water rushes through the flume. The water drops into a penstock and whirls around the turbine. Powerful streams of water squirt through nozzles and the mills reaction wheels spin at a high rate. Heavy wooden rods called pitmans connect the cranks on the reaction wheels to the frame above in the mill and carry the power to the mill. Years ago most flume lines were made of wood and subject to leaks.

The Snake Pipe Line at The Old Mill, Milford, Pa.

80 Mill Flumes, Sawkill Creek, Milford, Pa.

Mr. August Metz, Jr. is shown here with his first block of ice in 1925. Ninety 325 pound cakes of ice could be frozen at one time.

METZ ICE PLANT

The mill site on the lower dam on the Sawkill had a succession of owners beginning with the Wells brothers in 1750. These included Samuel C. Seely, a Revolutionary War veteran who acquired the property in 1793, the Biddises, the Dewitts, John Mott, for whom the Mott Street Bridge is named, the Klaers, and the Tuscanos. Beginning in 1915 the latter of these used the mill's power to manufacture jellies and cider that they marketed under the name Sunny Glen Farm. This proved a costly venture and in 1924 Alfred Tuscano sold the property to August Metz, Jr. Mr. Metz completely revamped the ramshackle mill and opened the first ice plant in the tri-state area.

METZ POWER PLANT FALLS, MILFORD, PA.

GLEN ACRES

Glen Acres consisted of "charming overnight and House-keeping Cottages" last owned by Doug and Eileen Callahan. The Callahans offered solitude and comfort in a rustic environment and touted their facility as close to shopping, churches, movies and swimming. The main house is still standing and is located in Dingman Township at the end of East Harford Street. The National Park Service now owns the property. However, long before the Callahans or Park Service were involved, this property was owned by George Bowhannon who kept a tavern, reputedly the first in Milford, and boarding house circa 1789.

New Bridge Over The Sawkill, Milford, Pennsylvania

NEW BRIDGE OVER THE SAWKILL

William Henn laments the construction of the new bridge: "Shortly before World War II, Highway 209, the Old River Road, was redirected over the lower glen by a massive concrete archway that was built with utter disregard for the natural beauty of the landscape. With the old iron bridge across the Delaware and the Mott Street Bridge limited to a five ton capacity, this viaduct was the ultimate link on the Old River Road that brought the woes of modern highway traffic to Milford. It was the harbinger of a roaring bedlam of monstrous trucks and recurrent accidents-some of them fatal-on the once tranquil thoroughfares of the Borough, completely obliterating the pastoral charm of the southern gateway to Milford."

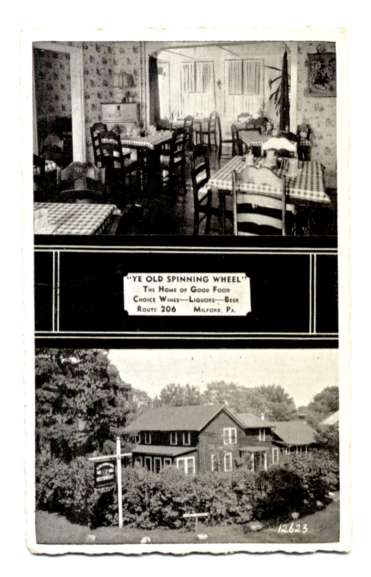

YE OLD SPINNING WHEEL

Ye Old Spinning Wheel was located at 536 East Harford Street across from the Metz Ice Plant. The restaurant and bar were on the first floor of the rustically charming house. This building was condemned and razed by the Federal Government.

YE OLD SPINNING WHEEL

A pamphlet called the "1941 Northeastern Pennsylvania Pocono Mountains and Delaware River Valley Vacationland" tells us the restaurant advertised: "Ye Old Spinning Wheel - Coffee Shop - Bar - Grill. Chicken - Steak - Vegetable Dinners. All Year. Mr. And Mrs. Detrick. Tel: 9280"

COYKENDALL'S POOL

In September, 1912 Professor Norman B. Coykendall, recognized as a world champion diver, beat "Dutch" Walter, a champion mile swimmer of Long Beach, New Jersey, in a mile swim contest. About 350 people watched the contest in a drizzling rain. Coykendall was to become a fixture at the Bluff House beach where he staged water sports and gave special exhibitions, often swimming while tied with heavy rope. Skip remembers seeing two of these special exhibitions. One involved Mr. Coykendall, whose body was tied with heavy ropes, towing a rowboat across the Delaware River by holding the tow rope in his mouth. In an equally amazing feat staged at Coykendall's pool, Skip watched as Mr. Coykendall, again encased in ropes, dove off the diving board through a hoop of fire to the bottom of the pool. There he removed the ropes and swam back to the top!

The swallows' nests, described on page 16, can be seen in this picture to the left and rear of the pool.

Coykendall's Pool, Milford, Pa.

RUTH HOWEY

He was also a pioneer in using swimming as therapy for persons afflicted or handicapped. Coykendall helped a Bushkill girl, Ruth Howey, overcome her disabilities due to infantile paralysis by putting her in the water and making her an aquatic star and popular exhibitionist.

Milford Hill at the Lower Mill, Milford, Pa.

219416

MILFORD HILL

According to a date written on the back of this card, this picture was taken in 1913. The Milford Hill pictured is the hill leading down to the former Metz Ice House. While this is simply referred to as Milford Hill on the card, all of the streets in Milford were given names by Judge John Biddis, a Circuit Court rider from Philadelphia. During his trips to the area that he would later purchase and designate as the town of Milford, he stayed at George Bowhannon's boarding house. He and George became friends and when it was time to name the streets of his newly established town Judge Biddis choose to honor that friendship. Thus he named George Street for his friend, Sarah Street for George's wife, Elizabeth Street for George's mother and Catharine Street for his grandmother.

SWALLOWS' NESTS

Located at the bottom of Harford Street where it meets the Delaware River there is an earthen cliff that provided a nesting place for hundreds of swallows each year. Jack Padalino, retired director of Pocono Environmental Education Center and lifelong birder, tells us they were bank swallows who ate airborne insects. Jack explained the swallows were colonial nesters who moved their sites periodically. This occurred in the 1970s when the birds stopped returning to the cliff. But according to an August, 1900 advertising booklet provided to the public by proprietor P.N. Bournique of the Bluff House, the swallows were very much in evidence at that time: "There are no disagreeable insects or malaria here, and the air is laden with the perfume of the pine." We can make the assumption that the swallows can be credited for the lack of insects, but not with the "perfume of the pine!"

"SWALLOWS" NESTS, MILFORD, PA.

HOTEL JARDON

Francis X. Jardon was born on October 23, 1854 in the village of Chalon Villard, France. In 1866 Francis came to America with his father locating first in New York City. There he secured a position as assistant to Louis Ragot, chef of Delmonico's. He worked as a chef at other establishments until he was selected as chef for the famous Princess Anne Hotel in Virginia Beach, VA. He opened the Hotel Jardon at 404 East Harford Street in Milford in 1886 where he ran a successful summer business. He closed the hotel in winter months to return to the Princess Anne.

Hotel Jardon, Milford, Pa.

from Mary

"HILLCREST INN," MILFORD, PA.

HILLCREST INN

In the 1920s Francis Jardon sold his Hotel Jardon to Mr. Thompson from New York City. Mr. Thompson renamed the hotel "The Hillcrest Inn" and continued in business until the 1940s at which point he sold it to Mr. Salvatore Lopez. The Lopez family operated the hotel until 1959 when they remodeled and opened the Hillcrest Nursing Home. This was sold to Felix and Carol Rosado and, subsequently, to Mr. Brennick. He converted it to a head trauma rehabilitation center. In the mid 1990s Hardie Beloff purchased the property. He modernized the building and opened the Belle Reve Senior Living Center.

VILLA INA, MILFORD, PA.

Villa Ina, Milford, Pa.   13413

The Villa Ina was built in February 1876 for the Meinke family who operated it as a boarding house. Today it is part of the Laurel Villa complex.

THE LAUREL VILLA, MILFORD, PA.

LAUREL VILLA

The Laurel Villa complex consists of five buildings and occupies ten borough lots at 310 East Harford Street. In the 1940s Anna and Herman Doscher owned the Laurel Villa in Milford as well as a delicatessen in Brooklyn. Florence Mulhauser's uncle was a partner in the deli business and eventually the Mulhausers joined with the Doschers to turn the summer boarding house into a thriving resort. In 1948 ownership passed to Carl and Florence Mulhauser.

THE LAUREL VILLA MODERNIZED

According to Cynthia Van Lierde in <u>Crossroads, Milford, Pa</u>: "It was under the progressive management of Herman and Anna Doscher and the Mulhausers that the greatest additions and improvements have been made. Rooms were modernized, with each room having its own private bath." It was one of the first places in Milford to install air-conditioning.

Laurel Villa, Milford, Pa.

H. Doscher, Prop.

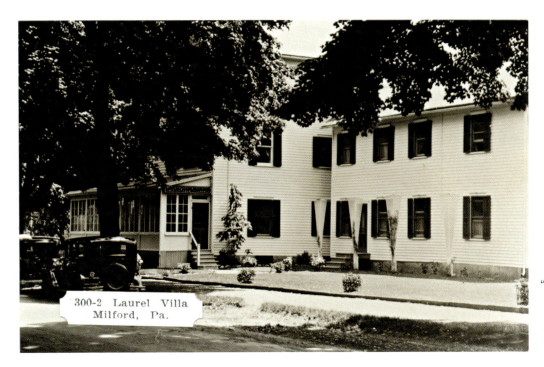

300-2 Laurel Villa
Milford, Pa.

CHEF CARL MULHAUSER

"Unexcelled cuisine" was advertised and provided by the chefs at the hotel throughout the years. That tradition continues today as Chef Carl Mulhauser, Jr. creates a perfectly prepared and eclectic menu.

— 19 —

A LAUREL VILLA VACATION

The Laurel Villa succeeded as a summer resort partially by providing a wonderful setting for families to enjoy a summer vacation. One family who discovered the benefits of a vacation there was that of Ernie and Mary Chamberlin and their children, Judy and David, of Oyster Bay, Long Island. In 1948 Mary and her family were invited by Mary's friend, Anita Luckenbill, to visit her at the resort. Anita's husband, Don, was the orchestra director at the Laurel Villa casino. The Chamberlin family enjoyed their vacation in the mountains and found it a relaxing change from their Long Island home. The family returned each summer until 1969 when they purchased a home in Milford. They became full-time residents in 1970 when Ernie retired. Ernie and Mary later moved to Lansdale, Pennsylvania but, along with daughter Judy and her husband, David Neave, returned to the Laurel Villa in August, 2002 to celebrate Ernie's ninetieth birthday.

THE ANNEX

The Annex was built in 1930 as a second guesthouse in the Laurel Villa complex. It was constructed in the same style as the lodge and is four stories high. Its construction allowed more guests to enjoy the beautifully kept grounds of the complex.

A recently added koi pond, soft outdoor lighting and gurgling fountains add magic to one's visit. We may thank Carl's wife Janice for these landscaping enhancements.

LAUREL VILLA CASINO

The casino, with its bar and large banquet hall, was built to accommodate large groups and to be used as a recreation hall for the guests. It quickly became a favorite gathering place for locals and provided the finest dance floor in Milford. Additionally many guests arrived from New York and New Jersey on midweek bus trips for a day's stay at the Laurel Villa. They could enjoy an excellent lunch, entertainment in the casino and a swim in the pool.

Laurel Villa Casino, Milford, Pennsylvania

SK 3808

LIVE ORCHESTRA

An orchestra, live bands or other entertainments were featured on weekends during the summer. The Laurel Villa Casino is presently the home of Dutch Country Treasures, owned and operated by Pat and Bill Bylsma and Andy and Melinda Hostetler.

LAUREL VILLA POOL

Ernie Chamberlin remembers that before the Laurel Villa had its own pool, the guests were given passes to swim at Bob's Beach. After it was built, the pool became a popular place to spend a relaxing day but it also served as a place where many local children learned to swim. Beginning in the late 1950s the Milford Lions Club sponsored a Red Cross swimming program and hired Bill and Betty Hendrian to serve as instructors. They continued the program for twenty-five years after which Roxanne Luhrs served as director. Carl Mulhauser's sister Lois was in charge of the pool for many years when it was open to the public and was a gracious hostess.

LAUREL VILLA COMPLEX

Cynthia Van Lierde concludes in her description of the Laurel Villa complex: "Modernization and adapting to changing recreation patterns have kept Laurel Villa from the decline suffered by many other boarding houses and hotels which were built in the same era."

DEL-A-VIEW

J.S. Wallace, a merchant in the village of Milford, built this house, now called the Del-A-View, at 300 East Harford Street for his wife, Elizabeth, in 1847. Their seven children were born in the house and the Wallaces owned the home for forty years. In the 1890s John Cornelius, owner of the nearby Sawkill House and one-time Pike County Sheriff, bought the house. After his death, his daughters, Annie and Betty, retained ownership of the house as a rental property.

MIR-MAR

In the 1920s movie stars Mildred Manning and her husband Augustus Phillips bought the house and renamed it Mir-Mar. She was a former Vitograph O. Henry Girl and he had the distinction of playing the original Doctor Frankenstein in the movie "Frankenstein" produced by Thomas Edison in 1910. Gus also acted in the last film shot in Milford in 1928, "Strength of the Weak."

Mildred's mother, Lillie Bailes, whose stage name was Lillian Langdon, resided in California but was a frequent visitor to Mir-Mar. She also took the opportunity when "East" to visit her cousin, Stephen Crane of Port Jervis, New York.

Mildred and Gus sold the property to the Conrad Diltheys. They named the house "Del-A-View" and ran it as a boarding house. A few years later the Diltheys sold the house to Charles Dimmick who continued to operate the boarding house business until 1963. At that time the house was purchased by Mr. and Mrs. Kurt Ostertag who have worked to preserve the character of their early Victorian home.

DEL-A-VIEW HOUSE
MILFORD, PA.

Del-A-View Guest House
Milford, Penna.

38278

GEORGE AND EFFIE GREGORY'S HOME

Located at 203 East Harford Street and built in the 1860s, this house has been described as an excellent example of Victorian architecture in the French Mansard style. In 1880 the home was sold to George and Mary Bull who, in 1920, sold the house to George and Effie Gregory. A Gregory family story tells us that in her eagerness to gain possession of the house, Effie Gregory paid the Bull's their full asking price! This was upsetting to George who informed his wife that he could have gotten it for $500 less. The home remained in the Gregory family until 1988. George and Effie's son, Pike County Prothonotary Rondolph "Dutch" and his wife, Janet, were the last Gregorys to reside there.

CENTURY 21

Godfrey Drake, Jr. recalls mowing the large lawn of this stately home at 205 East Harford Street in the 1940s for fifty-cents a mow! At that time it was owned by Silo and Daphne Klopman. Mr. Drake remembers his father's opinion that it was one of the best kept properties in Milford. In fact the Klopmans had in place an advanced irrigation system that allowed them to pipe water to their lawn and gardens.

Current owners Edward Raarup and Scott Eck made some interesting discoveries as they renovated the home and a carriage house located behind the home. They found a coin from 1890 nailed to a post, a pet's grave in the backyard designated as "Mack, 1923, Faithful Friend" and the remains of a large fountain, probably part of the irrigation system, in the front yard. Artwork courtesy of Ed Raarup - Century 21.

LEWIS CORNELIUS

The Sawkill House, a three-story structure with large porches built in 1823 by Lewis Cornelius, was reputed to be one of Milford's first hotels. William Bross, founder of the Chicago Tribune and one time Lieutenant-Governor of Illinois, who spent his boyhood in Milford, describes Lewis Cornelius as "probably the most widely known man in Milford. He kept both store and hotel in the house his family still occupy. Honest and socially an agreeable man, he was always popular. His hotel attracted customers from near and far...and Mr. Cornelius himself attracted the traveling public by his great size. At his death he weighed, as I remember, six hundred seventy-five pounds----probably considerably less than he would tip the beam at when in good health. But if people wanted to see him, they must give no sign that they came for that purpose for he would at once become invisible. In spite of his immense size, he always kept at the head of his business and no one could ever complain of negligence when stopping at his hotel."

Sawkill House, Milford, Pa

THE SAWKILL HOUSE

Lewis Cornelius died in 1841 and his widow, Elizabeth, sons James, William and John and daughters Catherine, Maria, Emily and Martha continued to run the sixty room, three-story house at 202 East Harford Street.

Notables staying at the Sawkill House throughout the years included American poet and playwright George H. Boker, Dr. Charles Neidhard, famous for his treatise on diphtheria, and the Drexel brothers of Philadelphia. Mary Pickford, Blanch Sweet, Harry Carey and Lillian and Dorothy Gish were also guests.

In 1937 the House was sold to E.H. Klein for $199. He demolished the front of the structure which had fallen into disrepair. The rear portion of the building was used for a long time by the Odd Fellows as a meeting hall. The building is currently owned by Godfrey Drake, Jr.

Sawkill House, Milford, Pa.

THE MAYFLOWER — MILFORD, PA.

THE MAYFLOWER

Advertisements for The Mayflower, which was located at 119 East Harford Street, proclaimed it was "a city hotel in the country." It listed the phone number to call for reservations as "Milford 5704."

THE MAYFLOWER HOTEL

While many of the resort hotels in the Milford area provided swimming opportunities for their guests in the nearby Delaware River or in streams adjacent to their properties, few had swimming pools.

The Mayflower was among those which could boast of having a swimming pool and tennis court. Fred Titus bought the hotel in 1954 and converted it to a private residence. Susan Titus Mickley lived there with her five brothers in a blended family from 1956 to 1962 when the family moved to Stroudsburg.

THE MAYFLOWER — MILFORD, PA.

COACHMAN'S INN

Graham D. Musselwhite and his wife, Lillian, purchased the Mayflower and renamed it the Coachman's Inn. Overnight accommodations came complete with "beauty rest mattresses" and they had plenty of guests. But what drew local people was the food. German cooking was their specialty and their sauerbraten was unequaled. The Coachman's Inn was destroyed by fire in the late 1970s. After the fire, the site remained vacant. The lot was recently purchased by the Pike County Library Board, and it will become the location of the Dorothy E. Warner Pike County Public Library.

DAVIS R. CHANT

Inscribed on a plaque attached to the house where Davis R. Chant Realtors has an office, at 106 East Harford Street, is the following: "Gulick/Hoagland House 1865. This residence erected on a lot Mary Gulick acquired from Cyrille Pinchot in 1844. In 1870 Rosencranse Bull acquired it from the estate of Mary Gulick Hoagland; it was passed down through the Bull family until purchased by Karl Wagner, Esq. in 1940." The plaque was presented to Mr. Chant, owner of the house, by the Historical Preservation Trust of Pike County. Photograph courtesy of Davis R. Chant.

DIMMICK INN, CIRCA 1900

Dimmick House, Milford, Pa.

Samuel R. Dimmick was born in Mansfield, Connecticut in 1793 and died in Milford on August 14, 1867. He enlisted from Mansfield during the War of 1812 and served until peace was restored. He came to Milford in 1826 where a sister and several brothers had already settled. Milfordites revered veterans and when he built his Dimmick House in 1828, locals, as well as visitors, afforded him a brisk business. The House was completely destroyed by a fire in 1856 but Mr. Dimmick rebuilt, electing this time to use bricks.

DIMMICK INN, CIRCA 1925

One of the more interesting stories connected to the Dimmick House is that of a visit made by Horace Greeley. According to Mathews' History of Wayne, Pike and Monroe Counties, Pennsylvania published in 1886, there was an eye witness to the incident who explains: "Horace Greeley had money invested in the Sylvania Society and was on his way to that point. The stage coach in which he was traveling broke down outside of town and the passengers, Greeley among them, walked into town on the muddy road. Mr. Greeley entered the Dimmick House and asked for the mud to be washed from his boots. Dimmick answered that he could accommodate himself at the pump trough outside.

DIMMICK INN, MILFORD, PA.

DIMMICK INN, CIRCA 1938

"Mr. Greeley had hardly begun when he was recognized by Cornelius W. DeWitt from his store across the way. DeWitt knew him for he was then the head and front of the Whig Party. DeWitt went over, shook hands with Greeley and, when told by him of the situation, at once ordered a halt, and taking Greeley by the arm, led him back to the barroom, and bringing him face to face with Dimmick, he said, 'Mr. Dimmick, I will make you acquainted with Horace Greeley.' Dimmick was dumfounded for a moment, but after recovering from his confusion said 'Is it possible-and it was Horace Greeley I sent to wash his own boots.' It is needless to add that Greeley's boots were taken off, washed and a pair of slippers was furnished and a place in the sitting room given to him." Horace Greeley returned many times as a guest at the Dimmick.

Dimmick Inn, A Modern Hotel at the Foothills of the Beautiful Poconos, Milford, Pike County, Pa. R. N. Friend, Prop.

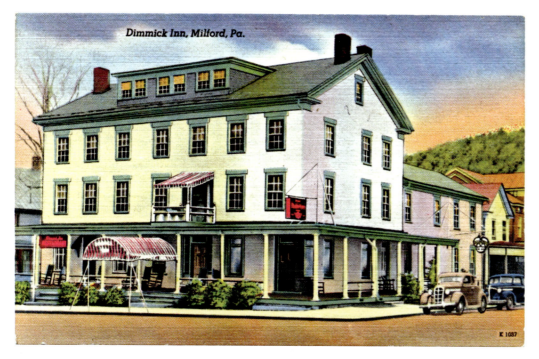

Dimmick Inn, Milford, Pa.

DIMMICK INN, CIRCA 1941

Miss Frances A. Dimmick, daughter of Samuel R. and Wealthy Dimmick, was born in Milford in 1831. As an adult, she was considered by the residents of Milford to be quite a "character." She wore masculine attire and, according to a news account of that period, "was not given to frills and frumperies but could cast a fly, drive a pair of four, ride a bronco side saddle or astride, and draw the sweetest melody from her 1721 French violin."

Lawrence Hoey and his wife, Ivah, together with his brother, John "Talley" Hoey and his wife, Marjorie, purchased the Dimmick Inn in 1955 from Richard and Gladys Friend. Members of the Hoey family owned and operated the Dimmick Inn, except for a period in the mid-1970s, until 1985. They sold the historic inn to Gerry Hansen and James Levell. The Inn is currently owned by Gerry Hansen and Edward and Karen Loeschorn.

BROAD AND HARFORD STREETS, 1919

Post Office Corner, Milford, Pa.

This is a view of the intersection of Broad and Harford Streets at the present traffic light. The Dimmick Inn is on the left; the old post office, built in the 1800s, and the new Forest Hall, built in 1904, are on the right. Please note the woman crossing the street. This photograph was taken in 1919, and although the "Roaring Twenties" are just around the corner when hemlines would rise dramatically, her dress is in keeping with the style of the day.

BROAD AND HARFORD STREETS, 2006

Fast forward to present day! This is The Gallery, a delightful shop owned by Michele Jaffe located in the old post office building at 101 West Harford Street. Photograph courtesy of Kristen Olson Murtaugh.

CRISSMAN HOUSE

The Crissman House was built circa 1820 by Timothy Candee. Mr. Candee built his large, two-story hotel on the northwest corner of Broad and Harford Streets and named it the Pike County House. The hotel was open year-round and contained a tap room, dining room and dance hall. Lodging was available for fifty guests. In 1853 Cyrus Crissman bought the hotel, renamed it the Crissman House and added a third story. The hotel was very popular with local organizations. In 1879 the Milford Ladies Club met downstairs and the Masons held their meetings in an upstairs room. In 1886 Mr. Crissman added a bowling alley.

CRISSMAN HOUSE, MILFORD, PA.

The Crissman House, Milford, Pa.

212326

CRISSMAN HOUSE

According to Beers' Commemorative Biographical Record of Northeastern Pennsylvania published in 1900, Frank Crissman "never seems satisfied unless he is making changes which will add to the comfort and convenience of his patrons and among his most recent improvements we may mention the introduction of acetylene gas for lighting the premises." Beers goes on to describe a model dining room containing a large fireplace over which is inscribed "As ancient is this hostelry as any in the land may be." Currently, the Rite Aid Drugstore occupies this location.

GREGORY'S GARAGE 1949

Greetings at Christmas

1949

Amos and Edith Gregory relocated Gregory's Garage from 310 Broad Street to 106-108 West Harford Street in 1947. After the death of Amos in March 1949, Edith Gregory successfully continued the management of the garage. However Amos Gregory's franchise to sell Chrysler automobiles came into question when Edith was sent a letter dated January 25, 1950 from the Chrysler Sales Corporation which stated "our management still has a matter of policy in which they do not wish to execute a new sales agreement with a business which is principally owned by a woman." To meet the Chrysler Sales criteria Randolph "Skip" Gregory was named president of the newly formed Gregory's Garage Inc. making Skip one of the youngest Chrysler-Plymouth dealers in the country. Edith was secretary/treasurer. The Chrysler-Plymouth dealership continued to be operated by Edith and Skip until 1985 for a total of more than fifty years. In 1994 the garage was remodeled and leased to the Pennsylvania Liquor Control Board who continue to operate a wine and spirits store there.

HARFORD STREET, LOOKING WEST

John Biddis, Sr. founded the town of Milford and named the streets. While some streets were named in honor of his friend George Bowhannon and his family, he named John Street for himself and Ann Street for his wife. Harford Street was named for John Harford, an earlier settler, who is credited with building the first house within the boundaries of Milford. Mill Street was named for the mills and Sawkill Avenue for the stream. The alleys running east to west were named for berries. Those running north to south were named for fruit trees.

27 Looking up Harford Street, Milford, Pa.

— 32 —

JAMES P. VAN ETTEN HOUSE

This was the home of James P. Van Etten at 111 West Harford Street. James and his brother John brought the first telephone lines into Pike County in 1895 when they formed the Van Pike Telephone Company. The phone lines ran from Port Jervis to Bushkill.

James' daughter Helen was the last member of the Van Etten family to live in the house. For many years prior to her death in 1957 she was the Director of the Pike Chapter of the American Red Cross. In the early 1960s the home was converted to an office building that became known as the Health and Welfare Building. The Pennsylvania Department of Health had offices on the second floor and the Department of Public Assistance had offices on the first floor. In 1983 Pike County District Magistrate Carolyn Purdue's court occupied the building. It was demolished in 1986 to make way for the current Wayne Bank.

HOME OF JAMES P. VAN ETTEN, MILFORD, PA.

Published By C. O. Armstrong.

HIGH SCHOOL, MILFORD, PA.   7009

MILFORD HIGH SCHOOL

A History of Milford High School, published in 1952 under the auspices of the Milford High School Alumni Association by an editorial board composed of George W. Turner, Class of 1901 and Norman B. Lehde, Class of 1932, recounts the education of Milford children from 1733 to 1952. As written records of schools of the 1700s were not kept, it is assumed parents taught their children to read and write. According to Mr. Turner: "It is also probable that the children later received some elementary instruction in small groups at the homes of some of the better educated families. In 1834 Pennsylvania enacted the Public School Act. From that time on Pennsylvania's school system took on the semblance of an organized social function."

MILFORD HIGH SCHOOL

HIGH SCHOOL, MILFORD, PA.

Records of 1877 kept by John Layton, County Superintendent of Schools for Pike County, show schools were in existence at Paupack, Dingmans Ferry, Milford, Minisink and Lackawaxen. In the late 1800s a rather pretentious building with a cupola was erected on the corner of East Ann Street and Fourth Street. It was called The Academy and Mr. Turner tells us: "generations of Milford children learned their three 'R's' there." Later this structure became the home of the Van Tassel family.

The first high school building was located on West Catharine Street, opposite the present Milford Borough Building. The building was torn down after a new high school was built on West Harford Street.

MILFORD HIGH SCHOOL

On January 10, 1903 the Milford School directors unanimously adopted a recommendation to build a new school. They stipulated that the building should cost no more than $15,000, be of modern style and character and have outside walls of native bluestone. Edwin Stanton Wolfe I, who also built Forest Hall and the Milford Borough Hall, was chosen as the builder. On Tuesday, September 6,1904 the new school opened. It housed both elementary and high school grades. In 1925 an addition was added and the school served grades one through twelve until 1956. Milford High School's last graduating class was 1956. In 1956 a newly constructed Delaware Valley Joint High School opened midway between Milford and Matamoras. The building on West Harford Street continued to serve as an elementary school until 1988. Today the building is owned by Sean Strub and Richard Snyder. A variety of businesses occupy the structure.

MILFORD HIGH SCHOOL TEACHERS

Ira C. Markley came to Milford in September 1923 to serve as Assistant Principal of the high school and to teach mathematics. He encouraged organized sports at the school and became a coach for basketball, and track and field teams. In 1925 he was promoted to Principal and in 1930 he became Supervising Principal, a position he held until retiring in 1962. Two Milford High School graduates, Frances I. Hankins, Class of 1922 and Katherine Middaugh Sheen, Class of 1925, accepted positions on the staff of Milford High School after earning their teaching certificates. Miss Hankins was a social studies teacher, Dean of Women, basketball coach and faculty advisor to the Pennsylvania Junior Historians. She retired in 1968. Mrs. Sheen, an elementary school teacher, taught the children of Milford for 45 years. At the biennial alumni banquets, Arthur Ridley, Class of 1952 and master of ceremonies, always reminds the alumni that the letters "MHS" stand for Markley, Hankins and Sheen!

HIGH SCHOOL, MILFORD, PA.

MILFORD HIGH SCHOOL BELL

A bell was placed in the Milford High School bell tower in 1904. The bell tolled daily to call the students to school at 8:45 AM, 8:55 AM and 9AM and again at 12:45 PM, 12:55 PM and 1PM. The bell came to be called the Milford Bell and was rung until 1979, when some members of the Alumni Association removed it and stored it in the barn of William and Bertha Fleming. The question of where to display the bell haunted the association. Someone heard U.S. Secretary of Education Lauro F. Cavazos was suggesting that each weekday should begin with the ringing of a school bell. Arthur Ridley, on behalf of the Alumni Association, contacted Secretary Cavazos and offered the Milford Bell. Secretary Cavazos accepted the gracious offer. The Dedication of the Milford High School Bell was held during American Education Week, on November 13,1989 with Arthur K. Ridley making the presentation. The bell is on permanent display on the plaza of the Department of Education Building in Washington D.C.

High School, Milford, Pennsylvania

THE DAUMANN AND WALTER HOME

In June 1907 George Daumann and his wife Martha Fieg purchased this corner lot at 500 West Harford Street and built their home. George was a carpenter who had also built the Malouk house on Seventh Street, the pergola for the water table at Grey Towers and homes at Twin Lakes and in Milford. After Martha's death in 1918, George married Martha's cousin Emile Fieg. Emile was a nurse who provided midwife services as well as personal care to individuals in need. George and Emile had two daughters, Virginia and Helen. Virginia married George Christian, a nephew of Jim Bull. In 1945 George Daumann sold the house to Jeanette and Othello Coppell who operated it as a boarding house they called The Lynn House. In 1951 Josephine Hougaz purchased the house. She sold it to Fred and Emma "Mag" Fieg Walter in 1959. Fred operated a heating oil business from their home. Fred and Mag raised their four children, Joe, Carol, Norma and Tim in the home. The Walter family sold the house in 1999. Today it serves the community as the home of Survivors' Resources.

THE ZALOOM HOUSE

In 1903 E.S. Wolfe built a small house for Madame Garnier at 504 West Harford Street. In 1923, when the home was purchased by George and Marie Zaloom, a transformation took place. The Zalooms enclosed porches and added the second story. They achieved the very popular 1920s Mediterranean look by applying stucco to the exterior of the building. It served as a pleasant summer home for the family, one of whom, Virginia, married a local boy, Warner Depuy. Mr. Depuy served his community well. He was a member of the House of Representatives, Secretary of Revenue for the Commonwealth of Pennsylvania, President of the First National Bank of Pike County and a longtime Pike County Commissioner.

MILFORD, PA.

FIRST CATHOLIC CHURCH

CATHOLIC CHURCH, MILFORD, PA.

In Mathews' History of Wayne, Pike and Monroe Counties, Pennsylvania he writes about the churches of Milford. Under the heading "Saint Patrick's Roman Catholic Church," he tells us that the first church was built in 1877 on the northeast corner of Eighth and James Streets. We learn that it was patronized primarily by workmen in the silver watch-case factory and their families. When that industry declined, services were seldom held.

Wendy Luhrs provided us with a booklet prepared by members of the congregation in celebration of their Fiftieth Anniversary held in 1996. It contains further historical information regarding the origin and growth of the church.

St. Patrick's Church, Milford, Pa

1906

BLANCHARD PRESS

CORNERSTONE LAID

While it has been determined that no written historical document allows us to know who designed or constructed the original church, it is a matter of record that the church cornerstone was laid on Eighth Street on Sunday, May 15, 1877. It was reported that the cornerstone was made of marble, weighed about five-hundred pounds and cost fifty dollars. Mentioned also is a reference to early Catholic services being held in the Revoryre's apartment above their bakery business on Broad Street.

MISSION CHURCH

Saint Joseph's Parish of Matamoras was officially established in 1892 by Bishop W. O'Hara, Ordinary of the Diocese of Scranton, Pennsylvania. Saint Patrick's Church was a mission church of Saint Joseph's Parish until 1946 when it was declared a separate parish by the Diocese of Scranton. Reverend Vincent J. Mahon began as pastor of Saint Joseph's in 1943. In 1946 he elected to leave Saint Joseph's and assumed the pastorate of Saint Patrick's.

FATHER MAHON

A plaque hanging in the front foyer of Saint Patrick's Church at 200 East High Street, now referred to as the Parish Hall, praises him: "Father Mahon's work in Saint Patrick's was magnificent! His work and vision translated goals into realities. He established this parish, built this church, rectory and established and built St. Vincent's in Dingmans as a mission. He began a catechetical center with a convent for Sisters of I.H.M. He planned development of the Mount Carmel section of the Milford Cemetery for the people of the parish." He retired in 1977.

CATHOLIC CHURCH, MILFORD, PA.

ST. PATRICK'S CATHOLIC CHURCH, MILFORD, PA.

50 Vantine House, Milford, Pa.

VANTINE HOUSE

The Vantine House was located at 90 Ninth Street. It served as one of the earliest hotels in the town of Milford. It was owned by Fred and Pauline Diem.

PROPRIETORS

The Diems offered the visitor "large rooms, fresh vegetables from the adjacent gardens, excellent cuisine and a beautifully landscaped property." The House could accommodate forty guests and the rooms ranged in price from $3 per day to $14 for a week.

When the hotel closed the building was converted into a Mediterranean style residence for Madame Saleen Moughabgab. It is presently owned by Mr. and Mrs. Ronald Parker.

VANTINE HOUSE, Fred Diem, Propr., MILFORD, PIKE CO., PA.

POND

A small pond next to the house complemented the pastoral charm of the location. It was created by damming the Vantine Creek.

VANTINE HOTEL, Milford, Pike Co., Pa.

VANTINE HOTEL GROVE, Milford, Pike Co., Pa.

GROVE

The Vantine House was situated on six partially wooded acres. Blue spruce, fir, maple and fruit trees provided cover and created a pleasant place in which to walk or rest.

SWISS CHALET

The Swiss Chalet, operated by Mrs. C.F. Matter Stanton, was a collection of summer cabins located at 613 West Harford Street. Today Alex Kresse's Auto Repair Shop is on this site which is across the street from Apple Valley Village.

SWISS CHALET   U. S. Route No. 6, Milford, Pa.   MRS. C. F. MATTER STANTON

PAL'S SERVICE STATION   PAL'S MODERN CABINS

PAL'S DINER

PAL'S — ¼ Mile West of Milford, Pa. on Route U. S. 6

PAL'S DINER

Ed Metzger tells a wonderful story regarding his acquisition of the Pal's property. When asked who Pal was, he responded that he had no idea! He does, however, remember being told that the diner on the property started life as the gondola of a zeppelin! He's never been able to find out if that is true, but he did find brass plates in the crawl space under the structure. These plates seemed to be holding it together and are probably consistent with those used on a gondola.

PAL'S DINER, MODERN CABINS AND SERVICE STATION, ¼ Mile West of Milford, Pa. Route U.S. 6. Phone Milford 9300. Cabins with hot and cold running water—Toilets—Showers—Innerspring Mattresses—Well Shaded— Cool Nights—Cabins heated in Winter—Excellent Food at Diner. A.A.A. Approved.

SERVICE STATION

Ed also vividly remembers going there as a boy in 1945 with his mother, who lived on Christian Hill, for a hamburger and finding the inside to be very narrow. He remembers a marble counter on the left side of the door and narrow booths. The bathroom was outside!

He knows the Wittekoks ran it for awhile as did Glen Musselwhite. When the property came on the market, he purchased it.

MODERN CABINS

There were some initial problems after he bought the property, as it had been closed for a time and required a lot of work to get it into shape. However, a bigger problem was that he couldn't cook! He went to see his friend, Norman Nicholes, who owned a motel and pancake house in Clarks Summit, Pennsylvania, for advice. Ed was thinking about contacting the Perkins Pancake House Corporation but Norman suggested he get in touch with Pillsbury instead. That turned out to be the right move, and the Pillsbury Company helped him establish his Pancake House.

Pal's Cabin Court
U. S. Route 6, Northwest Edge of
Milford, Pike Co., Pa.

APPLE VALLEY VILLAGE

OK. Now he had a pancake house but not a name! Ed explained how he selected the name. It seems years ago he was in California driving through the desert on his way to Las Vegas and saw a road sign for Apple Valley. He couldn't figure out how there could be an apple tree, let alone a valley there, so he drove to see it. At that time the town of Apple Valley consisted of a little motel and a radio station. (Later, that Apple Valley, California became home to Roy Rogers and Dale Evans!) His new property was in a valley where there were apple trees which belonged to the Pinchots. The name stuck and Apple Valley was born.

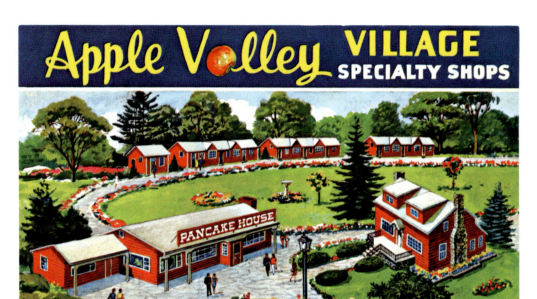

CANDY COTTAGE

While Ed was working at the George Washington Motor Lodge in Valley Forge, Pennsylvania he happened upon nearby Peddler's Village. He thought if some guy could create shops out of chicken coops, he could create cottages out of cabins. He took his mother, Helen, who had been involved with the project from the beginning, to Peddler's Village. She liked what she saw and agreed it could be done. The first cottage was rented to Mr. Atta who sold "Helen Elliott" candies. (Kitty Myer later had this shop.) Andy Zeigler opened a glass blowing shop and Ross Antiques occupied another cottage. Helen Metzger's gift shop, The Colonial, came under the management of Ed's wife, Gretel. She renamed it Temptuous Apple. Today, son Steve runs the restaurant and son Ted has a sporting goods shop where the gift shop used to be.

GATE HOUSE TO GRAY TOWERS

In his book <u>History of Wayne, Pike and Monroe Counties, Pennsylvania</u> published in 1886, author Alfred Mathews writes extensively about the Pinchot family. He tells us Constantine Pinchot was a prominent merchant in Bretielle, an island village about sixty miles from Paris, when his son Cyrille Constantine Desire Pinchot was born in 1798. When a young adult, Cyrille got caught up in the politics of the day and was an avid supporter of Napoleon Bonaparte. After Napoleon's defeat at Waterloo, Constantine, fearing reprisals, chose to leave France. In1816 Constantine, his wife Marie Augustine, his daughter Hortense and son Cyrille sailed for New York taking their stock of store goods with them. Constantine opened a store in New York City but relocated to Milford in 1818 where he built a house and store.

GATE HOUSE TO GRAY TOWERS. MILFORD, PA.

ENTRANCE TO GREY TOWERS

Constantine Pinchot's French Store offered a wide range of merchandise, was heavily patronized and very successful. His son Cyrille participated in the business and in 1824 was able to build a gracious home for his family on four lots at the corner of Broad and Harford Streets. Cyrille's first wife, Sarah, a daughter of Daniel Dimmick of Milford, died young without issue. His second wife, Eliza, a cousin of his first wife, was the daughter of John T. Cross, Esq. and Julia Ann Smith Cross. Both wives were grandchildren of DeAearts, whose father was Lord of Opdorf and Immerseele, in Belgium. Cyrille and Eliza had five children: Edgar, James, John, Mary, and Cyrille. When Constantine died in 1826, Cyrille and his mother, Madame Marie Pinchot, continued the business.

Entrance to Gray Towers, Milford, Pa.

LODGE HOUSE

Cyrille's son, James Pinchot, was born in 1831. As an adult James worked in New York City and became wealthy first importing and later manufacturing fine Victorian wallpapers. When his father died in 1873, he inherited the family homestead in Milford. He married Mary Jane Eno (from a monied New York City family) in 1864. They had three children, Gifford, Amos and Antoinette. Mary was well-schooled in manners and active socially. James had a keen interest in public affairs. He belonged to a number of prominent New York City and Washington, D.C. based organizations that nurtured his artistic and intellectual pursuits. According to historical information provided by the US Forest Service, members of these organizations were considered to be the "power that ran New York and the nation in the 19th century." James, with his abhorrence of wastefulness, became a mainstay of one of these organizations, the American Forestry Association. The Association sought, as early as 1875, to halt reckless destruction of natural resources by employing conservation management. After their college graduations, James encouraged his sons Gifford and Amos to become members of these groups.

The Lodge House leading to "Gray Towers," Milford, Pa.

Entrance to the Grey Towers and Road to Shohola, Milford, Pa.

ENTRANCE TO GREY TOWERS

At the entrance to Grey Towers is the Gate House, also known as the Lodge House or Garden Cottage. It was built in the same style as Grey Towers and is located on the Owego Turnpike. Prior to the construction of US Highway 6, the main road from Milford to the west was the Owego Turnpike.

You will have noticed two different spellings of Gray/Grey Towers. Ed Brannon, retired Director of Grey Towers, explained that "gray," the American spelling of the color, was used by the company that printed the postcards. Mary Pinchot, Gifford's mother, chose the name for Grey Towers using the English spelling of "grey."

GREY TOWERS

Grey Towers, built by James and Mary Pinchot as their summer estate, was completed in 1886. The home was designed by Richard Morris Hunt in the Norman-Benton style. It was modeled after LaGrange, Lafayette's country home in France.

The exterior of the building consists of fieldstone gathered on the estate. Pike County quarries furnished the bluestone that was used for corners, windows and door openings for strength and decorative purposes. The building, two-stories high with an attic, is eighty-one by fifty-two feet. The wing is twenty-seven by fifty-seven.

There are three turrets, or towers, on three corners of the main building, each twenty feet in diameter and sixty-three feet high. The home contains twenty-three fireplaces and forty-one rooms finished in imitation of the old baronial style. Grey Towers was built and completely furnished for $44,000.

GIFFORD PINCHOT

Gifford Pinchot was born in 1865. When he graduated from high school, Gifford's father suggested he pursue studies in forestry. James was concerned about the future of America's forests as much of the eastern forests had been burned to create farmlands, plundered of wood for construction and fuel or wasted by carelessness. Gifford loved the woods and everything about them so he took his father's advice and enrolled at Yale University in 1885. When he graduated in 1889, advanced education courses in the field of forestry did not exist in the United States. He went abroad to study at the L'ecole Nationale Forestiere in Nancy, France. When Gifford returned to the United States in 1892, he was hired by the Vanderbilt family, for whom he created the first example of practical forest management on a large scale at their Biltmore Estate in Asheville, NC. In 1898 Pinchot began the consolidation of the fragmented government forestry work undertaken by the Division of Forestry which lead to the establishment of the Bureau of Forestry now known as the US Forest Service. In 1903 Pinchot became professor of Forestry at Yale University.

Grey Towers, Milford, Pa.
Summer Home of Mr. Gifford Pinchot.

RESIDENCE OF GIFFORD PINCHOT

Pinchot formed a friendship with Teddy Roosevelt during Roosevelt's tenure as Governor of New York. The two had much in common and shared a love of the outdoors. In 1904 President Roosevelt appointed him Chief of Forestry, a position he held until 1910. During his period in office the Forest Service and the national forests grew spectacularly. In 1905 there were 60 forest reserve units covering 56 million acres. In 1910 there were 150 national forests covering 172 million acres. Gifford became President Roosevelt's most trusted advisor on matters of conservation, which Roosevelt considered one of the great accomplishments of his administration. Gifford Pinchot is generally regarded as the "father" of American conservation because of his great and unrelenting concern for the protection of the American forest.

"Gray Towers", Residence of Gifford Pinchot. Milford, Pa.

View from Gray Towers, Milford, Pa.

12459

VIEW FROM GREY TOWERS

Cornelia Bryce, daughter of Lloyd Bryce, a wealthy journalist and politician, grew up in Victorian circles. She was educated in private schools and traveled frequently with her parents to Europe. Cornelia was attractive, dressed in flamboyant clothes, and dyed her hair red. Cornelia became active in the Progressive Party, the party formed by Pinchot, Roosevelt and others, in 1912. She met Gifford Pinchot during the Bull Moose Campaign, so-called because Roosevelt declared himself as fit as a bull moose and ready to run against Taft and Wilson for the presidency. Cornelia's political interests began with women's suffrage, a cause she supported vigorously. She spoke out for birth control, educational reform, women's rights and child labor practices. During her husband's tenures as Governor she was one of the most politically active first ladies in the history of Pennsylvania. They married in 1914 and had one son, Gifford Bryce.

Milford Pa. from the towers

MILFORD FROM THE TOWERS

According to information provided in Forest Service literature, Cornelia's first impression of Grey Towers was of a dreary castle standing naked on a hill. Using much of her own money, she decided to "jazz it up." Cornelia combined rooms, added windows and redecorated extensively. The library was originally two rooms. Cornelia had a wall removed and added new teakwood floors, furnishings, shelves, cabinets and paneling.

The books presently in the library are the original Pinchot books. Forest Service Interpretive Specialist Chuck Croston tells us some are from the 1600s as James Pinchot was an avid book collector. Also in the room is a full-length portrait of three members of the Pinchot family. In 1872 noted French artist, Alexandre Cabanel, painted Mary Eno Pinchot with her children, Gifford, age seven and his younger sister Antoinette. They posed for the artist wearing Florentine costumes.

PINCHOT HOME

The tower room adjoining the library had been used by Gifford Pinchot as an office and remains filled with artifacts of his travels. Cornelia had converted the dining room and breakfast room into one large sitting room. A mural on the south wall of the sitting room was painted by Scandinavian artist N.H. Penning in 1799 and had originally hung in the Netherlands in The Hague. It was installed at Grey Towers in the 1920s. The mural, which depicts a nautical scene, was painted using a technique called *trompe l'oeil* or "to fool the eye." This gives the painting a three-dimensional effect. Also in the room is a portrait of President Kennedy presented to the Forest Service by Mrs. Jacqueline Kennedy.

"Grey Towers" (Home of Gifford Pinchot) Milford, Pa.

GREY TOWERS

Outside the French doors of the sitting room is a patio the family called the Marble Court. It is an outdoor room designed by Cornelia Pinchot as a natural extension of her home. The mosaic covering the ground has swirls of marble, simulating ocean waves. Beyond the patio is a building called the Letter Box. It was built for Gifford by Cornelia to serve both as an office and as an archive for his political papers. The Letter Box was recently restored as part of a Save America's Treasures project and Governor Pinchot's political papers were given to the Library of Congress. It is used for conservation education and small meetings. A pathway outside the Letter Box leads to an area used as an outdoor theater.

At the end of the pathway is the Bait Box. This was built as a playhouse for Gifford and Cornelia's son "Giffy." His father also called him "Mr. Fish" because of his keen interest in fishing. The Bait Box is now used for small conference groups.

The Grey Towers, Milford, Pa.

GREY TOWERS, HOME OF GOVERNOR PINCHOT, MILFORD, PA.

GOVERNOR GIFFORD PINCHOT

Gifford Pinchot, aided by the strong support of Cornelia, women voters and voters in rural counties, was elected to his first term as Pennsylvania's Governor in 1922. During his 1923-1927 term, Governor Pinchot's major goals were the regulation of electric power companies and the enforcement of Prohibition. He advocated "clean politics." He worked to eliminate the state's deficit, settled the anthracite coal strike, and was well-known for his accessibility to the public. Because a Pennsylvania law prohibited a successive term, he could not run for re-election. Four years later, however, he was elected to a second term. He served as Pennsylvania's Governor during the depression years. Pinchot was proud of "taking the farmer out of the mud." He provided work for men in the relief camps by having them build twenty-thousand miles of paved, country roads.

FULL VIEW OF GREY TOWERS. HOME OF GOVERNOR PINCHOT MILFORD, PA.

PRESIDENT JOHN F. KENNEDY DEDICATES

When Cornelia Pinchot died in 1960, her son, Dr. Gifford Bryce Pinchot, inherited Grey Towers. In 1963 Grey Towers was designated as a National Historic Landmark and the building and one-hundred acres were donated to the US Forest Service by Dr. Gifford B. Pinchot and Mrs. Amos Pinchot to be used as a center for conservation studies. On September 24, 1963 President John F. Kennedy dedicated the Pinchot Institute for Conservation Studies stating the work of Gifford Pinchot "marked a beginning of a professional approach to conservation resources." A crowd of twelve to fifteen thousand people gathered on the amphitheater hillside to hear President Kennedy's remarks.

GREY TOWERS TODAY

Today the US Forest Service, the federal agency founded by Gifford Pinchot, administers the home and grounds. The Pinchot Institute for Conservation Studies continues to hold conferences and seminars at the estate to help guide the future of conservation thought, policy and action. Under Director Ed Brannon a series of renovation projects was begun. In 1996 a new slate roof was installed. A multi-phase restoration and renovation project, started in 1998, necessitated the closing of the mansion for three years. This twelve-million dollar project included the restoration of all interior surfaces, the conversion of rooms to office space, a new elevator and structural modification of the wood flooring system. New landscaping, lawns, paved walkways and terraces were completed. The mansion reopened to visitors in the fall of 2001. Grey Towers is open to the public during the summer months.

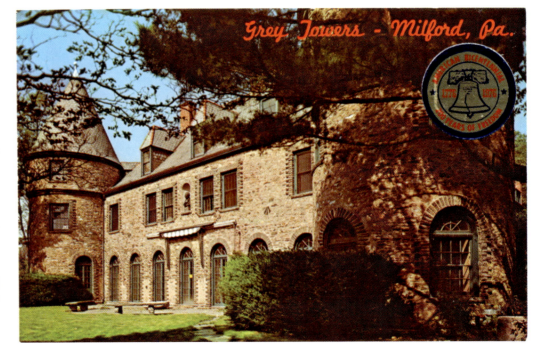

Grey Towers - Milford, Pa.

SAWKILL FALLS IN WINTER

At one time the Pinchot family owned 3,600 acres of land. This property encompassed the Sawkill Brook and watershed. The Sawkill Falls cascade a distance of ninety-feet into the deep gorge below.

FINGER BOWL

The tour of Grey Towers includes a special area near the Marble Court patio. It features a large stone pergola covered in summer by lush wisteria vines which protect guests from the elements as they gather around the Finger Bowl. The Finger Bowl is a unique water-filled stone table commissioned by Mrs. Pinchot after they returned from their trip to the South Sea Islands. Guests were seated around the table with dinner plates resting on the rim. Large wooden serving bowls, brought by Mrs. Pinchot from the Polynesian Islands, floated on the water and conveyed delicacies from guest to guest. Hollow glass balls floated on the surface of the water and guests could gently nudge them toward an unmoving serving dish to set it in motion. According to information provided by a staff writer at Grey Towers, one not-so- gentle nudge once sank a serving dish of turkey! This outdoor dining area is still used for seasonal social events.

Sawkill Falls in Winter, Milford, Pa.

HAPPY NEW YEAR '09

YALE FOREST SCHOOL

As Gifford Pinchot began his career in forestry he discovered trained foresters and schools with significant programs in forestry were in short supply. In 1900 Gifford's parents, James and Mary, endowed Yale University with $150,000 to start a post-graduate forestry school. The University agreed to host summer field camps to provide practical experience for their forestry students at the Pinchot estate in Milford. The first camp at Grey Towers opened in 1901 on sixty acres of forest land. It had a mess hall, lecture hall, clubhouse and an athletic field.

FORESTRY SCHOOL TENTS

The original camp was designed only as an introduction to forestry and almost anyone who was interested was welcomed. But by 1904 attendance at the camp was part of a required twelve-week professional course that culminated in a Master's Degree in forestry from Yale.

Students came from throughout the country and overseas. According to literature provided by Grey Towers, they were housed in approximately fifty tents and each tent was supplied with cots, a bucket, pitcher and washbasin.

CAMPER'S DAY

The students arose at 6:30 AM for breakfast. After eating they worked in the field running surveys, estimating timber volume, planting trees and learning aspects of applied forestry. Harry Graves, Yale's first Dean of Forestry, once said: "The object of the school was not only to give specific instruction but to build up a profession; not merely to teach men how to handle forest land, but to train them to be leaders in one of the most important economic movements of the time."

Yale Forest School, Milford, Pa.

CAMP GROUNDS OF THE YALE FOREST SCHOOL, MILFORD, PA.

SOCIAL ACTIVITIES

The Pinchots invited the young men to lawn parties, dinner parties and teas. They allowed the students to build a small dam on the Sawkill Brook to create a swimming hole. The campers swam there often, usually without benefit of a swimming suit. This drew complaints from strollers along the brook about swimmers in "nature's costume." Saturday night dances held at Forest Hall were very popular with the men and townspeople.

JUNIOR HALL

Everyone looked forward to the weekly campfires where they sang songs and told stories. Gifford Pinchot usually attended to the delight of the young men. The Milford Dispatch reported that they honored him as a leader and always greeted him with boisterous cheers. The men pictured here are seated in front of Junior Hall with Gifford Pinchot and a dog in the center of the front row. The graduate students started their field studies in the summer between their first and second year of the graduate program. They were referred to as Juniors. After completion of the program, they became Seniors. In 1926 the Forestry School moved their program to New Haven, Connecticut.

MILFORD EXPERIMENTAL FOREST

The Milford Experimental Forest is a 1,400 acre research forest established in 1901 by James and Gifford Pinchot and the Yale School of Forestry to study how to regenerate a new forest after the original forests were cleared in the late 1800s. The forest is on Pinchot family property surrounding the Grey Towers estate which extends across the Sawkill Creek and includes the former Yale School of Forestry camp off of Christian Hill. The property also crosses Route 6 West and borders Schocopee Road. In 1998 the Pinchot family in partnership with the USDA Forest Service at Grey Towers and the Pinchot Institute for Conservation Studies re-established the experimental forest. Peter Pinchot, grandson of Gifford Pinchot, was appointed Director. Present issues under study are deer management, reintroduction of the American Chestnut tree and prevention of the loss of the Eastern Hemlock tree.

PICNIC ROCK ON THE SAWKILL

The bridge pictured was the first bridge built over the Sawkill to connect Grey Towers to the Yale Forestry Camp.

PICNIC ROCK ON THE SAWKILL

This is a replacement bridge built later over the Sawkill connecting Grey Towers to the Yale Forestry Camp. This bridge was destroyed in 1955 by flood waters.

Sawkill Falls from Devil's Lake, Milford, Pa.

SAWKILL FALLS FROM DEVIL'S LAKE

To the left at the base of Sawkill Falls is a six to eight-foot wide gorge known as Devil's Glen or Devil's Kitchen. In conjunction with that area is a depression in the rock formation that collects water. This is referred to as Devil's Lake.

PINCHOT FALLS

According to the "Milford Magazine" of April/May 2004 and reprinted/quoted here with permission of Krista Gromalski, then editor and publisher: "The Pinchot Falls – also known as Sawkill Falls – is located adjacent to the US Forest Service – owned Grey Towers National Historic Landmark, the former home of Conservationist Gifford Pinchot. The falls remain privately owned by the Pinchot family, which has allowed public access to it for more than 100 years, until a few months ago. Currently (and hopefully temporarily) the falls are closed due to a family dispute."

Sawkill Falls, Milford Pike County, Pa.

FULL VIEW OF SAWKILL FALLS

This photograph below pictures Ralph R. Myer standing in the Sawkill Falls when he was in his teens. The postcard was postmarked in Milford, Pennsylvania at 6 AM, September 25, 1909. The photo was taken by his father, noted photographer J.A. Myer. J.A. Myer was a professional photographer who came to Milford in the summer of 1882. He erected a tent on West Harford Street and used it as his studio. In the winter he returned to Philadelphia. In 1897 he built his house and studio. His three youngest children, J. Edson, Clyde, and Vera were born in the home at 110 West Harford Street. Today the building houses the offices of the Pike County Chapter of the American Cancer Society.

Sawkill Falls, Milford, Pa.

No. 32341 Pub. by the Bazaar — Printed in Germany

RALPH R. MYER

G.E. Scheller took this photograph of Ralph R. Myer, again standing in the falls, some sixty years later. It was published by Ralph as a postcard and was for sale at the Myer Motel in Milford.

L'ERMITAGE, MILFORD, PIKE CO., PA.

L'ERMITAGE

This picture of what was then called "L'Ermitage" was taken in 1906. Beth Lovett has told us that her great-great grandfather, Henry Peck, originally owned the property, which was located off Schocopee Road at present-day 127 Evergreen Lane, originally called Hermitage Lane. Mr. Peck sold some of the property to Louis and Josephine Ragot in the late 1800s.

MAIN HOUSE

She adds: "The lower building, down by the brook, was the original L'Ermitage and later the upper building was established as Monte Cazar." The Ragots also added a swimming pool and "a powerful radio receiving set able to receive all the broadcasting stations far and near."

HERMITAGE MAIN HOUSE   MILFORD PA. 8

HERMITAGE

In 1923 an advertisement suggested one might stay at "an ideal vacation hotel situated 1000 feet above sea level amidst giant pines one mile from the town of Milford. The invigorating dry mountain air, cooled by numerous springs of pure water, is a blessing to those who desire rest and comfort during their vacation."

HERMITAGE COTTAGE

Eventually called the Hermitage, the English version of the French L'Ermitage, the hotel provided "an excellent French table." Beth Lovett tells us that festivities ended each evening with the French National Anthem sung by all present.

The Hermitage, Milford, Pa.

HERMITAGE

In 1923 L.F. Ragot listed his accommodations as "large airy cool rooms, all with hot and cold running water. Up-to-date bath accommodations, Smoking Room, Sitting Room, Dancing Room, Spacious Lawns, Piazzas and Balconies."

EVERGREEN ROAD

Mr. Ragot created the Hermitage Glen with paths through the forest. Beth Lovett remembers "a graceful walk down to the pond and nice summer benches."

Evergreen Road in the Glen   The Hermitage Milford P.

HERMITAGE GLEN

This postcard was sent by "Ada" to "Miss Grace Manning of 331 W. 29th Street, New York City." It was mailed from Milford on July 27, 1909 at 3:00 PM. She assures her friend that she is having a "glorious time" at the Hermitage.

The Hermit in Hermitage Glen, Milford, Pa.

THE HERMIT

Mr. Ragot was considered a creative man. He sculpted many faces, human and animal, from whose mouths flowed various springs. He also built a bridge over the stream and a summer cabin nearby.

LEGEND OF THE HERMIT

In his advertisement, Mr. Ragot promises "throughout the season we produce a very agreeable Lyric Poem of 'The Legend of the Hermit' in the Hermitage Glen."

CROWNING THE HERMIT

The lavish production involved much ceremony and concluded with the crowning of the Hermit. It was a unique activity enjoyed by guests of The Hermitage.

THE HERMIT

Very often Mr. Ragot's production of "The Legend of the Hermit" was open to the public. Proceeds from ticket sales in 1922 went to the Milford Fire Department, which allowed them to buy their first "motorized" truck.

The Hermit at the Hermitage
Milford, Pike Co. Pa.

No. 484.   National Art Views Co, N. Y. City.

In the Hermitage Glen,
Milford Pa.

ONE OF THE FOUNTAINS

In addition to the sculpture, Mr. Ragot had constructed a large sun dial. Beth Lovett points out that all of these items were "stolen from 1926 until the 1940s, as these properties were summer homes and easily accessible to anyone who wanted to 'help' themselves."

GROVE OVERNIGHT CABINS

The Grove Overnight Cabins, Wm. J. Lavery, Host.
1 Mile West of Post Office, Route U. S. 6
Milford, Pa. 874

The Milford Chamber of Commerce booklet of 1923 tells us: "Milford has no clap-trap cheap amusements, and nothing of the vulgar or shoddy. In the summertime it has every sort of recreation that is desirable in a resort that appeals to a high class, refined patronage." Fortunately, Milford, in addition to large resorts and hotels, also had some accommodations that a middle class could afford. Among these were the Grove Overnight Cabins located at 216 Route 6 and owned by the Lavery family.

This is the present location of Crawford Trailer Park.

SHERELYN MOTEL

Later overnight cabins gave way to modern motels such as the Sherelyn Motel constructed at 374 Route 6, west of Milford. William Bosler, Sr., William Bosler, Jr. and Evelyn Bosler built the motel in 1955 and named it for Bill and Evelyn's daughter, Sherelyn. Their establishment promised "Courtesy Coffee in Rooms, TV, Wall-to-Wall Carpets. Pool on well kept grounds. Restful...Relaxing. Open all year." The Boslers sold the motel in 1972 but this card pictures members of the family and friends enjoying the pool. Pictured are Sherelyn Bosler (foreground) and a photographer's model relaxing on the edge of the pool. Friend Rob Smith is in the pool. From left to right around the pool are an unknown guest, Bill and Evelyn Bosler, family friends Marie Giglia, Betty Lauer, Larry Giglia, Thelma Smith and Robert Smith.

SAWKILL POST OFFICE

This postcard was mailed from Milford on July 18, 1908. In Beers' <u>Commemorative Biographical Record of Northeastern Pennsylvania</u>, Sawkill is referred to as a village. It was located near Sawkill Lake on the upper Sawkill Road near the present New Jersey Y Camps and extended from Route 6 onto the upper Raymondskill Road to Frenchtown Road. Charles C. Bridge, owner of the Sunoco Gas Station on Route 6, now a tattoo parlor, tells us the Sawkill Post Office was located in the house of his grandfather, Charles Bridge at 600 Sawkill Road near the Y camps. Mr. Bridge was appointed to the position of postmaster in 1895. Charlie believes the post office closed in the early 1920s. A Protestant Church was located at what is now 252 Raymondskill Road. The nearby one-room Sawkill School educated children through the eighth grade. The Hoffman family also lived in Sawkill and Lorraine Gregory's grandfather Ira Hoffman was born there in 1874. One of the main attractions of the area was the excellent fishing on Sawkill Lake. Access to the lake was available from the Richard "Judd" Hoffman property until the early 1950s when the New Jersey Y Camps acquired the land.

Greetings from
Sawkill, Pennsylvania.

PEDERSEN HOUSE

Darlene Pedersen Harshman, widow of Warren Pedersen, told us Warren lived in this house with his parents, Gustave and Ingrid Pedersen, prior to his marriage. She suggested we look for an etched flagstone at the top of the steps in front of the house. Bill Leiser found it, and the stone tells us the house was built by L. B. Quick in October, 1884. L. B. Quick was Lucian Brink Quick, the grandson of Peter A. L. and Margaret Westbrook Quick. Peter Quick was the brother of Thomas Quick who was the first non-Native American to buy land, circa 1732, and settle in the area that would become the town of Milford. Lucian owned a dairy farm and pastured his cows and kept them in a barn across what was then the Owego Turnpike. Parts of the Owego Turnpike became Route 6 and the property once occupied by the barn is now owned by Bill and Pat Morcom whose home is at 521, Route 6. Lucian's house also served as a stagecoach stop and local lure tells us L. B. made it an enjoyable stop by providing the passengers with home brew processed by a still in his cellar.

SAWKILL PINES LODGE, MILFORD, PA.

SAWKILL PINES LODGE

I n the 1930s the New Jersey Federation of YMHA and YWHA Camps bought the property that had previously been known as the Sawkill Pines Lodge and established their camps. The Lodge was destroyed in a fire in the 1950s, but by then many other buildings had been erected to accommodate the campers.

SWIMMING CRIB, SAWKILL PINES, MILFORD, PA.

SWIMMING CRIB

T he swimming crib, an area defined by rope boundaries, was located in a small pond on the property close to the original lodge.

CAMP NAH-JEE-WAH

Camp NAH-JEE-WAH, a name established by the New Jersey Woman's Auxiliary of the YMHA that later became the YWHA, is the section of the camp used by the YWHA. In 2005 Mr. Leonard Robinson, Executive Director of the NJ YWHA and YMHA Camps, ordered an environmental impact study of the 1250 acres the camp owns. It was determined that because the Association had constructed all buildings on the property, such as seen in this card, on piers throughout the years, no earth was disturbed. Thus, little degradation has occurred to wetlands, lakes and streams. He and the Association were commended and proclaimed excellent stewards of the property.

STARTING THE DAY RIGHT AT NAH-JEE-WAH, FELIX FULD CAMPS, MILFORD, PA.

SAWKILL LAKE

Mr. Matthew Elson was Executive Director of the camps from 1950 to 1978. He credits Michael Stavitsky as the person who pushed the creation of the NJ YMHA and YWHA Camps. He also told us that two separate camps, NAH-JEE-WAH for girls and Cedar Lake for boys, existed for most of his tenure.

CEDAR LAKE CAMP

The lake on the property owned by the Y Camps is Sawkill Lake. The name Cedar Lake is a holdover from when a YMHA camp was established in the 1920s at a rented campground near Bear Mountain, NY. Felix Fuld was an affluent Newark businessman who gave generously of his time and money to support the camps at Bear Mountain and later at Sawkill.

CEDAR LAKE CRAFTSMEN, FELIX FULD CAMPS, MILFORD, PA.

A SHADY NOOK FOR STORYTELLING AT NAH-JEE-WAH, FELIX FULD CAMPS, MILFORD, PA.

SHADY NOOK

While both Cedar Lake and NAH-JEE-WAH Camps have always offered many diverse activities, Mr. Robinson found that in recent years children and parents wanted camps that specialized in athletics. In order to compete, the Y camps spent $8.5 million to revitalize the athletic fields and courts. Mr. Robinson says these are now "as nice as you would find in a private camp."

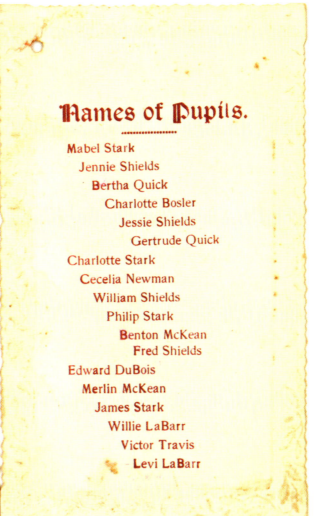

SAWKILL SCHOOL

The Sawkill School, one of seven one-room schoolhouses with eight grades used to educate the children of Dingman Township, was located five miles from Milford on Route 6 West across the road from Charlie Bridge's former Sunoco Gas Station. Leon "Mickey" Husson remembers attending Sawkill School for all eight grades. Walter Myer recounts that he and his sister, Marcella, began school there in 1933 when he was eight years old. Walter said he completed grades one through five in the three years he was there. Walter and Marcella lived on Frenchtown Road and were transported to school first by Judd Hoffman in an open Dodge touring car with side curtains and later by Charles Nitsche in a Model A Ford. Mr. Nitsche had removed the back seat from the Ford and installed benches. The children who attended this school later went to the Union School on Raymonskill Road until the new school on Fisher Lane was completed. This Dingman Township Consolidated School on Fisher Lane now houses the Dingman Township Administrative Offices.

AERIAL VIEW OF CAMP SAGAMORE

AERIAL VIEW OF SAGAMORE-ON-TWIN-LAKES, MILFORD, PA.   340

In 1885 Frank DeRilap purchased 800 acres near Twin Lakes and built a summer school for his "Legitimate School of Singing." The main campus of his school was in New York City where his students were studying to become professional opera singers. The students enjoyed the ambiance of country living and combined voice training with breaks for swimming, fishing and other outdoor activities. Mr. DeRilap died in 1907 but his wife maintained the house and property until 1929 when she sold it to the Lloyd family.

In the 1930s Edward, Burt and Brick Lloyd opened Camp Sagamore as a Christian adult summer resort camp.

The main entrance to the camp was located off Twin Lakes Road in Shohola Township.

SAGAMORE REUNION

To generate enthusiasm for return visits to the camp in the summer, the Lloyd family sponsored reunions. These were held in the fall, in midwinter and in the spring at the Hotel Pennsylvania in New York City. Two bands, playing continuous music, were enthusiastically received by over one thousand campers at each event.

Season's Greetings

Announcing . . .

SAGAMORE'S
WINTER REUNION AND DANCE
Friday, January 11, 1946
At the HOTEL PENNSYLVANIA—Keystone Room

33rd Street at 7th Avenue   All Subways at 33rd Street

There'll be Fun Galore for all.   Dress informal and bring your friends too! Refreshments.

Admission $1.46   Tax .29   Total $1.75

NEXT REUNION, SATURDAY, MARCH 2nd, AT THE PENN.
Send any news for The Spring Gossip Sheet to
Brick Lloyd, Milford, Pa. Thanx!

CAMP SAGAMORE

Sagamore had a theme "For the Fun! Try It!" They provided activities that encouraged people to get together and have fun. One such activity involved the camp orchestra. Members of the orchestra would meet very early one morning each week near the tower. They played lively dance tunes and went from one cabin area to the next waking all the campers. They encouraged them to get out of bed and, in their pajamas, join the parade! Most campers did and a fun time was had by all as they snake-danced throughout the camp!

READY FOR A CANTER, SAGAMORE-ON-TWIN-LAKES, MILFORD, PA.   309

SAGAMORE

Camp Sagamore was advertised as a "'No Style' Adult Bungalow Camp for Christian young men and women-single or married-and the older folks, too, on beautiful Twin Lakes near Milford, PA."

VIEW OF TWIN LAKES FROM THE TOWER.
SAGAMORE-ON-TWIN-LAKES. MILFORD, PA.

THE TOWER

Sagamore-on-Twin-Lakes near Milford was "A Beautiful 800-Acre Vacation Estate."

VIEW

The observation tower afforded guests magnificent views of the Big Twin Lake.

TOWER

Eddie Lloyd tells us the observation tower was originally near the George Washington Bridge. The Lloyds had the tower disassembled and reassembled at Sagamore in the 1930s. The tower, a wooden structure, was reported to be eighty-five feet high or, as described in the card below, eighty feet high. Either way, it was high!

85 Foot Observation Tower, Sagamore-on-Twin Lakes, Milford, Pa. 337

GOOD TIMES SQUARE FROM 80 FT. TOWER, SAGAMORE-ON-TWIN-LAKES, MILFORD, PA. 313

TENNIS

Tennis was promoted in a big way at Sagamore. Weekly tennis tournaments were held. All the weekly winners were invited back for a free Columbus Day Tennis Weekend to participate in the Tennis Championships. After this event the camp closed for the season.

— 73 —

GOOD TIMES SQUARE

GOOD TIMES SQUARE FROM THE DECK, SAGAMORE-ON-TWIN-LAKES, MILFORD, PA.   321

Everyone at Camp Sagamore, including management, had "camp names." Initiation night was held on Sunday nights at the Showboat at which time all campers were given their camp names. The campers used these monikers for the duration of their visit and in subsequent visits. Burt Lloyd was dubbed "Big Cheese" and Eddie Lloyd was called "Bugle." Mae Lloyd, Ed's wife, was referred to as "Spoon" and Milton Lloyd was known as "Brick." Ed Nemus, who had the horse concession, got "Rodeo." The camp lifeguards were called "Diver" and "Torpedo." "Goosestep" was assigned to the night watchman and Del Jordan, who had the canoe and sailboat concession, was hailed as "Skipper." Herb Moore, a frequent camper, was also known as "Strike" and his friend drew "Lucky."

Eddie and Brick Lloyd shared the responsibilities of running the camp. Eddie maintained the buildings and grounds and Brick handled the office.

DINING ROOM

The dining room could accommodate four-hundred campers for breakfast, lunch and dinner. On holidays the number could increase to five hundred. All campers had the opportunity to preselect their meals from a varied menu. Meals were served at the same time each day and the efficient serving staff were able to serve all within an hour. Eleven campers were seated at each table and a staff server was responsible for the same two tables at each meal. Sharon Kelly of Milford Township remembers her Uncle Ernest "Buck" Arnold was a chef at Camp Sagamore after he was discharged from the Navy.

A SECTION OF OUR SPACIOUS DINING ROOM, SAGAMORE-ON-TWIN-LAKES, MILFORD, PA.   342

BOY MEETS GIRL

Skip and Lorraine's friend, Herb Moore, vividly remembers his vacations at Camp Sagamore. In 1939 Herb heard about the camp, called and made reservations for one week. He enjoyed his week at the camp and liked participating in the activities. He returned the following summer for two weeks. After that he made reservations for the same two weeks each summer during which he became reacquainted with friends from the previous summer. Most of the campers and staff were young, single adults ready and willing to meet members of the opposite sex. In this "boy meets girl" atmosphere, Herb met Doris.

After WWII, Doris lost her job at the Gyroscope Company on Long Island and found a summer job at Camp Sagamore. Herb and Doris fell in love and married in 1947. Herb's work took them to foreign countries to live but when they retired in 1968 they chose to return to the area they loved. They built a house in Sagamore Estates and lived there until 1993 when they relocated to Florida.

HIKING PATHS, TENNIS AND THE OUTDOORS

Many of the campers were from urban areas and were delighted with the camp's abundant trees and forest paths. Tennis was an important activity at the camp and the courts were some of the finest in the area. Campers could play on one of the three clay courts or use the macadamized court.

TWIN LAKES FROM RECREATION HALL. CAMP SAGAMORE, MILFORD, PA.

BEACH

Camp Sagamore imported white sand from the New Jersey Shore to create its private beach on Big Twin Lake. The sand was shipped by boxcar load on the Erie Railroad to the train depot at Shohola. A local contractor, Joe Boehm, trucked it to the lakeside. Big Twin Lake provided opportunities for water recreation that helped to make Camp Sagamore a successful enterprise for many years.

BRINK PONDS

When Camp Sagamore, or Sagamore-on-Twin-Lakes, opened for business in the 1930s, the name Twin Lakes had been established. However, as Pike County Historian George Fluhr explains: "The Twin Lakes were originally two unconnected bodies of water called Big Brink Pond and Little Brink Pond. They were named for Hermannis Brink who settled there shortly after the American Revolution. Brink was a lumberman who had an 'up and down' saw mill on the Twin Lakes Brook near its outlet from the lake. Later a second mill called Black's Mill was built on the brook near the point where it is crossed today by the Twin Lakes Road. During the 1800s the two ponds were popular, although remote, hunting and fishing spots."

THE SHOWBOAT

The Showboat, the building pictured in this card, was the center of entertainment for the guests. Nightly activities in the Showboat varied. Sunday night was initiation night. Monday night dances were popular and the camp's seven-piece orchestra played a wide selection of dance music. Tuesday night was Cabaret night. The Husson brothers or another local talent, Phil Judd, made Wednesday night special by calling and providing the music for square dancing. Guests could relax and listen or dance to the orchestra music on Thursday evenings. Friday night, amateur night, was eagerly anticipated. Guests showed off their talents as did Eddie Lloyd. He had a wonderful singing voice and it was felt he could have sung professionally. Saturdays found guests departing and arriving and a welcome dance was held in the evening. Church services were provided in the Showboat on Sundays. In later years, a piano bar was an added attraction. Brick Lloyd frequently played to entertain the guests.

SWIMMING AND BOATING

Del "Skipper" Jordan had the concession for canoes and sailboats. Canoeing or sailing for most campers was a relaxing time. Sagamore was located in the southeast corner of the Big Lake. Guests who were more adventurous took on the challenge of canoeing down the lake to find the channel between the lakes and make their way to the Little Lake.

Although Sagamore had a motorboat, it was only used for emergencies. It was called the "crash" boat and was employed to rescue anyone who capsized a canoe or sailboat.

In 1927 the Twin Lakes Property Owners Association (TLPOA) was formed to help preserve the quality of water and life at Twin Lakes. TLPOA held their 60th Anniversary celebration in the Showboat in August 1986. It was one of the last major functions held in the Showboat. In 1937 the Pennsylvania Legislature passed a law restricting the use of gasoline and electric motorboats on Twin Lakes. This law helped to prevent the degradation of the lake water and fostered a peaceful and quiet atmosphere.

THE COZY CAPTAIN'S LOUNGE

The cozy Captain's Lounge was upstairs in the Showboat next to the dance floor. During the 1930s and 1940s Camp Sagamore had some very strict rules – no alcohol was served and a rigid curfew was enforced. The orchestra stopped playing at 11:30 PM. It was not uncommon for some campers to leave around 10:00 PM to look for "firewater." They could choose between Harley Hinkel's Bar or the Cos-Mid Inn operated by Beth Nikles' father and mother, "Cos" and Dorothy Costello. With the strictly enforced curfew, the campers had to drink fast and get back to camp by midnight. If the night watchman, "Goosestep," caught them out after the curfew, they were confronted by Brick Lloyd. If they apologized to him for breaking curfew they were allowed to stay, or, if they chose to disagree with him, they were asked to leave camp.

RECREATION ROOM

Rainy day activities included reading and board games.

THE BAR AND LOUNGE

This bar was built at the top of the hill by the office. Herb Moore tells us that when he and Doris returned for a stay in 1951, Sagamore was still operating as a camp. However there now was a bar serving alcohol and no curfew was enforced. He says it gave the camp a different atmosphere.

GIFTS

The gift shop was popular with campers and visitors. Sharon Kelly remembers she and her sister, Diane, being given Indian dolls purchased there.

A BUNGALOW AT CAMP SAGAMORE, TWIN LAKES, PA.

CABINS

Cabins used by the guests were located in three different areas of the camp. One cluster of cabins provided lodging for married couples. Another group, located at the bottom of a hill and by the lake, were reserved for male campers. The women's cabins were located at the top of the hill. The men and women cabins were dormitory style and ten campers were assigned to each cabin. The cabins had no bathroom facilities and campers had to walk to a designated shared bathroom. The cabins were sparsely lighted and unheated. Weekly rates began at $21 for deluxe accommodations.

Each assembly of cabins had a designated camp name. Two of those used were Mountaineers and Millionaires.

ALWAYS SOMETHING DOING

The young adult campers enthusiastically embraced the many activities offered at the camp. They could participate in team sports such as volleyball, basketball and baseball or challenge themselves at the archery range. Water sports included canoeing and sailing. Bicycle trails were well defined as were those for horseback riding. The horseshoe court was a favorite and indoor ping-pong was enjoyed in fair or foul weather. Weekly individual competitions were held in all the sporting events and the winners were invited back for a free weekend in the fall.

NEVER A DULL MOMENT, ALWAYS SOMETHING DOING AT SAGAMORE-ON-TWIN-LAKES, MILFORD, PA. 306

HONEYMOON BUNGALOWS AT SAGAMORE

Honeymooners were welcome! In keeping with the camp's theme of "for the fun of it," jingle bells or old cowbells would be tied to the bottom of the honeymooners' beds.

HONEYMOON BUNGALOWS, SAGAMORE-ON-TWIN-LAKES, MILFORD, PA.   322

ONE OF THE MEN'S BUNGALOWS, SAGAMORE-ON-TWIN-LAKES, MILFORD, PA.   310

CHIEF

Camp Sagamore was an immensely popular tourist retreat in the 1940s. At that time there were more than sixty buildings including cabins, offices and halls for recreation and dining. The appeal of a camping vacation was popular until the early 1960s. The camp closed in 1961 and the property was sold in 1964. A portion of the property would become present-day Sagamore Estates.

The word sagamore means "a subordinate chief among the Algonquians of North America" and roads in the future Sagamore Estates would bear Native American names.

FIRST CAMPERS AT TWIN LAKES

AEROPLANE VIEW OF CAMP SHAWNEE, TWIN LAKES, PIKE COUNTY, PENNA.

Camp Shawnee was located near the western shore of the Little Twin Lake. Prior to the establishment of Camp Shawnee, George Fluhr tells us about the first campers at Twin Lakes: "In 1886 the Wells family of Port Jervis purchased property at the lake and began going there on regular vacations. Each summer, at Port Jervis, they would fill a railroad boxcar with tents, canoes, cooking utensils, food, clothing and blankets. They would arrange for it to be brought to a siding at Parker's Glen where they would be met by a horse and wagon in which they traveled up to the lake." Eventually the Wells family constructed a summer home. Presently, Peter and Alice Jane Loewrigkeit own this property, located at 132 Between the Lakes Road. By the turn of the century several families had established summer homes, or as they called them, "camps," at the Brink Ponds. In 1894 Stephen Crane, author of the Civil War novel The Red Badge of Courage, spent the month of August at Camp Interlaken (between-the-lakes) camping in tents with twenty-seven friends.

CAMP SHAWNEE

In 1921 Samuel D. Parry established a boy's camp for "young Christian gentleman" on the west shore of Little Brink Pond and named it Camp Shawnee. It could accommodate eighty-five boys and boys from age six to sixteen were eligible to attend. The boys were divided into two groups, the Browns and the Whites. These groups competed with each other in sports. Track and field events were held. Swimming competitions and canoe races were staged. After supper the boys played games of softball or capture the flag.

Barry Culin was hired as a riding instructor but, in 1928, was promoted to Camp Director. In 1932 he married Janet, Mr. Parry's daughter. John Moore and Willard (P.D.) McCullough were campers who became camp counselors and, in later years, Twin Lakes property owners. The camp flourished until World War II, but closed in 1944.

The building pictured in the postcard was the main house at Camp Shawnee. The Parry family lived on the second floor. The first floor contained the camp kitchen and the large porch was used as the camp dining room.

Camp Shawnee, Twin Lakes, Pa.

CULIN COTTAGES

When Camp Shawnee closed in 1944, Barry Culin decided to turn the camp buildings into housekeeping cottages. He called his business Culin Cottages. After Barry's death in 1954, Janet Culin continued to rent the cottages. She later sold the property to her niece Betty Miller and husband, Bob Miller. They continued the business but renamed it Shawnee Cottages.

In 1979 a group of eight people represented by Roy Perper and Ed Nikles bought the thirty-two acre business. The group obtained subdivision approval and built roads. A tennis court was added, the softball field was moved and the beach created. Twin Lake Preserve was established.

Along the shore at Camp Shawnee, Twin Lakes, Pa.

DURHAM'S LOAFERS LODGE

The information on the back of this card tells us it is "Durham's Loafers Lodge, Twin Lakes, Pike Co, PA." Aura May Durham is writing from Winter Haven, Florida to her friend, Ethel Wolf, of Harford Street, Milford to tell her she will be in Milford April 5 or 6, 1963. She is asking her friend to make reservations for her for the Historical Society Dinner.

This card affords the reader a good view of Big and Little Twin Lakes. It is also quite interesting to note that Aura May Durham is the great, great, great granddaughter of Israel Wells. The ancestral line is Israel to Nathan to Henry B. Wells to Joann Wells Sawyer to Aura May Sawyer Durham to Aura May Durham.

On the Road to "The Watson",
Twin Lakes, Pike Co., Pa.

WATSON HOUSE

Circa 1891 the Watson family of Port Jervis, NY purchased five acres of land on Little Brink Pond. Like the Wells family, they soon replaced their camping tents with summer cottages. Their son, L.B. Watson, an avid outdoorsman, took the concept of a summer sojourn at the pond one step further. In 1905 he built a small lake-front hotel that would eventually become one of the largest in the area.

GUESTS

In the ad in the "1906 Summer Homes An Illustrated Guide to Summer Homes in Pike County, Pennsylvania on the Erie Railroad" we are told: "The Watson on the shore of Twin Lake. 50 guests; per week $7 to $10; children, servants and season rates on application; per day $1.50; 4 miles from station; conveyance 50 cents." The station being referred to here is the Parker's Glen Railroad Station.

ROAD NEAR "THE WATSON"   TWIN LAKES, PA.

1937

POST OFFICE

Mr. Watson's hotel and the area around Big and Little Brink Ponds continued to attract a growing number of summer visitors. Mr. Watson decided the area needed a post office to accommodate them. When filling out an application for one, he was asked to give the name of the village. He did not think Brink Ponds accurately described the lakes, so he wrote in Twin Lakes. The name Twin Lakes had been previously used by the Wells family to describe the area.

"The Watson"
Twin Lakes, Pike Co. Pa. Aug 15th to 29th/08

EXPANSION

According to George Fluhr: "By 1911 additions had been made. Watson's Hotel, by then known as the Watson House, more than tripled its original size. It could boast of hot and cold water at the end of each hall, and oil lamps and a water pitcher and bowl in each room. (The privy was still outdoors.) With 42 rooms it could accommodate 120 people with prices ranging from seven to ten dollars a week. As chef they hired Frank vanCampen, who had previously worked for the Pinchot family in Milford and who would later accompany Theodore Roosevelt on a trip to western United States."

The Watson, Twin Lakes, PIKE COUNTY, Pa.

GIFFORD PINCHOT

Gifford Pinchot, later Governor of Pennsylvania and noted conservationist, stayed at the Watson House. With fellow students of the outdoors, he practiced techniques for determining the size and depth of the lakes. Experiments were also conducted to calculate the amount of water in the lakes. Always concerned about the danger of fire while he slept, Pinchot kept his horse tethered to his second floor window in case escape from the hotel was necessary.

"THE UPHEAVAL"

George Fluhr also tells us: "In 1916 Lionel Barrymore and Libby Knowlton arrived at the Watson House to make a movie called The Upheaval. Young Brant Watson was paid fifty cents to row a bear and its trainer across the lake to the movie set location. It was a hot day; the bear became excited, bit his trainer, and chased an actress off the dock. Watson, frightened by the scene refused to row the bear back. Watson also had the job each evening of driving Lionel Barrymore to Milford to use the nearest long-distance telephone. Barrymore was very concerned about his polio-stricken son."

Twin Lakes seen from the Watson, Pike Co., Pa.

ANOTHER SEASON

In an invitation to visit, Mr. Watson writes: "Announcing Another Season. The Watson again offers you a most cordial welcome and an invitation to visit this delightful and attractive mountain resort. The house is situated on the shore of beautiful Twin Lakes, at an altitude of 1500 feet. Here you will find relaxation, entertainment, and a degree of sociability seldom found elsewhere. By appointment, we meet trains stopping at Parkers Glen, Pa; also Short Line Bus Station at Sawkill, Pa. Tri States Bus Line meets trains at Port Jervis, N.Y. and brings guests direct to the house. Most direct auto route from New York is via Branchville, N.J. and Milford, Pa. Five miles west of Milford on route No. 6 turn right at Twin Lakes sign."

"THE WATSON." OVERLOOKING TWIN LAKES. PIKE COUNTY, PA.

SEVENTY FIVE YEARS

The Watson family welcomed guests to the Watson House for nearly seventy-five years. The hotel closed in 1967 and was dismantled in 1969. Some of the lumber was reused during the construction of the Kindgom Hall of Jehovah Witnesses located on Route 6.

AUGUST TAMPIER

Spring Brook Mountain House, August Tampier, Propr., Shohola Falls, Pike Co., Pa.

Tom Coleman, Jr. shared information about the Spring Brook Mountain House. He, as a young man, remembers August Tampier as a man in his 80s with a "big white beard." Tom also remembers August Tampier's daughter, Josie. She helped her father run the boarding house and married one of the boarders, Victor Maeran. Mr. Maeran later became a Dingman Township Roadmaster. The Spring Brook Mountain House was on Spring Brook Road on the right at the top of a hill about two miles from Route 6. At the bottom of the hill on the left was the schoolhouse. The House burned and the schoolhouse was converted to a private residence.

WEHEINGER'S BAR AND GRILL

Wehinger's Bar and Grill was located on Route 6 West at a junction locally called Roosevelt Corners. Thomas C. McKean and his wife Joan A. remember that Tom's father, Cleveland McKean, had the roadhouse built in the 1920s. The establishment consisted of a bar, restaurant, gas station and, in a separate building, a boarding house. The boarding house was located to the immediate west of the building pictured here but burned in the 1950s. Cleveland and his wife, Jennie Pedley McKean, operated the business for some time during which Jennie's chicken dinners became widely popular. Later, Cleveland leased the business to his sister Florence Wehinger and her husband George. They continued to offer good food and added Schmidt's beer. Mel's Tavern now occupies the building.

BUBBLING SPRINGS • 1044 ROUTE 6

In 1944, Frank and Mary Agnes Hazen bought the Bubbling Springs property from George Cadoo. Their daughter, Mary Veronica Hazen, and their son, James, who became postmaster after World War II and later a fish and game warden, and their son, Eugene, who was a PennDOT foreman, helped with the businesses. They had a restaurant, gas station and post office. In those days, before I-84, Route 6 was heavily traveled and the Hazens had a successful establishment. Mary Veronica remembers when an ambassador to India stopped in with his young son. His son wanted and received a boat ride on the Bubbling Springs Pond.

Bubbling Springs
Shohola Falls - Pa

Red Brook Farm, Shohola Falls, Pa.

RED BROOK FARM • 840 ROUTE 6

Hank Arneburg owned Red Brook Farm. He operated a restaurant, gas station, post office and rental cabins at the property on Route 6 West, eight miles from Milford. He sold the business to Joseph Weidner. The Weidner family had two sons, Joseph Paul, known as "Paul" in his youth and by "Joe" as an adult, and David. Tom Coleman remembers Paul with whom Tom was a schoolmate. The Weidners sold the property to Mike and Ada Kruk. They rebuilt the main structure and operated it as Red Brook Restaurant.

Jim and Helen Martin bought the property. Jim has the J&M Motorcycle Shop and Helen operates an ice cream stand called "The Ice Cream Stop."

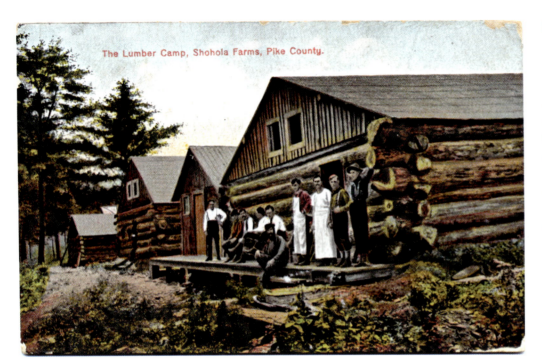

The Lumber Camp, Shohola Farms, Pike County.

PENNSYLVANIA COAL COMPANY

In a conversation with Lucy Brooks regarding the history of the Shohola Falls area, we concluded Garret Hart owned a lumber camp near the present day dam on the Shohola Waterfowl Preserve. Lucy remembers cabins on the side of the road that lead away from the lake. The late Ross Kleinstuber, former Dingman Township Historian, tells us the Pennsylvania Coal Company bought 800 acres near the Rattlesnake Creek in 1890. "While coal was elusive, the timber on the property was of prime value." It is therefore possible the lumber camp was owned by the Pennsylvania Coal Company. Either way, the plan was to cut logs, store them during the winter in the pond and float them down the Shohola Creek to the Delaware River in the spring.

SHOHOLA FALLS POST OFFICE

Lucy has documents that show Garret Hart was commissioned in 1890 as Postmaster for the Shohola Falls Post Office. She believes the post office may have been located, for a short period of time, in the home she and her husband Kenny now own next to the log cabin post office structure.

Garret Hart owned the house at the time and lived there with his mother, Nellie, and wife, Gertrude. After Mr. Hart became ill and could no longer function as Postmaster, the post office was relocated to Red Brook Farm and Hank Arneburg took over as Postmaster. Later, when Mr. Arneburg sold the Red Brook property, the post office was moved to the Hazen's at Bubbling Springs. Eventually, it was moved across Route 6 to Warncke's Five Gables Bar & Restaurant, now Peter's Restaurant owned by Peter Jajcay at 1023 Route 6.

Post Office, Shohola Falls, Pa.

OWEGO TURNPIKE

This "Transportation, Old and New Way, Shohola Falls, Pa" picture was probably taken on the old Owego Turnpike which was built in 1804. The road ran from Milford to Owego, NY. Owego is derived from an Iroquois word AH-WA-GA which means "where the valley widens." George Fluhr tells us that Grant Irwin, in his article on the Owego Turnpike, says that US Route 6 roughly follows the Owego Turnpike route with some exceptions. One of these happens in Milford where the Owego Turnpike goes past Grey Towers and Route 6 takes a less steep curving path out of town.

Transportation, Old and New Way, Shohola Falls, Pa.

ROOSEVELT HIGHWAY BRIDGE OVER SHOHOLA FALLS CREEK, NEAR MILFORD, PA.

120476

ROOSEVELT HIGHWAY

In 1926 work was begun on the Grand Army of the Republic Memorial Highway, also known as Route 6 and also known as Roosevelt Highway, in honor of Theodore Roosevelt. It is the longest US route in the country. It traverses 3652 miles and terminates in California. The opening of this road was celebrated in Milford with a dinner at the Bluff House on July 9, 1927. W.E. Anderson of Hawley was toastmaster. Gifford Pinchot and Judge Shull gave speeches.

Lucy Brooks says this is the "old" bridge which followed a difficult curve in the road. She remembers when a tractor-trailer crashed into the side of the bridge and dumped its cargo of hundreds of cans of Maxwell House Coffee into the Shohola Brook. People came from miles around to salvage the coffee cans, most of which were not damaged in the accident. She and her husband knew of a pool in the stream, headed in that direction and ended up with an impressive supply of free coffee!

THE KNOB

73 Looking down Broad Street from Post Office, Milford, Pa.

The Knob, seen here at the end of Broad Street, has always been a favorite blip on Milford's southern horizon. In 1898 during the Spanish-American War there was great patriotic fervor in Milford. Flags were raised daily in all parts of town and, led by Thomas and Lance Armstrong, funds were raised to erect a sixty-foot high flagpole on the knob. From this pole flew an American flag measuring twenty feet by thirty feet. In more recent times the Milford Lions Club has established a tradition of putting a lighted star on the Knob for Christmas and a lighted cross for Easter.

LOU DE BERLHE'S GARAGE

Straight ahead in this picture below the Knob was the location of Lou de Berlhe's Garage. In 1904 Louis de Berlhe, who had previously run a bicycle repair shop at 110 Broad Street, began specializing in auto repair. He also became an agent for Cadillac and Northern, selling their automobiles. It is interesting to note that those who bought Mr. de Berlhe's cars, as well as others, were now subject to regulations. One stipulated that the automobile must be registered with the county prothonotary and a speed limit of eight miles per hour was set for boroughs. Auto operators also had to stop at the signal of a driver of a horse drawn vehicle until the latter had passed. Additionally, a horn or other audible device had to be sounded at crossings.

Broad Street, Milford, Pa.

HORSELESS CARRIAGE

Norman Lehde writes in the Heritage: 250 book regarding the citizens of Milford and the automobile as the 1800s end: "The people of Milford were already seeing changes take place. On June 1, 1899 the first automobile, a Winton, driven by W.W. Scranton of Scranton, Pa., the father of former Governor William W. Scranton and the grandfather of the present Lt. Governor, made an appearance in Milford. This horseless carriage which could attain a speed of fully 30 miles an hour was a novel attraction at the time and even a subject of some ridicule. But the handwriting was on the stable door."

VIEW OF BROAD STREET, MILFORD, PA.

PINCHOT HOMESTEAD

Cyrille Pinchot built a home for his family at the corner of Broad and Harford Streets in 1824. The house is the oldest Pinchot dwelling in Milford and three generations of Pinchots made it their home.

From
Susie
Sept. 6. 1905

Homestead Free Library.

LIBRARY

Cyrille Pinchot died in 1873 and his son James inherited the Homestead. James lived with his wife Mary and their three children Gifford, Antoinette and Amos at Two Gramercy Park in New York City. They used the Homestead in Milford as a summer home until 1886 when their new summer home, Grey Towers, was completed.

Later, reflecting the same generosity toward his community displayed by his family in the past, James Pinchot decided to turn the Homestead into a public library. Ed Brannon, retired Director of Grey Towers, tells us the building was used as a library from 1903 to 1926 by Yale University School of Forestry summer camp students. During this time Harry Graves, Yale's first Dean of Forestry, had his summer office on the second floor.

LIBRARY BOOKS

The Pinchot family was committed to the idea of a well stocked, free public library for the people of the Milford area. This generosity included a donation of new books. According to the May 10, 1901 edition of "The Pike County Press" James asked Reverend C. B. Carpenter to help him achieve this goal: "Reverend C.B. Carpenter was in New York last week to select books for the Milford Library to be established by James W. Pinchot and has purchased about 1,200 volumes."

Homestead Free Library.

HOMESTEAD FREE LIBRARY

Circa 1902 Mrs. Amos Pinchot, the former Gertrude Minturn, helped organize the library. She stocked the shelves with the books donated by James and Mary as well as with volumes from other members of the the Pinchot family. She assisted in the furnishing and decorating of the rooms and turned the warm and welcoming Pinchot family homestead into an equally appointed Homestead Free Library.

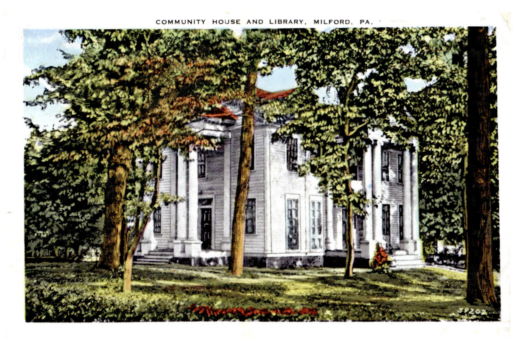
COMMUNITY HOUSE AND LIBRARY, MILFORD, PA.

COMMUNITY HOUSE

According to Cynthia Van Lierde in "Historic Sites of Milford," all other heirs to the Pinchot homestead relinquished their interests to Gifford Pinchot and on July 1, 1924 Gifford deeded the home to the newly formed Community House Association. The Association accepted responsibility for maintenance of the house and property and agreed with the stipulation that the home would continue to function as a free public library. In 1928 the Pike County Commissioners recognized the library as a county institution and began a yearly donation that would assist with its growth. A law enacted in 1931 by Governor Gifford Pinchot made state funds available to libraries assuring that growth would continue. In 1980 an organization called Friends of the Library was formed with Mary Sabel serving as President and Miriam Siegel serving as Vice President for the purpose of promoting and expanding services offered by the library. This group continues to host fund-raising activities.

The Community House, corner of Broad and Harford Streets, Milford, Pa. was built in 1824 as the private home of the Pinchot family.

Today it is the home of the Pike County Library and the Historical Society.

PIKE COUNTY HISTORICAL SOCIETY

COMMUNITY HOUSE ASSOCIATION

J. Edson Myer had written a chronicle of the Community House Association for the Heritage: 250 book published in 1983. The Association had begun sixty years before when a group of citizens contributed $100 each to form the charter. Mr. Myer mentions two of the charter members, Miss Ethel Noyes Barckley and Frank P. Ludwig. He goes on to mention many of the officers of the Community House Association Board of Trustees as well as their accomplishments. The present board officers are: Jennifer Bennett, President; Arthur Ridley, Vice President; Jane Ridley, Secretary and William Fleming, Treasurer. The community House Association depends on donations to maintain the building and grounds.

COMMUNITY CHRISTMAS

Each December the Community House Association gives the community a chance to come together and start the celebration of the Christmas season. There is a tree lighting ceremony, a sing-along and refreshments.

NORMANDY COTTAGE

The Normandy Cottage was built in 1903 by James Pinchot for his son Amos. It was constructed on land which had originally sustained the Pinchot family garden. Cyrille's wife Eliza had taken great pride in the family flower garden and is historically noted as the propagator of what is now called the Milford Rose. The original rose bush was brought from Grasse in southern France to New York City by friends of the Pinchot family. Eliza was given a part of the bush which she planted in her garden. Every summer she gave cuttings from the bush to friends and neighbors and soon the Rose of Grasse flourished in many Milford gardens. It was eventually referred to as the Milford Rose and the small fragrant pink blooms can still be seen in Milford today.

TUDOR REVIVAL

The Cottage is considered to be Tudor Revival and is architecturally and texturally interesting. The roof has fish-scale slate shingles while blue stone is used for the chimney and corners. The walls are made of rubble stone with half-timbering stucco. The overhang features glass decorations believed to be bottoms of glass bottles.

87 Normandy Cottage, Milford, Pa.

Normandy Cottage and Pinchot Homestead Free Library, Milford, Pa.   12729

FIRST POST OFFICE

On January 1, 1803 Milford became the site of the first post office established in what was then Wayne County. A bluestone building designed by the architectural firm of Hunt and Hunt was erected at the northeast corner of Broad and Harford Streets to serve as the Milford Post Office. Hugh Ross, who later became an occasional preacher at the Methodist services and whose voice could be heard one-half mile away, was named as postmaster. The postal rates were based more on the distance a letter was to be carried than its weight. The rate for a letter consisting of a single piece of paper was, with less than 40 miles to travel, 8 cents; less than 90 miles, 10 cents; less than 150 miles, 12 cents; less than 300 miles, 17 cents; less than 500 miles, 20 cents and more than 500 miles, 25 cents.

MILFORD POST OFFICE

A 1923 advertisement for the United States Post Office at Milford, PA tells us Walter V. Dingman was Postmaster and August Metz, Jr. was assistant. The incoming mail schedule was 9:45 AM, 11:00 AM, 1:00 PM and 6:45 PM. The outgoing mail schedule was 8:05 AM, 11:00 AM, 1:15 PM and 3:20 PM. The postal patron was urged to "Buy Treasury Savings Certificates."

K 2667. Post Office and Forrest Hall looking up Broad St., MILFORD, Pa. (Germany)

PROHIBITION

Prohibition ended in 1933 and on Thursday, April 5 of that year postal employee Charles Hanna and garage operator Dorie Fuller drove to Allentown, PA to buy the first legal beer. One minute after midnight they procured a keg and brought it back to Milford!

FOREST HALL, MILFORD, PA.   6306

Published by C. O. Armstrong.

Forest Hall. Milford, Pa.

With best wishes from Lillie Bridge.

No. 1225 Moore & Gibson Co., New York. Germany

YALE UNIVERSITY

After the Yale Forestry School summer camping program had begun at Grey Towers, it became apparent that classrooms and a lecture hall would be needed for the students. James Pinchot wanted to site the hall next to the post office building on Broad Street. In order to accomplish this he purchased two existing buildings located next to the post office building on Broad Street.

Broad Street, Milford, Pa.

FROM BROAD TO HARFORD

One of the buildings had been used as a barber shop and the other as a telegraph and telephone office. Both of these buildings were relocated to West Harford Street. One, located at 107 West Harford Street, was used for many years by Violet Terwillger Clune as a newsstand and telegraph office. It presently houses The Velveteen Habit, a dress shop owned by Mariama Law. The second building was destroyed in a fire.

Forest Hall and Post Office, Milford, Pa.

FOREST JOINS POST OFFICE

Once again James Pinchot used the architectural firm of Hunt and Hunt to conceive plans for Forest Hall. Friends of James Pinchot, they had designed Grey Towers as well as the post office building, next to which the hall would be built. The building contract was awarded to E.S. Wolfe in 1904. Mr. Wolfe was contractually instructed to make the new building correspond to the existing building.

FOREST HALL

According to Cynthia Van Lierde in "Historic Sites in Milford:" "Specifications called for the floors to be on the same level. Second story windows were to be of the same height and width. Niches in the new building were to follow the design and detail of niches in the Post Office Building. The entrance to the new building was to be similar in detail to the Post Office entrance, but to have double doors. Cellar steps were to be made of four-inch bluestone, as were the chimneys. The chimneys were to be carried full size to the bottom of the cellar. Another dummy chimney was to be built on the end of the wall next to the Post Office Building and to be started at the roof lines and run up."

Forest Hall on Broad St., Milford Pa.

No. 32548. Published by the Bazaar. (Printed in Germany).

K. 3101 Forrest Hall Building and Post Office Milford Pike Co. Pa.
Artino post cards New York City, & Germany.

SLATE ROOF

Fieldstone for the structure was purchased from the Foster Hill Farm and slate for the roof was secured in Newton, New Jersey at Slateworks. The three medallions on the front of Forest Hall reflect the Pinchots' fields of interest. They are the likenesses of Bernard Palissy, artist, sculptor and philosopher, Andre Michaux, who studied and wrote about the trees of North America in the Nineteenth Century, and the soldier-statesman Lafayette.

Please note that Forest Hall never had a red roof. When this postcard was printed and hand tinted in Germany, the artist gave it a red roof.

FOREST HALL, MILFORD, PA.

PIKE COUNTY HISTORICAL SOCIETY

When the Yale Forestry School summer program was moved to New Haven, Connecticut in 1926, the Pinchot family allowed the community to use the building. Various events were held there and in 1930 the newly formed Pike County Historical Society opened their museum in the building. Governor Pinchot served as honorary president and each of the thirteen municipalities in Pike County had a representative at the initial meeting on April 29, 1930. They had collected more than two hundred historical items for display and the public was invited to come to Forest Hall on Saturday afternoons to see the artifacts.

Forest Hall is presently owned by Reggie Cheong-Leen and Peter Spielhagen. They operate an antique shop on the second floor.

FOREST BUILDING AND BROAD STREET, MILFORD, PA.

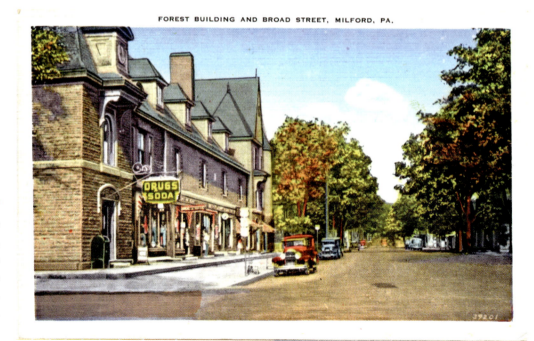

STRIPPEL'S DRUGSTORE

In 1934 Chester Strippel opened his drugstore in a part of the post office building located at 202 Broad Street. His store had a soda fountain where both children and adults enjoyed the many treats offered by Mr. Strippel. When the post office relocated, Mr. Strippel expanded his store and ran his successful business until 1967. Today the Up River shop, owned by Kevin Holley, is located in Strippel's original store.

GRAND UNION

The Globe Store opened in the Forest Hall building on March 8, 1922. This store was later acquired by the Grand Union Company and was operated under the management of Frank Murphy. Mr. Murphy hired fifteen year old Norman "Red" Helms of Milford to stock shelves. Red was a dedicated employee who stayed with the company for more than fifty years. In 1961 the Grand Union relocated to the site of the current Rite Aid Drug Store. Frank Murphy retired in January 1970 and Red was named manager. A new Grand Union was built in 1979 at 501 West Harford Street from which Red retired in 1995. Red's younger brother Lee, also hired by Frank Murphy, worked as a grocery manager for the Grand Union Company for thirty-six years. Other businesses once located in the Forest Hall building include Luhrs Hardware and Bridals by Vicki. Today the building is home to The Artery Fine Art & Fine Craft Gallery and the Dona-Helene Hair and Nail Salon.

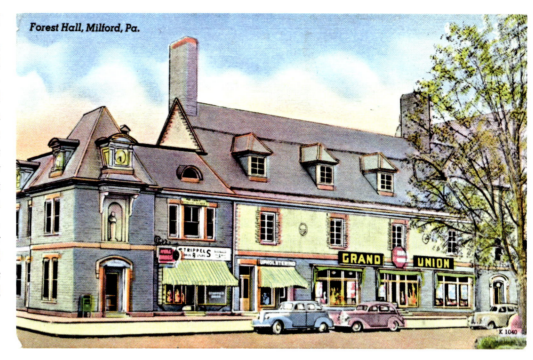

Forest Hall, Milford, Pa.

The Grace Bakery and Donut Bar
Milford, Penna.

REVOYRE BAKERY

Norman Lehde, in his Pike County History, recalls: "On December 16, 1929, Joseph A. Revoyre died at the age of 59. Never married, his death was the first break in the family-operated bakery in Milford after 56 years." The Revoyre Bakery at 221 Broad Street became the Grace Bakery under the ownership of Rudy and Grace Schleutermann who expanded it to include a Donut Bar. When the Schleutermann family relocated to Flordia, Dietrich and Jean Paul operated their Paul's Pastry and Coffee Shop at the location. In 1987 John Brennick bought the property and replaced the existing structure with a three story brick building. Mr. Brennick ran a facility for people recovering from head injuries and he used the building as classroom space for his clients. When Joe Biondo later bought the property the building was designated as the Biondo Building and became the home of Arthur K. Ridley, Esq. Law Office. The Center for Developmental Disabilities, CDD, founded by Marion Almquist, also has an office in the building.

VIEW OF BROAD STREET, MILFORD, PA.

BEN KYTE'S STORE

On the right-hand side of this card you will see the entrance to Ben Kyte's General Store at 225 Broad Street. Coffee, sugar, oatmeal and crackers were kept in large barrels, as was molasses. Apparently molasses was one of the most challenging products to sell. People brought their own jugs that had to be filled via a spigot on the molasses barrel, also known as a hogshead. There was no way to fill these jugs without the proprietor getting the sticky stuff all over his hands!

TITUS REAL ESTATE

Allen Titus, a real estate agent and insurance broker, had an office at 222 Broad Street. He was married to Gene-Anne Buchanan, great-great granddaughter of George (Bowhannon) Buchanan. Gene-Anne, a Cornell University School of Business graduate, helped her husband with his business. Mr. Titus was also an airplane pilot best known for his aerial photographs of the Milford area.

EMMA WOLFE'S TEA ROOM

In an advertisement Mrs. Wolfe called her establishment a "French Tea Room." She offered "a la carte service" and "Table d'Hote Dinner." In 1952 Harry and Emma Wetmore leased the business and continued in the tradition of Emma Wolfe. Lorraine Gregory remembers this second Emma, who was well known for her sweet rolls and homemade pies. John Misenhelder remembers farther back to when the building housed Benedict's Specialty Store. He can recall the ad they used one Christmas: "A Merry Christmas and many more are the wishes galore from Benedict's Specialty Store."

MILFORD COFFEE SHOPPE

In 1963 Kate and Elmer Herring, who had a summer home not far from Milford on the Delaware River, sold their Sweet Shop in New Jersey and bought the former tea room. Mr. and Mrs. Herring successfully operated the Milford Coffee Shoppe on Broad Street for ten years until relocating to the edge of town. The First National Bank subsequently bought the property and had the building razed in September 1972.

FIRST NATIONAL BANK OF PIKE COUNTY

In 1900 Ebenezer Warner persuaded four Milford men to join with him to apply for a charter to establish the First National Bank of Milford. Henry B. Wells, owner of the Bluff House, Adam D. Brown, proprietor of the Homestead, William Mitchell, owner of Mitchell's General Store, and Robert Warner Reid, grandson of Ebenezer, agreed to do so and the First National Bank of Milford became a reality.

The original bank office was located in a section of the T. Armstrong and Company General Store now known as the Bloomgarden Building. In 1907 the bank was moved to Forest Hall. In 1929 they moved to their newly completed building at 224 Broad Street.

The building is presently the home of Wachovia Bank.

THE LUNCH WAGON

Raymond McCollum is credited with establishing the first diner in Milford at 301 Broad Street. After operating it for a short time, he sold the business to Clarence and Mrs. Glen Musselwhite on March 12, 1928. They passed the management of it to Graham and Lillian Musselwhite.

Mrs. Ethel (Glen) Musselwhite says that this picture of the Milford Diner is as it looked in 1946.

Local people originally affectionately referred to the Milford Diner as "The Lunch Wagon." Photo courtesy of Matt Osterberg.

MILFORD DINER, CIRCA 1948

Graham and Lillian Musselwhite advised the public in their ad that "Johnnie says 'the food is Pike County's finest.'" "Johnnie" referred to John Ridley, a short-order cook at the diner.

The Musselwhites originally kept the diner open twenty-four hours a day, every day. Many Milfordites took advantage of the good food and late hours by stopping in for an early breakfast after a Friday or Saturday night out. It was not uncommon to hear "meet you at the diner" as a late night function in town came to an end.

The diner was also a popular stopping place for tractor-trailer drivers and before Route 209 was closed to most truck traffic, big rigs would be parked all along Broad Street.

THE DON BUDGE GRAND SLAM

The next generation of Musselwhites, Danny and Colleen, helped to keep the diner in the family for many years. The Musselwhites fostered a friendly, family atmosphere that combined with good food and good service to ensure return customers. One of the "regulars" who ate at the diner was world renowned tennis champion Don Budge. Mr. Budge had a home in Dingmans Ferry and his frequent visits to the diner inspired Danny Musselwhite to add "The Don Budge Grand Slam" meal to his breakfast menu. It consisted of two pancakes, two sausage links, two eggs, two strips of bacon, two pieces of toast and coffee. Don Budge and fans were present at a ceremony held at the diner when John Phelps presented the Musselwhites with a tennis racquet-clock he had made in Budge's honor.

The Musselwhites built the new diner pictured here in 1973. Presently the diner is owned by Peter and George Rigas and George Cattes. They advertise their business as the place "where good friends meet to eat."

FIRST PRESBYTERIAN CHURCH

PRESBYTERIAN CHURCH, MILFORD, PA.

According to Bill Attick, writing for the <u>Heritage-250</u> book: "On April 18, 1822, a petition, signed by Jacob Quick, Francis Smith, John Lafarge, John Brink, George Bowhannon and D. Jayne, was presented to the state for a charter for 'The Presbyterian Congregation of Milford.' It was enrolled in Harrisburg, February 12, 1824."

First Presbyterian Church. Milford, Pa.

No. 1257   Moore & Gibson Co., New York.   Germany

CORNERSTONE LAID

Credit is given to Moses Bross for conducting prayer meetings in the Pike County Court House, now the Pike County Sheriff's office. On September 25, 1825, Reverand Grier of the Presbytery of Hudson preached a sermon and ordained three ruling elders: James Wallace, Moses Bross and Jacob Quick, Esq. Eventually, the County Court House became too small for the growing congregation. This resulted in the original Presbyterian Church being built where the manse is presently located. On March 23, 1873, the congregation decided by "unanimous vote to build a brick church, but to incur no debt." The present church site was chosen and on September 1, 1874 the cornerstone was laid with appropriate ceremony.

BELL AND CLOCK

On November 30, 1886, the Honorable William Bross, Lieutenant Governor of Illinois, who had spent his childhood in Milford, gave the church a bell. It was in memory of his father, Moses Bross, one of the founders and first elders of the church. The bell was made by Mc Neely and Company of Troy, New York. Mr. Bross also donated a tower clock made by the Seth Thomas Company of New York City in memory of his "beloved and venerated" mother.

FIRST PRESBYTERIAN CHURCH, MILFORD, PA.

SANCTUARY

On January 11, 1965, a Building Advisory Committee was formed to make recommendations regarding renovations to the First Presbyterian Church of Milford. Serving on the Committee were Chairman Bob Fish, Edith Gregory, Ronald Gregory, Lucille Stroyan, Roger Woltjen and Reverend Arthur Meissner. Renovations of the first and second floors were advised and undertaken. A recommended educational wing was added to the back of the building.

In this beautiful sanctuary on June 14, 1969, Red Helms walked his sister Shirley down the aisle to be united in holy matrimony with Raymond Orben, Jr. The Reverend Frederick Allen performed the ceremony.

Christopher Odgen took this picture of the interior of the sanctuary of the church in December 1974.

GREGORY'S GARAGE

In 1928 Amos Gregory, George's son and Skip's father, established an automobile repair business and gas station at 310 Broad Street.

CHRYSLER-PLYMOUTH DEALERSHIP

In 1934 Amos Gregory added a Chrysler-Plymouth dealership. He continued his business at this location until 1947. In March of 1947 Amos moved the garage and dealership to a new building at 106-108 West Harford Street. His brother Rondolph "Dutch" Gregory continued to operate the Mid-Town Garage at 310 Broad Street until 1977.

HERBST'S DRUG STORE

Fred J. Herbst operated The Rexall Store, Home of Jonteel, at 312 Broad Street after the building had been relocated from 403 Broad Street. According to an advertisement from 1918 Jonteel was a very popular talcum powder "perfumed with the costly odor of 26 flowers" which was sold in a black and gold tin for twenty-five cents. The store offered "Kodaks and Films, Cigars, Cigarettes and Tobacco, Soda Water and Home Made Ice Cream." Mr. Herbst also stocked stationery, Waterman's fountain pens, paperback books and four brands of popular boxed candies, including Whitman's. In later years the building became home to the A&P, McCollum's Market, Heater's Market, Village Market and Hartman's Market. Jorgenson's Deli is now at this location.

BROWN BUILDING

In 1888 A.D. Brown, owner of the Homestead Boarding House, built the Brown Building located at 314 to 324 Broad Street. He had a "Dry Goods/Groceries/Crockery/Hardware" store according to his ad in the Milford Dispatch of December 9, 1897. The First National Bank of Pike County, established in 1900, was in the building as well as A.D. Brown's office for his lumber business. In 1902, A.D. Brown sold the building to Mr. and Mrs. Louis Krawitz. In 1918 Jake Krakower took over "The Milford Bargain Store" and sold "ladies, gents and childrens" clothing and shoes. He and his family operated the store until 1934 when Mr. Krawitz's daughter Claire and her husband, Jonas Anchel, assumed ownership. The family retained ownership of the building when Claire's sister, Gertrude, and Gertrude's husband, Henry Bloomgarden, purchased the building in 1960. They continued to operate a department store and the building became known as the Bloomgarden Building. When Mrs. Bloomgarden retired in 1988, she sold the building to Tom and Jean Hoff.

"KRAKOWER'S" DEPARTMENT STORE.

MILFORD, PA.

HERBST THE DRUGGIST

Marion Wolfe Steele tells us about her grandfather, Fred J. Herbst, the druggist who served the town of Milford for forty years in three different locations. In 1925 his business at 312 Broad Street was moved across the street to 317 Broad Street to its third location.

Pharmacist Herbst was an admired local character who was easily recognizable as he wore his trademark black skullcap in the pharmacy. Herbst's homemade ice cream, a town favorite, was available in many flavors at the marble soda fountain. The secret family recipe for the ice cream was made using rich cream from the Foster Hill farm owned by his son-in-law Julio A. Santos. Fred's daughter Marion followed in her father's footsteps and became a pharmacist. She was the first woman pharmacist in Pike County when she joined her father's business. When Mr. Herbst died in 1944 Richard Williams purchased the business and redecorated the store.

WILLIAMS' APOTHECARY

Pharmacist Williams was fond of Pennsylvania Dutch Folk Art and used it to decorate. He also displayed his collection of antique pharmaceutical equipment and patrons enjoyed the individuality of the store. Mr. Williams retired in the 1950s and the building was used to house the Milford Post Office. Bill Leiser worked there part time and remembers Ray Orben, Sr. was postmaster and John Misenhelder, assistant postmaster. Other full and part time employees included Ron Gregory, Phil McCarty, George Williams, Ann Hinkel, Art Badoud, Knute Purdue and Clyde Canouse. The post office relocated to its present building at 200 West Harford Street in the 1960s, and Leonard Mattar opened Leonard's sundry store in the building. Carol Ann Sklar presently operates her Carol Ann's Linen Closet at the location.

SAWYER AUTO & REPAIR CO., MILFORD, PA.

SAWYER BUILDING

According to Norman Lehde in his Pike County History book, after World War I: "Henry Sawyer, active in the Pike County Chamber of Commerce, erected a garage and machine shop on the corner of Broad and Catharine Streets in Milford." Mr. Sawyer maintained furnished rooms on the second floor which he rented to tourists. He later converted these rooms to apartments.

SAWYER'S MOTOR INN AND FRENCH TEA ROOM

The Women's Christian Temperance Union, which had been active in Milford for many years, hoped the "tea" room would replace the "bar" room in town! Throughout the years several individuals including Raymond McCollum, Ethel [Mrs. Clarence] Musselwhite, Emile and Edna Rover and the Karl Sassman family had a restaurant business in the tea room area of the building. In September 1981 a fire seriously damaged the building; the second floor was never rebuilt after the fire. In the 1960s the area was converted to retail space. Golden Gifts Jewelry and Clockworks presently occupy the space.

Motor Inn and French Tea Room, Sawyer Building, Broad and Catherine Sts., Milford, Pa.

17,168

SAWYER'S TOURIST HAVEN

Sawyer's Tourist Haven offered everything for the visitor! His establishment was unique in that it provided automobile repair as well as food and lodging.

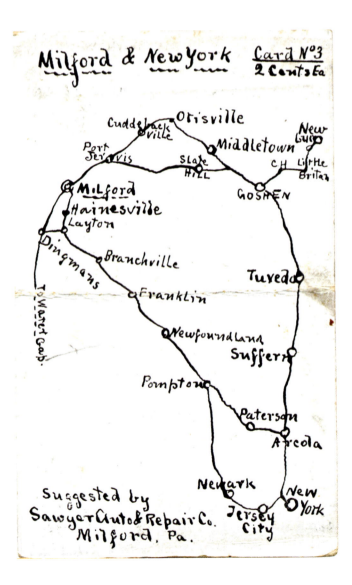

MILFORD TO NEW YORK CITY

According to Norman in the Heritage:250 book: "The stables disappeared and garages, to take care of the increasing auto traffic, opened. Learning to drive the automobile became almost mandatory and a new generation took eagerly to the steering wheel as the teamster, with his special skills, receded farther and farther into the shadows."

— 114 —

HOTEL FAUCHERE, MILFORD, PA.

LOUIS FAUCHERE

Operation of a boarding house and restaurant business at the present location of the Hotel Fauchere seems to have begun circa 1848. Jacob Sands had an establishment there which he sold to David VanGorden, who in turn sold it to Desire' Culot, a French chef circa 1852. When Desire' Culot retired he sold the business to Louis Fauchere. Fauchere had been a chef at Delmonico's in New York City. He was born in Verkey, Switzerland on March 4, 1823 one of thirteen children. His father died when he was two and one-half years old and Mathews' history book tells us he "was reared by his mother up to the age of fifteen when he began his apprenticeship as a cook, being afterward employed in various prominent hotels in Switzerland." Louis and his brother, Alphonse, came to America in 1851.

MARIE VICTORINE FAUCHERE CHOL TISSOT

On November 16, 1846, Louis married Rosalie Perrochet daughter of Francois H. Perrochet, a prominent Swiss distiller, and his wife, Henriette in Switzerland. Rosalie's aunt was married to the aforementioned Desire' Culot. Thus, in 1867, when Louis had the means to do so, he moved his family to Milford, worked as a chef for Mr. Culot and eventually bought the business. When Louis Fauchere died in 1893, Louis and Rosalie's daughter, Marie Victorine and her husband, Henri Tissot inherited the business.

Marie's first husband, Alfred Chol was a noted comedian who died in Paris in 1875 while on a business trip. They had four children: Louise, Louis, Rose and Warren. Marie married Henri Tissot in Brooklyn, New York on November 6, 1886.

HOTEL FAUCHERE & COTTAGE
MME. TISSOT, PROPRIETRESS, MILFORD, PA.
8887

HOTEL FAUCHERE

According to Beers in his <u>Commemorative Biographical Record of Northeastern Pennsylvania</u>, published in 1900: "In 1880 he built the present handsome and commodious hotel, containing twenty-four sleeping rooms and other apartments, including a beautiful dining-room at the rear of the house enclosed with glass and commanding a pleasing view. There are two cottages on the premises, one of frame, with six rooms, and the other of brick, with twelve rooms." Vicki Ciesielski, the great-great granddaughter of Louis and Rosalie Fauchere, told us the six room cottage, later called the Broome Cottage, was moved across the alley from the hotel and used to house employees. The Brick Cottage at 110 East Catherine Street was built by Louis for use by his friends and former employers, the Delmonico family.

Hotel Fauchere and Annex, Milford, Pa.

Hotel Fauchere and Annex, Milford, Pa.

THE ANNEX

In 1906 Louis Fauchere's grandson Warren Chol bought the home of Doctor H. E. Emerson located next door to the Fauchere Hotel at 403 Broad Street. It became known as the Annex. Warren Chol, his wife, Bessie Heller Chol and their four children Marie, Margaret, Louis and Ann lived there. Norman Lehde tells us in his <u>Pike County History</u> book: "In the fall of 1918 the flu epidemic caused the closing of amusement establishments, saloons, schools and other public places. A wedding between Margaret Chol and Corporal Andrew Spotts, scheduled for October 12 at the Episcopal Church in Milford had to be transferred to the home of the bride." Thus, Vickie Ciesielski's parents had the distinction of being married in the living room of the Fauchere Annex. The building had many subsequent owners and uses but present owners Sean Strub and Richard Snyder will incorporate the Annex as part of the Hotel Fauchere complex. They plan to honor the original owner and call it The Emerson House.

HOTEL FAUCHERE, MILFORD, PA.

CHEF FAUCHERE, FRENCH CUISINE

One of the signature dishes prepared by Louis Fauchere when he was the chef at his hotel was Chicken Marengo. He made it in honor of Napoleon Bonaparte, a great French hero who on June 14, 1800 had led his army in a decisive battle defeating the Austrian Army at Marengo, an Italian province of Piedmont, south of Turin. Napoleon considered it his greatest victory and associated the chicken dish made for him by his chef Dunand after the battle with a good luck talisman. After Louis' death Rosalie asked that their descendants never serve Chicken Marengo again as the honor of preparing it had belonged to Louis. Another special recipe perhaps first concocted by Louis Fauchere at his hotel was Lobster Newberg. The true origin of this dish is not apparent but food historians tend to agree the dish was perfected by Master Chef Caesar Chippani who worked at the Hotel Fauchere from 1926 until 1968.

HOTEL FAUCHERE, CIRCA 1940

According to an account by Victorine Spotts Ciesielski, named for her great-grandmother, Marie Victorine Chol Tissot, the following generations carried on the traditions of Louis Fauchere: Her grandparents, Warren and Bessie Chol; their children, Marie Olsen, Margaret Spotts, Victorine's mother; Ann Metzgar and Louis Chol. All worked to keep the Hotel Fauchere operating as a viable and profitable business in Milford. "Miss Marie" Olsen took the leadership role in managing the business and Master Chef Caesar Chippani flawlessly recreated Louis Fauchere's French cuisine. When the Fauchere closed in 1977, Louie Chol, Jr. was the hotel manager.

THE CASINO, HOTEL FAUCHERE

Victorine Ciesielski also tells us Warren Chol built the Casino at 106 East Catharine Street in the 1920s to serve as the Fauchere's dance hall. A dance band consisting of five or six instruments played five nights a week. Her cousin Helen Heller was in charge of the Casino kitchen. Guests could buy drinks at a small bar and nibble on house specialties such as Welsh rarebit and chicken salad. The big windows were pushed open for ventilation and Chinese lanterns were hung to provide festive lighting. In the 1940s the Casino was used for special events such as the annual St. Patrick's Church Farewell Party held each September. The building was razed in the late 1970s. The recently enhanced area will now serve as a parking lot for guests of the Fauchere.

The Casino, Hotel Fauchere, Milford, Pa.   13603

RESTORATION OF THE FAUCHERE

Throughout the years the Fauchere attracted wealthy, famous and fashionable people. The hotel registers reveal that among others were Sarah Bernhardt, Francis X. Bushman, Mary Pickford, Mitch Miller, Ogden Nash, Robert Young and Pennsylvania Governors Scranton and Shapp. The hotel closed in 1977. The Fauchere's historic contents and property were sold at auction in 1979. Lew Miller purchased the property and reconfigured the interior into office spaces. In 2001 Milford businessmen Richard Snyder and Sean Strub purchased the property. After a long and costly restoration of the hotel, a grand reopening was held on August 18, 2006. The Fauchere now features the Delmonico Restaurant on the main floor, the Bar Louis on the lower floor and sixteen lavishly appointed guest rooms on the upper two floors. Photograph courtesy of Jim Levell.

ORIGINAL HERBST'S DRUG STORE

This photo was taken by Eddie Rupp in 1906 in front of Herbst's Drug Store when the store was located between the Hotel Fauchere and the Emerson House [the Annex]. Fred J. Herbst established his drugstore in the former office of Dr. Henry E. Emerson in 1904. The banner in the window is advertising "Hot Soda" a concoction of hot water and baking soda offered as a cure for a stomach ache.

Looking down Broad Street, Milford, Pa.

BUILDING MOVED

In 1906 Skip's grandfather, George Gregory, purchased the Herbst Drugstore building from Warren Chol and moved it to 312 Broad Street. Skip remembers Everett Warner who lived upstairs over the drugstore telling the story of how he continued to sleep in his apartment each night even as the building was being moved!

CIVIL WAR VETERAN

This is a picture of Civil War Veteran Jacob "Jake" Schorr taken in front of the Alpine House. He drove a stagecoach for the John Findlay & Son Company and later had a livery service of his own. Jake and his wife Mary Stichler had six children; Jake, John, Frank, Lulu, Fanny and Leonard. Jake's daughter Fanny was married to Sheriff Ernest C. Wood. Leonard, the youngest son, left Milford and became Captain of the Garden City Long Island Fire Company. He and his family returned to Milford each summer for camping vacations and eventually purchased a summer home. In 1952 Leonard retired and he and his wife Louise moved to that home on Route 209 South across the road from Lorraine's family. Skip and Lorraine have always considered Len and Louise to be very special friends.

Three "Old Residenters," Milford, Pa.

THE ALPINE HOUSE

The original part of this building located at 400 Broad Street and later called the Alpine House was probably built in the late 1700s. It was known as the Old Plank House and used as an inn. Years later Netti Rupp kept an old-fashioned barroom there that featured sawdust on the floor. After Prohibition was enacted, Netti Rupp was forced to close the bar. Norman Lehde tells us the first chain store in Milford, the A&P, used the building in the 1920s. In the 1930s the building was owned by Marie Chol and her husband Ollie Olsen. They used it as their residence but Mr. Olsen also operated a beauty shop and subsequently an antique store in a portion of the home. In the 1960s after Mr. and Mrs. Olsen died Mrs. Olsen's sister Ann Metzger rented the building to the Pike County Area Agency on Aging. In 1985 Charles Lieberman and Richard Berger purchased the building and used it to house their law offices. The building was destroyed in a fire in 1988. Mr. Lieberman and Mr. Berger had the present Alpine office building constructed on the site.

EAGLE HOUSE,

MILFORD,

Pa.

R. R. Station,
Port Jervis, N. Y.

Even after the advent of the automobile, many patrons of local establishments continued to favor traveling by train to our area. They would disembark in Port Jervis, New York where they would be met by a vehicle provided by their hotel. They could also opt to use the auto stage line.

THE SWITZERLAND OF AMERICA.

Situate on the Bank of the Delaware River with picturesque scenery. Its surroundings have numerous Falls and Lakes. Falls: Sawkill, Raymondskill, Bushkill, Dingman's and Shohola, falling over rocky precipices of about 500 feet. Lakes: Sawkill, Brink, Log-Tavern, Silver and Porter's. Mountains averaging a height of 1500 feet above sea level, as High Point, High Knob, Utter's Peak, Round Top. Blue Ridge and Delaware Water Gap. Parks and Glens: Blooming Grove, Ottenheimer's, Cumming's, Shohola and Milford

Drives and Cycle Roads, Fishing, Boating and Hunting not to be excelled in any country.

Connected with said house is all modern conveniences for Bathing.

Terms reasonable and within limits of all who desire to spend the Summer vacation in a quiet town.

For further information address Box 102, Milford, Pa.

MODERN CONVENIENCES

The card tells us: "Connected with said house is [sic] all modern conveniences for Bathing." Bathing or modern, sanitary bathrooms was obviously a concern of visitors and such facilities a selling point for an establishment.

EAGLE HOUSE, CIRCA 1900

W hile not calling the area "The Switzerland of America," the Milford Chamber of Commerce does point out in its 1923 brochure: "The picturesque village rests on an elevation six hundred feet above sea level."

 The front portion of the building at 405 Broad Street was called the Eagle House. The attached portion at the rear of the building at 407 Broad Street was called the Eaglet. It ceased business as a boarding house and eventually became the residence of Doctor Ernest Kipp and his sister Ann Foster. Skip purchased the property in 1958 and converted it to office space.

EAGLE HOUSE, CIRCA 2005

M r. Robert Fish, an employee of the Federal Government as Delaware Rivermaster, had his Geological Survey Office in the building for thirty years. Bob shared information regarding his job as a Rivermaster. Historically the Commonwealth of Pennsylvania, the states of New Jersey, New York and Delaware have all had proprietary designs on the Delaware River. In 1954 by decree of the United States Supreme Court, a division of benefits each state could expect was decided. River masters were mandated by the decree and hired by the government to make certain the benefits specified in the decree were enacted. In 2005 Skip sold the building to John "Duke" Schneider.

UNION HOUSE

Centre Square Hotel, Milford, Pa.

In 1887 the Union House, owned by George Frieh, despite the best efforts of the Milford Fire Department, burned to the ground. He replaced it with the Centre Square Hotel. He had come to the Milford area to work on his father's farm in Dingman Township in 1881. Having worked previously as a chef, he was interested in running his own hotel. He married Louise J. Beck on January 11, 1888. She was a native of Milford whose father, Ernest J. Beck and mother M. Frederika Beck, were proprietors of the Vandermark Hotel. Her brother, John Beck, built Beck's Hotel in Milford. After Mr. Frieh died on June 8, 1899, Louise and their daughter, Pauline, took over the management of the Centre Square Hotel.

TERWILLIGER HOUSE

Mrs. Amanda Beck Terwilliger owned the Terwilliger House next to the Centre Square. She was Louise Frieh's sister and the two of them each had a successful business. It is said both establishments served excellent food, enhanced by the use of herbs and condiments grown in a large garden in the rear of the hotels. People from Port Jervis, as well as other areas, would bicycle to the hotels where bicycle racks were provided. In 1944 Bob Phillips, Sr. bought both hotels, combined them into one, and named the melded establishment the Tom Quick Inn. Mr. Bob Phillips, Jr. tells us while the first floors of the two hotels connect, you can walk from one hotel into the other, the upper floors do not. In order to reach the upper floors of each building you need to start on the ground floor of each and go up separate stairways! He and his wife, Joyce, operated the inn from 1950 to 1975. In 1976 Richard and Pam Lutfy bought the Tom Quick Inn and ran it until 2004.

TOM QUICK INN

These cards show the Tom Quick Inn's cocktail area, then called the Arrowhead Lounge. The main dining room was called the Pow Wow Room. The advertisement on the back of the card promises "food we are proud to serve" and "firewater."

TOM QUICK LOBBY — INDIAN PRAYER

The back of this card contains an old Indian prayer; "O Great Spirit, Maker of men, forbid that I judge any man until I have walked for two moons in his moccasins."

BACK BAR

This bar area of the Inn was referred to as the Back Bar and served as a gathering spot for Happy Hour during banquets. Individuals were invited to engrave their name into the wall using an electric wood burning tool. These names reflect a great diversity of background, career choices and nationalities.

BANQUET ROOM, CIRCA 1948

The Inn's banquet room under the capable management of Joyce Phillips and, in later years, Dick and Pam Lutfy was the favored place to hold weddings, fire company celebrations and community events. Chef Harold Castle, in charge of the kitchen staff for more than thirty years, was well known for the excellent food he served at these functions. This post card shows the banquet room set up as a gaming room providing guests with evening entertainment.

PIKE COUNTY COURT HOUSE

The Pike County Court House was built in 1872-1873. The contract was awarded to A.D. Brown. He was allowed $26,096 to build it. Later he was allowed additional funds for extra work that brought the total cost to $45,000.

COURT HOUSE, MILFORD, PA.

NEW PIKE COUNTY COURT HOUSE

The Milford Dispatch at that time reported: "Work has actually been commenced on the New Court House; between 30 and 40 men being employed excavating for the basement. The building is to be of brick and located directly in the rear of the present Court House which will be continued in use until the new structure is completed. The extreme length of the front of the building including the wings will be 120 feet and the depth of the main building 104 feet. The offices and vaults of the several officials will be located on the first floor, while the second story of the main building will be fitted up for the Courtroom...the jury rooms being located in the wings. The judges, attorneys, and criers rooms will be directly in the rear of the Court Room. The main audience room will be about 90 feet in length by 53 feet in breadth, perhaps a little more than one fourth of which space will be set apart for the Bench and Bar. All the details of the building have not been positively agreed upon, but the above is sufficiently accurate to give a general idea of the plan which will be adopted."

Court House, Milford, Pa.

212320

CIVIL WAR MORTARS

On September 21, 1942, Commissioners Lloyd J. Gumble, John W. Hornbeck and Asa B. Martin decided to sell the Civil War mortars, procured by Joseph Hart in 1896 when he had been a Member of Congress, for scrap metal. They planned to use the money for civil defense expenses. While the mortars had been delivered to Milford from Port Jervis, New York in 1896 without a problem, a tragedy occurred when trying to remove them. On October 22, 1942, Jacob A. Mencoff, President of The Port Jervis Trucking Company, while trying to move the mortars, had one of them topple over on him, crushing his left side. He was rushed to St. Francis Hospital in Port Jervis where he died.

FLAG POLE

When America entered World War I, the purchase of a flagpole for the Court House lawn was authorized for the "showing of the colors."

MILFORD HONORS ITS SERVICE MEN AND WOMEN

Please note the two bronze plaques on the courthouse. The larger plaque between the doors was presented by a group called the Village Improvement Association to Pike County to honor the men and women who had served their country in World War I. The dedication ceremony took place on October 11, 1930. The Gettysburg Chapter of the National Society Daughters of the Union 1861-1865 presented the smaller plaque to Pike County to honor Veterans of the Civil War. The ceremony was held November 11, 1936. Discernable in this picture on the far right is a signboard displaying a Roll of Honor list of people from Pike County who had served in World War II. Ralph Myer hand lettered this and other signboards that were placed on the Courthouse lawn.

Pike County Court House, Milford, Pennsylvania

COURT HOUSE, MILFORD, PA.

ELECTION BET

According to Norman Lehde in the Heritage:250 book: "After the 1928 presidential election, Louis Pulice lost a bet when Hoover was elected. He pushed Leonard Supplee from Milford to Halfway House and back again in a baby carriage. Supplee, who had backed Hoover, had a milk bottle, a cigar and a contented smile. The trip took two hours and there were many spectators along the way."

AMOS GREGORY

Milford Borough

REPUBLICAN CANDIDATE FOR

ASSOCIATE JUDGE OF PIKE COUNTY, PA.

respectfully solicits your vote and
support at the

PRIMARY ELECTION ON TUESDAY, SEPT. 9, 1941

VOTE FOR

RONDOLPH D. GREGORY

Milford, Pa.

Candidate for

ASSOCIATE JUDGE

**Your Vote and Support Respectfully Solicited
at the General Election November 8, 1949**

GREGORY FAMILY POLITICIANS

The Gregorys had a family tradition of "throwing their hat into the political ring" and many members of the family have been elected to diverse positions throughout the years. George Gregory, Skip's grandfather, served as Pike County Sheriff from 1901 through 1904. Skip's father, Amos, served as Associate Judge from 1941 through 1949. His Uncle Rondolph also held the office of Associate Judge from 1949 until 1971 and served as Pike County Prothonotary from 1972 through 1984.

COMMISSIONER RANDOLPH A. GREGORY

Skip served as Chairman of the Pike County Board of Commissioners from 1988 until 1992. He was instrumental in purchasing land in Blooming Grove Township as a site for the Pike County Jail and other offices. Commissioner Gregory had previously served as Mayor of Milford from 1979 until 1985.

**RANDOLPH A. GREGORY
REPUBLICAN CANDIDATE**

FOR

**PIKE COUNTY
COMMISSIONER**

Primary May 19, 1987

PULL LEVER 5C

YOUR VOTE AND SUPPORT WILL BE APPRECIATED

— 129 —

COMMISSIONERS DEPUY, CRELLIN AND DUFFY, 1978

Pike County Prothonotary Rondolph "Dutch" Gregory chauffeurs Commissioners Warner Depuy, Jim Crellin and Jim Duffy in a parade in Milford.

COMMISSIONERS GREGORY, GILPIN AND JONAS, 1990

Skip is driving his fellow commissioners Willis Gilpin and Margaret Mary Jonas in his 1924 Chrysler Touring Car in a parade in Milford.

PRESIDENT JUDGE HAROLD A. THOMSON

Harold A. Thomson, Jr. served as Pike County District Attorney from 1971 until 1977. In 1977 he was elected to the position of judge of the 43rd Judicial District serving Monroe and Pike Counties. He took the oath of office on January 2, 1978. Because he served both Monroe and Pike Counties his time was divided between Stroudsburg, the County Seat of Monroe County and Milford, the County Seat of Pike County. Both counties were experiencing a growth in population. In 1981 the Pennsylvania legislators and Governor responded to this growth and created the 60th Judicial District for Pike County. Judge Thomson was sworn in as President Judge of the new 60th Judicial District on August 2, 1982 making him Pike County's first full time judge. He retired on January 3, 2003 and on January 4, 2003 became a Senior Judge. He continued to be assigned full time to the Pike County Court until the election of a new judge for the 60th District took place.

HAROLD A. THOMSON, JR.
PRESIDENT JUDGE
COURT OF COMMON PLEAS
60TH JUDICIAL DISTRICT OF PENNSYLVANIA

FAX: 570-296-6054
E-MAIL: court60@ptd.net

PIKE COUNTY COURTHOUSE
MILFORD, PA 18337
570-296-6216

JOSEPH F. KAMEEN
PRESIDENT JUDGE
COURT OF COMMON PLEAS
60TH JUDICIAL DISTRICT OF PENNSYLVANIA

PIKE COUNTY COURTHOUSE
FAX: (570) 296-6054
E-MAIL: court60@pikepa.org

410 BROAD STREET
MILFORD, PA 18337
(570) 296-6216

PRESIDENT JUDGE JOSEPH A. KAMEEN

Joseph A. Kameen served as assistant district attorney from 1994 to 2000. In 2000 he was named first assistant district attorney. During his tenure he tried more cases than any other prosecutor and holds the County record for the highest conviction rate. He was elected as a Republican Committeeman-at-large in 2002. President Judge Joseph A. Kameen took the bench on January 2, 2004.

In 2005 the Pennsylvania Legislature enacted a bill signed by the Governor that provides for a second Pike County Judge to be elected in 2007.

Pike County Jail and Court House, Milford, Pa.

220891

PIKE COUNTY

The territory which is recognized today as Pike County was, at one time, part of a much larger designation of land called Bucks County. This comprised most of the Eastern portions of Pennsylvania from Philadelphia north to Scranton. Ultimately, Bucks County was subdivided, and Pike County, named for Zebulon Montgomery Pike, a famed American general and explorer, was formed. Pike County was officially designated on March 26, 1814 and a scramble began immediately as to the location of the County Seat. According to Norman Lehde: "One must recognize the importance of being a county seat to a small rural community in the late eighteenth century. It just about insured permanent status for the community. Such designation assured not only the erection of county buildings and law offices, but created a need for lodging facilities for jurors and other persons involved in court business. This was a time of slow travel often seriously affected by weather conditions."

COUNTY SEAT

There was a great deal of controversy involved in the selection of the Seat and many towns in the newly formed county petitioned the Commonwealth of Pennsylvania for the honor. But the citizens of Milford stopped talking, opened their purses and quickly donated $1,500 toward the cost of building a court house. Judge John Biddis donated the land; newly elected County Commissioners Hezekiah Bingham, Cornelius Case and John Lattimore levied taxes and hired Daniel Dimmick, Jacob Quick and Samuel Anderson to build it. They used local stone in the construction and it has the distinction of being the second oldest courthouse in the Commonwealth. When construction of the new courthouse was completed in 1873, this building was converted for use as the county jail.

Pike County Jail, Milford, Pa.

HANGING

There was only one court-ordered hanging at the jail. Herman Schultz, a resident of New York City, had followed his estranged wife, Lizzie, to a boarding house in Shohola where she was working. An argument was heard between the two and she was found dead from a single gunshot wound to her head. A jury found Mr. Schultz guilty and he was hanged in the jail, with the rope attached to the roof rafters, at 11:15 AM on Tuesday, December 7, 1897.

On a lighter note, in August of 1923, three prisoners, Eugene Panza, John Goodal and Lawrence Carnivale, "escaped" from the jail. A half hour later, Sheriff Wood found the three hiding in the cupola!

JAIL, MILFORD, PA.

MA AND PA JAIL

When the courthouse was converted in 1873 to serve as the jail, some steps were taken to make the accommodations in the building comfortable for the resident warden and his family. Retired Sheriff Harry Geiger remembers the Pike County Jail as one of the last ma and pa jails in Pennsylvania when the warden/chief deputy lived with his family at the jail. Historically the wife of the warden prepared meals for her family and the prisoners. Harry tells us, "the prisoners ate what we ate." Many of these wives were good cooks and some inmates expressed a desire to stay even after they had served their sentence.

In recent years, some of the men who served as warden were Bill Bradley, Levi Cole, Bob Kurtz, John McCarthy, Frank Breitfeller, Harry Geiger and Tom Carey. In 1978 during the tenure of Warden Carey, the family bedrooms were converted to space to house the work release rehabilitation program inmates. The warden and his family would no longer live in the building.

COURT HOUSE, HIGH STREET, JAIL.
MILFORD, PA.

PUBL. BY
C.O. ARMSTRONG

JAIL OPERATIONS

Sheriff Phil Bueki began his career as a Deputy Pike County Corrections Officer in 1980. He provided us with information regarding the use of the space in the jail. On the first floor were two holding cells, a kitchen where the meals were prepared, a correction officer's desk and a visiting area with three booths. Each booth was equipped with a two-way phone and a plexiglass partition. Communication was achieved via the phone and no direct contact between a visitor and the inmate was allowed. Upstairs were four maximum-security cells. Each cell could hold two prisoners. There were no facilities for women. Opposite the four cells were three bedrooms arranged with bunk beds for use by the inmates in the minimum security work release program. Each bedroom could accommodate up to eight men. By 1989 the Pike County Jail was deemed overcrowded and a system of transporting Pike County prisoners to other facilities became necessary. Plans were undertaken to find a location for a new jail.

COUNTY JAIL, MILFORD, PA.

SHERIFF'S OFFICE

The Pike County Jail was one of the longest continuously operating jails in the Commonwealth of Pennsylvania. In 1998 under the directions of McGoey, Hauser, and Edsell Consulting Engineers, the Pike County Jail was completely renovated into a fully functional office for the County Sheriff. Administration areas, holding cells and physically-accessible bathrooms were created.

In December 1995 a new Pike County Jail facility opened on Route 739 in Blooming Grove Township. It can accommodate 277 prisoners.

irca 1832, George Biddis, a son of John Biddis, carved a six-foot white pine trout to serve as a weather vane on the original courthouse. One hundred years later the weather-beaten trout was donated to the Pike County Historical Society and Ralph Myer was given the job of carving a replacement. He used a piece of ponderosa pine from Chance Rowe's Lumber Mill and finished his carving with gold leaf. This trout proudly served until 2002 when Commissioners Harry Forbes, Gerry Hansen and Karl A. Wagner, Jr. with the financial backing of the Historic Preservation Trust of Pike County authorized a new trout. Bob Hartman replicated the fish and it was painted by fourteen-year-old Kevin Delonas, an art student under the tutelage of Valerie Meyer. The new weather vane was situated on top of the cupola in 2003 using a ball bearing rotation system designed by Michael Lamoreaux of the McGoey, Hauser and Edsall engineering firm. Photograph courtesy of Kristen Olson Murtaugh.

VIA WATERING FOUNTAIN 1911

In Milford in the early 1900s a group of citizens, concerned with the beauty and sanitary conditions of their resort town, formed the Village Improvement Association. At their meeting on June 21, 1904 Mrs. J.H. (Adelaide) Van Etten was elected President and Mrs. Robert (Katherine) Barckley was named Secretary. In 1911 the group paid for the construction of a stone-watering fountain on a public lot originally donated to the town by Judge Biddis at the corner of Broad and High Streets. The fountain was set at the curb to allow horses to drink from the watering trough on the front while people could get a drink from the fountain in the rear. The fountain was moved back from the sidewalk in the 1980s.

Upper Broad St. showing the V.I.A. Fountain, MILFORD, Pa.

WAR MONUMENT, 501 BROAD STREET

In the spring of 1930 the members of the Village Improvement Association, under the leadership of Mrs. Lila Huddy, decided to order a plaque to be placed on the Court House that would enumerate and honor those who had served in World War I. This was accomplished and the plaque was dedicated in a ceremony on October 11, 1930. However, as in any small town, there was a splinter group who favored a monument over a plaque. These folks prevailed upon "Marble King" August Kiel to donate the marble and a monument, located across the street from the jail and ironically in front of the house where the Huddy family lived at 501 Broad Street, was erected.

WAR MONUMENT IN VILLAGE SQUARE, MILFORD, PA.

DEDICATION

The inscription on the monument reads: "Dedicated in Honor and Memory of the Soldiers and Sailors from Pike County Penna. Who answered our Country's call to Arms in Wars of our Nation."

Vera E. Myer took this photograph at the unveiling of the monument which was held on July 4, 1931 with Governor Gifford Pinchot serving as Master of Ceremonies. August Kiel is pictured on the left-hand side and Governor Gifford Pinchot on the right-hand side of the photograph. The boy on the left is Raymond Orben Sr. who would serve his country in World War II. The monument was restored by Mt. Laurel Post 8612 in 1991.

VANDERMARK HOTEL

The Vandermark Hotel, believed to have been built circa 1785, was used as a tavern and boarding house. It was especially popular with Pike County people who lived in the townships and opted to stay in town when called for jury duty. Emmett Steele operated the hotel in the 1930s and 1940s and liked to host hunting parties. He encouraged the hunters attending to display their trophies of deer and bear on the front porch of the hotel! Joseph and Peg Gagnon were the last owners of the hotel before it was torn down to make room for the new Pike County Administration Building.

PIKE COUNTY ADMINISTRATION

On March 29, 1984, contracts were awarded by Commissioners Willis Gilpin, James Crellin and Donald Brink to build a Pike County Administration Building. The contracts awarded totaled $2,390,610. The new building was dedicated and opened to the public on November 14, 1985 at 10:00 AM.

— 137 —

MCLAUGHLIN HOME

According to Lori Strelecki, Curator of the Pike County Historical Society, the McLaughlin home, located at 608 Broad Street, was built in 1904 for wealthy Hoboken, New Jersey businessman Dennis McLaughlin. The twenty-two room mansion known as The Columns served as a summer home for Dennis McLaughlin, his wife Theresa and their three children, Edward, Marie Dorothy and Theresa. The family sold the home in the 1940s and several businesses were subsequently established. Henry Platt ran the White House Restaurant and Bar from the building. Elmer Herring had a nightclub/restaurant business at the location. In the mid 1960s the Veterans of Foreign Wars and American Legion purchased the building and established their Vet's Club. In 1983 the Pike County Historical Society purchased the home to serve as their museum. The building once again became known as The Columns.

THE LINCOLN FLAG

On display is the Lincoln Flag and other gifts from the Struthers family. Jean (Struthers) Newell was a teacher in Milford in the early 1900s. Her grandfather, actor Thomas Gourlay, was in charge of the repertory company that presented "Our American Cousin" to President Abraham Lincoln in Ford's Theatre in Washington, D.C. on that fateful night of April 14, 1865. After the President was shot, Mr. Gourlay placed the flag beneath Lincoln's head to ease his transport from the theater. Passed from generation to generation and finally to the Society, this bloodstained flag has touched Pike County's history and has a place of honor in its museum.

HIAWATHA

Also on display at The Columns, in an enclosed glass portico, is the Hiawatha. The Hiawatha is an Abbott and Downing Concord Stage Coach used in the Milford area in the 1860s for the transport of people and mail. Purchased originally by John W. Findlay, Sr., the coach remained in the possession of the Findlay family until 1953 when they donated it to the Pike County Historical Society. The Society raised the $18,000 necessary to restore the coach and it appears today as it did when built in 1840.

Welcome to

Milford Manor
CELLAR
The Room of Perfect Cocktails

SMORGASBORD
COFFEE and DESSERT
$3.75

Closed Tuesday   **Dancing**

THE CELLAR

The Milford Manor Cellar is the name Elmer Herring and his partner gave to their restaurant/night club they operated at The Columns. In addition to offering "The Room of Perfect Cocktails," they provided a smorgasbord for their patrons.

OLD STAGE COACH "HIAWATHA" MILFORD, PA. *1932*

STAGECOACH

According to William F. Henn's book "Westfall Township, Gateway to the West," in regard to the Hiawatha: "Emblazoned on each door of the stage coach was a colorful shield showing an Indian in a canoe, a scene from which was derived the fictional name of HIAWATHA OF THE DELAWARE. When fully loaded, 22 passengers were crowded into the vehicle including those "up" on the roof. There was also a driver and a brakeman. The mail was carried underneath the driver's seat. Two wooden side panels could be raised for ventilation. The coach was supported by strong lengthwise leather straps of several thicknesses, providing a back and forth motion (in contrast to side to side motion as with axle supported springs). At the rear, leather straps supported a trunk rack. A special breed of slender horses, known as "roaders," hauled the vehicle, sometimes 3 teams being used for a given load. Stage dogs, running with the coach underneath the carriage, embellished the rustic scene."

AUTHENTICATED

In 1996 after extensive research, the Lincoln Flag was authenticated to the satisfaction of the Pike County Historical Society by Joseph Edward Garrera. Many Lincoln scholars contributed to the conclusion Mr. Garrera reached.

The "Lincoln Flag"
Displayed at The Columns-
Museum of the Pike County Historical Society
Milford, Pennsylvania

COLLINWOOD INN

The Collinwood Inn and Cottage, located at 605-607 Broad Street, shown here in 1929, was owned by the Bessett family. They made it known that the establishment was "Officially Inspected And Approved By Publicity Travel Bureau." The Inn was later operated by Howard F. Haas, an actor and singer whose stage name was Frank Howard, and his wife Constance.

BED AND BREAKFAST

Jim May told us his parents Maurice and Peg May purchased the Collinwood Inn in 1939. During the summer tourist season they operated the Inn as a bed and breakfast with guests usually staying one night. In the off season the Inn became a boarding house. Individuals living in other parts of the county would rent rooms by the week while working at their job in Milford. Marie Hoffman remembers boarding at the Collinwood when she worked for Attorney Karl Wagner, Sr. Other regular boarders were Ed Parsons, Louise Emery, Adeline Smith and Pat Gavoille. The Mays charged $2 per day which included the room, breakfast and dinner. In 1975 Mrs. May sold the property to Bill Strong and Bruce Earlin. They expanded their Milford Motors automobile dealership by creating a parking and display area for their cars after the Inn was razed.

THE COLLINWOOD INN & COTTAGE
MILFORD, PA.
OPEN ALL YEAR   F.E.&.C.I.BESSETT
OWNERS

OFFICIALLY INSPECTED AND APPROVED BY PUBLICITY TRAVEL BUREAU

Collinwood Inn, Owned and managed by F. E. & C. I. Bessett. Tourist—Transient—Permanents—Meals served. Open all the year. Phone 162, Milford, Pa. Pike County. Routes 6 and 209.

MONUMENT OF
TOM QUICK THE INDIAN SLAYER
MILFORD, PA.

TOM QUICK

The first documented account of a non-Native American to settle in the area is that of Thomas Quick the third. His father, Teunis Thomassen Quick, a Hollander immigrated to New York City in the 1630s. On August 26, 1732 Thomas Quick bought two acres of land along what is now the Vandermark Creek from Solomon Davis for fifteen pounds. Quick was a millwright by trade and he cleared the land, built a house, barn and gristmill. He and his wife, the former Margite Dekker had nine children. His son Tom, born in 1734, was the first white child born on the site of what would become Milford.

There are many stories about Tom Quick the fourth. According to Alfred Mathews: "In December of 1796 Tom Quick, the "Indian Slayer," died. He was buried in the Rose Family Cemetery two miles south of Matamoras. Soon after his burial the local Indians dug up his corpse, cut the body into pieces, and sent a piece to each of their villages.

Monument to Tom Quick, the Indian Slayer, Milford, Pa.

THE RED REVENGER

These remains were to be kept as evidence that the "Red Revenger" was dead and the indians [sic] need no longer live in fear of his vow to kill them all. Legend has it however, that unknown to the indians [sic], Tom Quick had died of smallpox. The recipients contracted the disease and thus the "Indian Slayer" killed more indians [sic] after his death than before it."

While the first story is fictional, this is not: In 1889 the Reverend Abraham S. Gardner, pastor of the First Presbyterian Church of Milford, led a campaign for the erection of a monument to the early settlers of Milford to be located on Sarah Street near the Vandermark Creek. William Bross, one time Lt. Governor of Illinois, who had spent his boyhood in Milford, provided the funds for the monument.

Monument to Tom Quick, The Indian Slayer. Milford, Pa.

ROSETOWN

Tom Quick's remains were removed from the Rose Family Cemetery and placed beneath the monument with a great fanfare. Hundreds of people attended in tribute to the early settlers of the area. Reverend Gardner delivered a very long speech in which he praised the virtues of these settlers and dismissed Tom Quick's later retaliations against Native Americans saying that Tom Quick was " an outgrowth of the period in which he lived" one hundred and fifty five years ago.

 Since that time, the monument has been known as the Tom Quick Monument. The monument, as of this writing, is in storage.

Upper Broad Street, Milford, Pa.

AUTO STAGE LINE

On March 27, 1906 a meeting was held at the Crissman House to discuss the establishment of an auto stage line between Milford and Port Jervis. By June, the Delaware Valley Transportation Company had been formed. They procured a Mack van with five rows of seats and planned to purchase another vehicle later in the summer. Paul N. Bournique was President of the company; John C. Warner, Vice-President; B.E. Brown, Treasurer; and Percy Lyman, Secretary. The line ran a schedule of two trips daily to Port Jervis. Private arrangements could be made for special excursions.

Auto Stage Line leaving, Milford, Pa.

TO PORT JERVIS

Before the 1930s, when leaving Milford, traffic crossed over the Vandermark Bridge at the end of Broad Street and continued on the Milford-Port Jervis Road. The Milford-Port Jervis Road or Old Milford Road was constructed in 1867 and runs behind the Milford Motel and Luhrs Ace Hardware Store. This road predates the highway we know as Routes 6 and 209 which was built in the mid 1930s. Routes 6 and 209 continue at the end of Broad Street into Milford Township.

FREDERICK VAN DERMARK

Amy Leiser, Director of the Monroe County Historical Association and her volunteer staff members Evelyn Smith and John and Mary Lenz found a rare book in the museum at the Stroud Mansion in Stroudsburg, PA. It was published in 1942 by members of the Van der Mark family and contains information regarding Frederick Van der Mark, Jr. for whom the Vandermark Creek is named.

Frederick Van der Mark was born in Marbeltown, NY in 1733. He married Mary Oosterhout of Kingston, NY. On May 10, 1784 Frederick bought one-hundred and three acres from Joseph Rider and moved his family to the Milford area. He built a home on the Mudder Kill near the Delaware River. In 1786 he was on the tax list for Upper Smithfield Township [Milford], Northampton [Pike] County. He was taxed on a dwelling, grist mill, saw mill, one-hundred acres of land, two horses and two cattle. We know the mills had been owned by the Quick family from 1733 until 1754 because "Quick" mill was specified on the Vandermark deed.

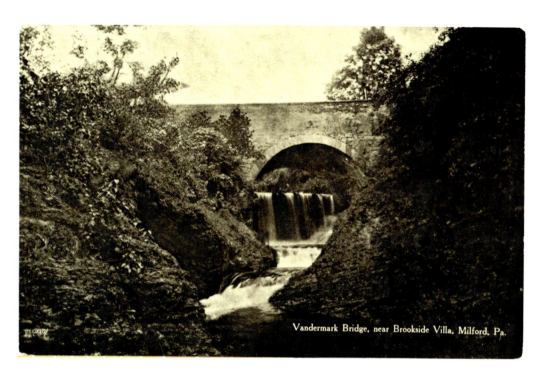

Vandermark Bridge, near Brookside Villa, Milford, Pa.

Stone Bridge on Vandemark Creek, Milford, Pa.

VANDERMARK BRIDGE

Mathews tells us the Vandermark house was the third house built in what is now Milford. Circa 1793 Frederick, Mary and their son James all died in the house as a result of consumption (tuberculosis). On January 16, 1794 Loderwick, the eldest son and heir of his brother James who had died without issue, sold the property to Judge John Biddis of Philadelphia. "Milford" was about to be born!

Although the exact date is unknown, it is apparent the Mudder Kill, along which the Quick family had settled, became known as the Vandermark Creek during Frederick's lifetime. Thus, in 1867 the Vandermark Bridge was built by Master Mason S. T. Van Auken at the behest of then Commissioners William Brodhead, S. D. Van Etten and Jacob Hornbeck. Catherine Vandermark, daughter of Frederick and Mary, had married Tobias Hornbeck circa 1788. Commissioner Jacob Hornbeck was a descendant. The bridge is still owned by the County and in 2002 was placed in the Historic Preservation Trust of Pike County.

BROOKSIDE VILLA

One of the original boardinghouses still standing in Milford is the Brookside Villa. It is located near the corner of Broad and Sarah Streets on Constitution Avenue. According to Diane Robacher Besson, writing for "Historic Sites in Milford": "Toward the end of the last century Milford was becoming a resort center of eminence. Inns, hotels, and boardinghouses proliferated. In tune with the times the spacious old farmhouse of John and Louisa Ross Brodhead was renovated by their daughter, Kate VanWyck, to accommodate summer guests and was named the 'Brookside Villa.' The 1000-acre Brodhead tract included the rich farmland lying along the Vandermark and extended to the Delaware River."

Brookside Villa, Milford, Pa.

ACCOMMODATIONS FOR 25

In 1904 Happy Theodora VanWyck Benner inherited the property from her mother, Kate. In 1912 Happy sold it to Tobias Nelson. In 1916 Oscar and Nell Wells purchased the property from Tobias Nelson. Two years later, when Oscar died, Nell inherited the property. Her ad in the 1923 Milford Chamber of Commerce booklet mentions "accommodations for 25, all modern improvements, cool, comfortable house" and "fresh milk and vegetables from our farm." Her rates were $18 to $25 per week.

Brookside Villa, Milford, Pa.

13594

SUMMER COLONY

In 1926 the Drake Holding Company of Mt. Vernon, New York, in which Louis A. Rudolph, a former Milford resident, was active, bought Brookside Villa and the surrounding farmland from Mrs. Nell Q. Wells. The intention was to form a summer colony community with a clubhouse and a private beach on the Delaware. The plan never came to fruition.

Brookside Villa, Milford, Pa.

BIRD'S-EYE VIEW OF MILFORD, PA., SHOWING KNOBB IN THE DISTANCE.

RIDGE VIEW

This view is from the top of the ridge, now designated as Greenwood Hills, that lies behind Brookside Villa. The wide street pictured is Broad Street looking toward the Knob. The Erie Railroad Directory of Attractions published in 1910 describes the Knob as rising one thousand feet. "A foot path leads to its summit, which is a favorite outlook with summer boarders, as the country for forty miles around is brought beneath the gaze. A stretch of meadow slopes from the base of the Knob to the Sawkill Creek."

THE HOMESTEAD, MILFORD, PA.

HOMESTEAD

Abram D. Brown built his home in the 1880s on the Vandermark Creek. Throughout the ensuing years he built additions onto it and by 1906 The Homestead could accommodate 120 guests. It was an imposing four story structure with tree shaded, covered porches on two levels. Mr. Brown charged $8 to $12 per week for adults and $6 for children. His ad states "rates for servants on application." He also advertised all modern conveniences and promised the air temperature at the home was "several degrees cooler than any other part of Milford." Mr. Brown suggested guests bring their own liquor but promised icy water from the Sherman Spring located one hundred feet from the piazza.

HOME COOKING

The Schultz family purchased The Homestead in 1923 and advertised "Home Cooking a feature." They also offered a large dance floor and swimming in the Vandermark Creek.

The Homestead.

No. 3 Moore & Gibson Co. N. Y. Germany

SENIOR HOME

In the late 1930s the Methodist Church bought the hotel and property to use as a home for senior citizens. Extensive renovations were necessary to accomplish this and fund-raising efforts failed to meet their goal. In March 1975 an arsonist's fire destroyed the hotel.

The Homestead.
Milford, Pa.

208.565 JV

On the Vandemark Creek,
Milford Pa.

SWIMMING AREA

A dam was built on the Vandermark Creek to provide a swimming area for guests of the Homestead.

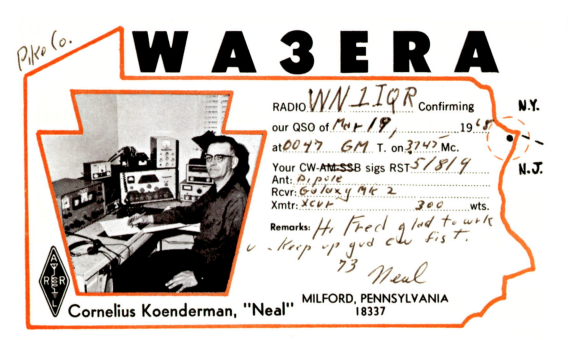

WA3ERA

Piko Co.

RADIO *WN1IQR* Confirming
our QSO of *Mar 18,*   19*68*
at *0047 GM* T. on *3747* Mc.
Your CW-AM-SSB sigs RST *5/8/9*
Ant: *Dipole*
Rcvr: *Galaxy MK 2*
Xmtr: *XCVR*   *300*   wts.

Remarks: *Hi Fred glad to work
u - Keep up gud cw fist.
73 Neal*

N.Y.

N.J.

Cornelius Koenderman, "Neal"   MILFORD, PENNSYLVANIA
                                              18337

HAM RADIO

Mr. Koenderman was a popular "ham" radio operator who lived on Bennett Avenue. The Radio Act of 1912 enabled the government to issue Amateur Radio licenses, and operation of "ham" radios became a popular activity.

HUNTERS INN

This house was located on the right-hand side of Routes 6 and 209 as one enters Broad Street from Milford Township. At one time it was called The Anchorage and, later, Hunter's Inn. Ultimately it was used as a residence by famed science-fiction writer Damon Knight. The Inn was destroyed in a fire in 1979 but we are left with a lovely legacy of lilac bushes on the site.

MILFORD MOTEL

The Milford Motel is located at the eastern edge of Milford. It advertises "Modern rooms beautifully furnished and decorated, each with tile bathroom, inner spring mattresses and individual room heat control."

AMENITIES

It mentions that "swimming, boating, fishing, churches, stores and restaurants" are nearby.

MYER MOTEL, CIRCA 1945

The Myer Motel located at 600 Routes 6 and 209 was built in 1945 by Ralph and Matilda Myer. The motel was situated on four acres of land that abutted the Delaware River. The Myers maintained a private beach on the River for their patrons.

Myer Cabins, Milford, Pa.

MYER MOTEL, CIRCA 1960

In 1952 Ralph remarried and he and his wife, the former Audubon Winfield, continued to run the business until they were both in their eighties. The Myers advertised exceptionally large and luxurious rooms. Each room had a television, individually controlled hot water heating, wall to wall carpeting, bathtub, shower and separate dressing area.

COUNTRY MOTIF

In 1975 their artistic daughter Audubon Cox used her knack for decorating to impart a country motif to the decor. This ambiance caused many guests to comment that the motel was their "home away from home."

MYER MOTEL, CIRCA 1982

In 1995 Audubon Cox' son Craig and his wife Sharon became the third generation to assume operation of the business. Perhaps their children Courtney and Cody will continue the tradition.

— 153 —

ELMER'S FAMILY RESTAURANT

In 1973 Milford Coffee Shoppe owners Elmer and Kate Herring bought Squire Durr's Coffee Shop at 586 Routes 6 and 209. They renovated the building and established Elmer's Family Restaurant. Kate's special interest in health food fueled the addition of The Honey Bee Health Food Store in 1976. In 1981 a new dining room was added and in 1983 beer and wine became part of the menu. For many years, Elmer and Kate generously held a Community Day when all proceeds on that day were given to various local charities. These included the Heart Association, Salvation Army Children's Camping Program and the Center for Developmental Disabilities. Balch's Restaurant is now located in the building once occupied by Elmer's Restaurant.

the ONE route 6 and 209

ARCHITECTURAL GEM

Famous Architect Peter Bohlin of Bohlin, Cywindski and Jackson of Wilkes Barre who worked on the design of Microsoft's Bill Gates home designed this building located at 540 Routes 6 and 209. Zitone Construction built the structure for Joe Biondo. The trees on the wooded lot on which it is built provide a natural sound barrier from the noise of the traffic on the highway. Artwork courtesy of Joe Biondo.

SANTOS DAIRY FARM

In 1941 Julio and Marion Santos purchased Al Tuscano's 238-acre farm at 569 Routes 6 and 209 in Milford Township. In addition to corn, wheat and grazing fields, it contained a large apple orchard and twenty acres planted with 27,000 currant plants. The Tuscano's had used the fruit to produce cider and jelly at their mill. After the purchase the property became known as the Santos Farm.

Julio continued his Foster Hill Dairy Farm, also located in Milford Township, at the new location. He had a herd of thirty-five cows and one of thirty heifers. Each herd had its own barn. He stayed in the dairy business until 1967 when governmental policy changes forced him to discontinue the production of milk. He continued to grow corn and wheat and raise cows and pigs for market. He maintained a flock of one hundred chickens whose eggs he sold to the public. He used an "honor system" to sell the eggs which allowed the customer to go into the cellar, pick up a dozen eggs and leave the money in a container. Photograph courtesy of Jim Levell.

SANTOS FARM

Julio and Marion's three children Cecile, Ted, and Julio H. grew up on the farm. Julio H. chose to help his father in the business. Julio continued to farm with his son's help until he was ninety.

On July 6, 1996, the Milford Township Board of Supervisors declared a "Julio A. Santos Day" to honor his accomplishments during the ninety years he lived and worked in the township. On that day township, county and state officials congratulated Julio on his seventy-eight years of farming. Julio also served his community as a charter member of the Milford Township Planning Commission. In 1977 he was named to the Nation's Voting Hall of Fame when recognized by President Reagan for having a perfect voting record for fifty years. Julio died on November 17, 2004 at age ninety-eight. Photograph courtesy of Jim Levell.

MAPLE SHADE FARM

Hankin's Maple Shade Farm was located at present day 552 Routes 6 and 209. The building was last used to house a business called the Browsery. The River Rock Inn, owned and operated by Ken Pisciotta, is behind the former Browsery.

CASINO

The Milford Airport Casino was located in the vicinity of Luhrs Ace Hardware Store.

SQUARE DANCE AT MILFORD AIRPORT CASINO

MILFORD, PA.

WEDNESDAY, JANUARY 7, 1931

Music by Bill Cook and His Pike County Folks from Bushkill, Pa.

Come and bring your friends.   Dancing to late Hours.

———o———

WEDNESDAY NIGHTS—Old Fashion Square Dancing Only.

SATURDAY NIGHTS—Round Dancing—Only Waltz's and Fox Trots.

A prize of $2.50 in gold given for best waltz.

SWISS INN

The Swiss Inn was located at 190 Old Milford Road. The Inn was owned and managed by the Groslimond family. Chef Groslimond had worked for the Fauchere Hotel under Chef Louis Fauchere. When he felt experienced enough to do so, he opened his own restaurant.

388-2 SWISS INN
MILFORD, PA.

JOE AND PAULA WALKER

Joe and Paula Walker bought the Swiss Inn in 1946 and operated the restaurant until 1950 with their daughters Theresa and Anita serving as waitresses. In 2004 Geoffrey Peckham opened his Hazard Communication Systems business on the site of the former Inn.

NEW EVERGREEN

The new Evergreen opened on September 3, 1969, on Routes 6 and 209. It was built by the Moglia family to enable them to continue their family operated Italian restaurant. On December 31, 1986 Dick and Pam Lutfy purchased the restaurant and continued its operation until 1992. In 1993 the Lutfys renovated the building and Director Pam Lutfy opened her childcare center, the Sunshine Station.

EVERGREEN'S MAIN DINING ROOM

Pictured is the main dining room of the Evergreen Restaurant which had an adjacent bar and lounge. There was a large banquet room with a bar in the basement where many banquets and weddings were held.

THIRSTY DEER

Billy and Arthur Paul MacArthur opened the Thirsty Deer Snack Bar and Campground in the 1950s. It was located close to the Delaware River on Routes 6 and 209 near present day River Beach Campgrounds.

ANOTHER THIRSTY DEER

The snack bar building has since been demolished. However, a new Thirsty Deer snack bar is located within Ruth Jones' River Beach Campgrounds.

HALF WAY HOUSE, CIRCA 1910

According to William Henn, there were two Half Way Houses on the Old Milford Road. In 1820 John B. Quinn, son of William Quinn and Sally Bowhannon Quinn, built the first at Deep Hollow Brook also known as Quick's Creek. It was at the juncture of an early mountain road descending from Shohola called Cummings Road. His establishment became a favorite stopping place for the carriage, stage and wagon trade. In 1875 James Cummings bought the inn and changed the name to the Cummings House. This postcard pictures the second Half Way House.

Half Way House on Milford Road, Pike Co., Pa.

HALF WAY HOUSE

In 1875 John Quinn built his second Half Way House located on the Old Milford Road about one-half mile east (toward Matamoras) from the first Half Way House (Cummings House). In 1895 Maurice Zann owned the inn when it was destroyed by fire. Maurice rebuilt the inn into a modern and attractive hostelry of twenty-three rooms.

Half Way House between Milford, Pa., and Port Jervis, N. Y.

EVERGREEN, CIRCA 1947

Toward the end of World War II, Ubaldo "Pete" Moglia bought the property. He invited his brother, Emile, and Emile's wife, Louise, to relocate to Milford and help him run the business.

On August 26, 1946 Emil, Louise and their two son's Adolph, age 13 and Emil, age 12 arrived to work with Pete. They refurbished the old building, named it the Evergreen and opened the first Italian-American restaurant in the area. According to a newspaper article written by Joseph A. Cusack and published by the Union Gazette on April 13, 1961 their specialties included veal parmagiana and scallopini, chicken cacciatora, lasagna and osso bucho. All dishes were prepared using culinary techniques learned in their youth in Parma, Italy.

EVERGREEN, CIRCA 1955

In the spring of 1947 the Evergreen Lodge opened with a new look. A wall had been removed and an addition built. A shuffleboard was provided for entertainment and soon a shuffleboard league was organized. The league gained in popularity and a second shuffleboard was added.

Those not wishing to play shuffleboard could instead watch the first television offered to the public in the area. There was a standing-room only crowd when the Joe Lewis verus Jersey Joe Walcott fight was televised. The Moglia family also installed a sound system that provided their guests with soft background music and an air-conditioning system which ensured comfortable dining.

EVERGREEN, CIRCA 1961

Pete left for Florida in 1950 and Emile's family operated the business. Emile worked in the kitchen and Louise greeted customers and served as bartender. In 1947 Emile was injured in a car accident and his son Adolph became a waiter. When Emil, Jr. returned from the service in the 1950s, he began helping in the kitchen. Adolph relieved Louise at the bar. Emil's wife Arlene helped in the kitchen and Adolph's wife Jean was in charge of the wait staff. In 1961 Adolph and Emil, Jr. became partners in the business. The construction of Interstate 84 forced the restaurant to close on July 20. 1969. It was razed and buried under the highway.

BEAR MURAL

Part of the renovations to the restaurant, completed in the spring of 1961, included a mural painted behind the bar. Mr. Moglia hired Arthur Von Ignatius, a local artist and father of famed local artist Harriet Cotterill, to paint the mural. Harriet tells us her father had worked in New York City painting backdrops for Minsky's Burlesque as well as the Metropolitan Opera House. All who visited the Evergreen loved that mural!

TOM QUICK'S OLD HOME

Although these post cards are labeled "Tom Quick's Old Home on Delaware River, Pike Co., Pa.," by all historical accounts this structure was not "on the Delaware River" nor was it "Tom Quick's home!" According to Mathews: "His headquarters in the summer were generally at the house of Showers, near Mongaup Island, or at a hut near Hagen Pond, where he hunted and trapped. He never married."

Tom Quick's Old Home on Delaware River, Pike Co., Pa.

TOM QUICK'S OLD HOUSE ON DELAWARE RIVER, PA.

JACOBUS ROSEN KRANS HOUSE

Mathews also tells us: "In his old age he was looked upon as a hero by the pioneer hunters and trappers. He died at James Rosencrance's in the year 1795 or 1796 and was buried on his farm." Henn tells us this is a picture of the Jacobus Rosen Krans house where Tom Quick died. He also points out that these farm homesteads were located on the only "thoroughfare" of the area, the Mountain Road or as we know it today, the Old Milford Road.

TOURIST VILLAGE MOTEL, CIRCA 1954

This postcard tells us the Tourist Village Motel is "owned and operated by Mr. and Mrs. Geo. Numrich." It boasts "20 acres of wood lands, nestled on the Delaware River in the beautiful Pocono Mountains."

TWENTY UNITS

Now "owned and operated by Mr. and Mrs. E. Austen," "twenty modern units" are promoted. The tourist is promised air conditioning and a television in each room.

DINER

At this point, one may call owners Hal and June Meredith at 491-9861 for a reservation. They offer a "diner on premises."

PETS WELCOME

Muriel, Jane, and Bob Kleber, the next owners, describe their "eighteen modern units" and indicate that pets are welcome. They also offer a "beach and picnic area on the Delaware."

VILLAGE DINER, CIRCA 1956

According to the information provided on this postcard, the Village Diner is located midway between Milford, PA and Port Jervis, NY on Routes 6 and 209, or, as the post card also proclaims, "At the Northeastern Gateway to the Pocono Mountains." Originally the Tourist Village Restaurant built to match the architecture of the Tourist Village Motel next door occupied this location. During the flood of 1955 the restaurant was surrounded by water when a fire erupted. Fireman could not reach the building to fight the fire and it was totally destroyed.

TEA ROOM ATMOSPHERE

A new diner built in 1956, was owned and operated by Glen and Ethel Musselwhite. They promised seating for ninety-six and extolled their establishment as: "The Diner With The Tea Room Atmosphere." In 1990 the business was sold to Dimitros Pagelos. Mr. Pagelos continues to own and operate the diner.

DELAWARE VALLEY HIGH SCHOOL, CIRCA 1957

The Delaware Valley Joint School District came into being in 1954 with the consolidation of the Milford Independent (Milford Borough and Milford Township), Matamoras Borough, Dingman, Delaware and Westfall Townships. When the Delaware Valley Joint High School opened in September 1956 it was the final step in the merging of Milford and Matamoras High Schools into one high school. In 1968 Shohola Township became part of the district making the consolidation complete with the name changing to Delaware Valley School District. The Class of 1957, the first graduating class, had forty-four members with the total district enrollment less than one thousand.

The population of Pike County is increasing so rapidly that it is considered to be the fastest growing county in Pennsylvania. This is reflected in the school enrollment today. There were 425 students in the graduating class of June 2006. As of August 2006, the number of children enrolled in the Delaware Valley School District was 5,694.

BLUE SPRUCE MOTEL

Jackie Cole Mackey grew up at the King Cole Cabins built in the late 1930s by her parents, Harry and Lydia, better known as "Jean," Cole. Harry, a Prudential Insurance agent, and Jean had a dream to build a motel. While continuing to work for Prudential Insurance, he began fulfilling their dream by building one cabin at a time until there were fifteen units. When their tourist business increased, he tore down the rear cabins and built a modern motel. In 1964 Martin and Helen Dymeck bought the business and changed the name to Blue Spruce Motel. The motel, which was open all year, offered some units with efficiency kitchens and eight-channel cable TV. The Dymecks transferred the business to their daughter, Debbie Innella. In 2005 the Blue Spruce Motel was demolished to make way for Lowe's.

BEST WESTERN INN

Most of the hotels, boardinghouses, and motels which have been described up to this point were "smallish," unique and family owned and operated. The Mickey Hunt family brought the first chain hotel to Pike County when they built the Best Western Inn at Hunt's Landing. Best Western International, Inc. is the world's largest hotel brand with more than four thousand hotels in eighty countries.

LOU DOBBS

At a Pike County Chamber of Commerce Dinner held at the Inn, Skip and Lorraine Gregory welcomed guest speaker Lou Dobbs of CNN fame.

E 6926 Pocono Farm, Matamoras, Pa.

POCONO FARM

Frederick A. Rose was born in Hartford, Connecticut in 1789. In 1828 he purchased the old Rosencrance farm and a portion of the VanAuken farm on Old Milford Road. His son, Elijah, married and had children, one of whom was James Cole Rose, born in 1840. William Henn tells us: "James C. Rose, another son of Elijah, left the parental home in 1866 when he married Elizabeth Martin and lived on a farm further up on the Old Milford Road. When his father died, he purchased the interests of fellow heirs and became the owner of 250 acres of choice land along the Delaware which he integrated into POCONO FARM, recognized as one of Pike County's foremost resorts."

1903 FLOOD

In the late 1800s a fire destroyed the resort but it was rebuilt. The flood of 1903 did damage as described in the Milford Dispatch: "The water came into the first floor of Rose's Pocono Farm House and his woodpile and several hundred bushels of apples were scattered along the roadway for some distance. Corn on the Mapes and Rose Farm was washed away." In 1924 a second fire once again destroyed the building but it was replaced and by 1926 C.H. Diehl was the proprietor of the sixty room Pocono Farm House. During World War II, the farm house served as a dormitory for the flying cadets at the Matamoras airport. In 1944 Elmer and Mildred Masurack bought the property and renovated and revitalized the business. Their Pocono Lodge also served as home to Elmer and Mildred Masurack and their three children Elmer, Jr., Joyce and Dolores.

POCONO FARM, MATAMORAS, PA.

20406

POCONO LODGE

Elmer and Mildred Masurack's Pocono Lodge could provide accommodations and three meals a day for eighty five guests. Amenities for the guests included a beach for swimming and boating on the Delaware River in the vicinity of the present golf driving range. Elmer Sr. maintained a farm with an assortment of animals including horses, which guests could use for horseback riding. Shuffleboard and tennis courts were available.

Elmer Sr. also operated Elmer Masurack's Produce road stand on Routes 6 and 209 as well as Pocono Farms Produce which provided a delivery service of fresh fruits and vegetables.

Over the years the Masurack children became an integral part of the business. Mildred died in 1974 and Elmer in 1981 but the Lodge continued to be operated by the family until it was sold in 1986. The lodge was renovated and Lewis and Marsha Adimari established Golden Acres, an assisted living facility that was in operation until 2004.

POCONO LODGE SWIMMING POOL

In 1958 the Masuracks built a swimming and wading pool at Pocono Lodge. Bob Rhoades was the lifeguard. This was the only public swimming pool in the Matamoras / Westfall area and under the direction of the American Red Cross hundreds of area children learned to swim. In 1960 the Masuracks added a pavilion to serve as a snack bar and to provide an area for dancing. Dance bands such as the Storm Kings played every Thursday night for the teenagers of the community. In 1968 the pavilion was renovated to accommodate Elmer Masurack's Produce Store which had to be relocated because of the construction of Interstate 84. About the same time eleven cottages and a house previously owned by George Kleist and located across from the Westfall Firehouse were moved and placed around the pool. Dolores Kolvenbach operated the pool from 1981 until 1986. She sold the property in 1986. The new owner tore down the cabins and filled in the pool.

HOT DOGS AND SAUERKRAUT

In the 1930s Pio and Assunta Colaiaco established Westfall Gardens which offered a wide range of services to local residents as well as the traveling public. They sold beer, coffee, milk, tea and ice cold Coca-Cola at their roadside snack bar. They also had "Hot Franks" and hamburgers were their specialty. Skip and Lorraine remember stopping to enjoy their hot dogs and sauerkraut.

346-2 Westfall Garden, Looking South
Matamoras, Pa.

347-2 Westfall Garden, Looking North
Matamoras, Pa.

STANDARD GAS STATION

Their Standard gas station offered free air and a comfort station. The attendant's hand invites the public to drive-in.

344-2 Westfall Garden
Matamoras, Pa.

FIRST DRIVE-UP SERVICE

Mrs. Alteo Colaiaco, daughter-in-law of Pio and Assunta, recalls that at one time the snack bar was amended to include a drive-up window. People could stay in their car, order their food and have the food passed to them through the window. Mrs. Colaiaco believes this was probably the first drive-up food service in Pike County.

345-2 Picnic Pavilions, Westfall Garden
Matamoras, Pa.

MAKE YOURSELF AT HOME

The Colaiacos added cottages and a separate shower house to the property. This made it possible for the traveler to visit and picnic for a few hours or spend the night.

WESTFALL GARDENS

The Colaiaco family continued to improve their full-service Westfall Garden complex with the addition of motel units. This postcard depicts the complex circa 1938.

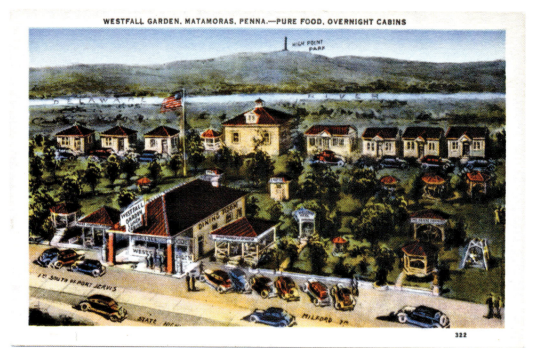

WESTFALL GARDEN, MATAMORAS, PENNA.—PURE FOOD, OVERNIGHT CABINS

WESTFALL GARDEN RESTAURANT

In 1959 Pio and Assunta's son Alteo Colaiaco opened the Golden Steer Restaurant. It featured a complete American and Italian menu and was very popular with local residents as well as tourists. The Golden Steer is now called the Appl Grill and is owned and operated by John Altadoma.

— 173 —

MANSION HOUSE

Proctor's Farm House, or Mansion House, was built by George Proctor circa 1902. It was located on Tenth Street, between the Old Milford Road and Cedar Lane. According to William Henn: "The three story frame structure, built to accommodate 150 guests, was designed with 50 outside sleeping quarters on the second and third floors, and the kitchen, dining room and dance hall on the ground floor."

Proctor's Farm House, Matamoras, Pike Co., Pa.

Mansion House, Matamoras, Pa.

VALIANT FIREFIGHTERS

The Mansion House was owned by Paul Holz when it was destroyed by fire. According to the Port Jervis Gazette of May 8, 1928: "While the Matamoras fire department and three companies from Port Jervis were responding to the alarms, aroused neighbors rushed to the scene and saved most of the furniture on the first floor and part of the sleeping room equipment. Fifty minutes after the first alarm, the entire building was a roaring mass of flame. The odds against the firefighters was overwhelming. The combined fire companies stretched 1,800 feet of hose across the fields, and with pressure supplied by the pumper engine, were able to direct one solitary stream of water on the building, all to no avail. Chimneys on either end of the building toppled in and the electric circuits and telephone wires were burned through. The estimated loss was $25,000.00, partly covered by insurance."

HOPE EVANGELICAL CHURCH

HOPE EVANGELICAL CHURCH, MATAMORAS, PA.

In 1891 Matamoras had a population of approximately 1,500 people. Most of these families were members of Protestant denominations who traveled to Port Jervis to attend services. In the fall of 1891, people representing these denominations, Dutch Reformed, Methodist, Episcopal, Presbyterian, Baptist and Evangelical Associated, "waived their denominational ideas, joined hearts and hands in a movement, out of which grew the religious organization known as the Hope Evangelical Church." The church, which was built for approximately $3,000, was dedicated in the spring of 1892. Today Pastor Reverend Robert C. Grieve commutes from Waldwick, NJ to conduct Sunday worship service for a small congregation.

BARROUGH HALL, MATAMORAS, PA.

MATAMORAS BOROUGH HALL

Although Matamoras Borough Hall at 10 Avenue I was not built until 1916, the first meeting of the Matamoras Borough Council was held on February 21, 1905. Charles A. Snyder was appointed Chief Burgess (we now use the term "Mayor"). The Councilmen were: Archibald C. VanEtten, Alfred Devlin, B.C. Toten, L.L. Hornbeck, W.N. Lawrence, William H. French and A.D. Vanderwort. Richard Gassman currently serves as Mayor of Matamoras.

St. Joseph's Church & Rectory, Matamoras, Pa.

52357

ST. JOSEPH'S CHURCH, CIRCA 1905

According to information provided by Michele Ricciardi Bensley, the first Catholic services were held in Pike County in 1813. During the period prior to the establishment of the Diocese of Scranton, Pike County was part of the Arch-Diocese of Philadelphia and was served by various priests traveling by horseback from New York to Philadelphia. The Diocese of Scranton was established in 1868.

ST. JOSEPH'S PARISH

St. Joseph's Parish, Matamoras, PA was officially established as a parish in 1892 by Bishop William O'Hara, Ordinary of the Diocese of Scranton. Father Joseph W. Treis was appointed by the Bishop as the first permanent pastor. The parish served all of Pike County. St. Joseph's was the mother church and the missions were St. Mary's in Lackawaxen, St. Patrick's in Milford, Mt. Calvary Chapel in Parkers Glen with Stations at Shohola, Mast Hope and Pond Eddy. Mass was not celebrated every Sunday at all of these locations. A lack of priests and the vast distances involved made it impossible to do so. Mass was celebrated at St. Joseph's every Sunday and once a month at the other locations.

ST. JOSEPH'S CHURCH AND RECTORY.   MATAMORAS, PA.

ST. JOSEPH'S CHURCH DEDICATION

In 1896 St. Joseph's Church in Matamoras was dedicated. It had been built according to plans drawn by Father Treis on the site of the present rectory.

Father Raymond O'Neill served as Pastor of St. Joseph's from June 1948 to September 1975. During his tenure, a new St. Joseph's Church was built on the corner of Third Street and Avenue F. The dedication took place on June 28, 1970. Father O'Neill officiated at many weddings, including the wedding of Jane McGoey and Lee Helms, on December 19, 1964. Their children, Mary René, Albert, John and Dawn were all baptized by Father O'Neill.

Catholic Church and Parsonage, Matamoras, Pa.

ST. JOSEPH'S R. C. CHURCH AND RECTORY, MATAMORAS, PA.

CENTENARY CELEBRATION

Father John Turi replaced Father O'Neill in 1975. Skip had the honor of walking his daughter, Randi Marie, down the aisle of St. Joseph's Church on her wedding day, May 20, 1989. Randi Marie Gregory was married to Lt. Michael Short, USN, with Father Turi officiating. Father Turi has baptized all of Randi and Mike's children, Michael, Mary Kate and Corry Gregory Short. St. Joseph's Parish Centenary Celebration was held on Sunday, May 31, 1992. Following a Mass of Thanksgiving, a gala ball was held at the Best Western Inn. Jim Burnett was Master of Ceremonies and Matamoras Mayor Joseph Ricciardi issued a proclamation in honor of the 100th Anniversary of St. Joseph's Church.

M. E. CHURCH, Matamoras, P.

MATAMORAS METHODIST CHURCH

Shirley Basham and Pastor Glenn Scheyhing provided the following information: On June 1, 1891, a charter was granted to the Epworth Methodist Episcopal Chapel of Matamoras, Pennsylvania to hold services of worship. Later that year a meeting was held to elect Trustees. C.D. Angle was chosen to act as President, C.F. Langton was chosen as Secretary and G.H. Langton was elected to the position of Treasurer.

M. E. CHURCH, MATAMORAS, PA.

METHODIST CHURCH CENTENNIAL

In 1991 the United Methodist Church of Matamoras celebrated their 100th anniversary. On Sunday, June 23, 1991, at their special worship service celebrating this birthday, they honored Russell Skinner and Gladys Lyon as the "longest living members," Harold Lyon as the "oldest living member" and Michelle Reaggs as the "youngest member." They continued the celebration with a family oriented picnic at Matamoras Airport Park.

52338　High School, Matamoras, Pa.

This is the school we go to. Dora B

FIRST MATAMORAS SCHOOL

A.J. Quick built the first Matamoras grade school in 1879 at the corner of Avenue G and Third Street. Forrist Mc-Caslin relates: "In 1892, Peter Drake was appointed as Principal. He must have been an unusually accomplished youth at age eighteen and is believed to have been the youngest Pennsylvania principal." This building served as a school until a new one was completed in 1924. Bill Clark, Jr., Class of 1952 and Matamoras Alumnae Historian, reports that there was a "procession of school children in late 1924 who moved books to the new school." The late Hazel Coykendall MacDonald Petitti recalled that move. She said the books were loaded onto sleighs which she and the other children pulled through the snow from the old school to the new school. She and Bill Clark, Sr. were in the first graduating class of 1925. The Pocono Order of the Eastern Star later owned the building and the New Life Christian Fellowship owns it today. It is used as a church and Christian Day School.

MATAMORAS HIGH SCHOOL

Bill Clark, Jr. states that C.D. Wolfe of Port Jervis, New York built the Matamoras High School which was located on the corner of Sixth Street and Avenue H. It was built circa 1923 at a cost of $100,000. Five hundred students, grades one through twelve, were enrolled and in 1939 more classrooms were added. The Matamoras Alumni Association was formed in 1927 and has met every year since. Gloria MacDonald Foss, Class of 1951, recalls that in 1950 Milford students were bussed to Matamoras for Latin and Home Economics, while Matamoras students went to Milford for French and Industrial Arts (Shop). Bruce Cuddeback, of Matamoras, was bussed to Milford for Shop. Gloria Foss and Joyce Decker Phillips went to Milford for French classes. Art Ridley and Lee Klaer were in their class. The last class graduated from Matamoras High School in 1956. It then served as an elementary school until 1988. In 1996 it was demolished and replaced by a senior citizen housing unit, Delaware Run.

MATAMORAS HIGH SCHOOL, MATAMORAS, PA.

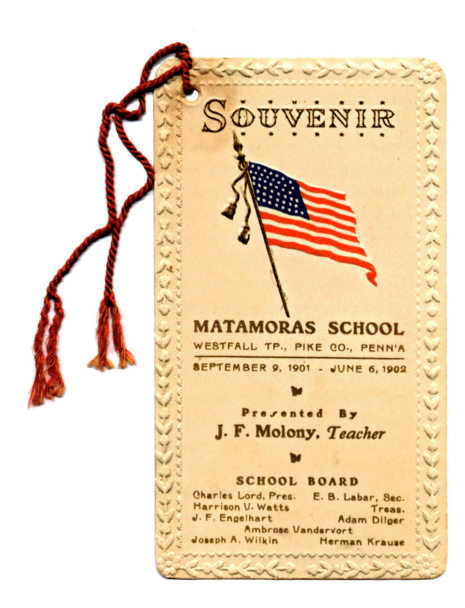

SOUVENIR

MATAMORAS SCHOOL

WESTFALL TP., PIKE CO., PENN'A

SEPTEMBER 9, 1901 - JUNE 6, 1902

Presented By

J. F. Molony, *Teacher*

SCHOOL BOARD

Charles Lord, Pres.   E. B. Labar, Sec.
Harrison V. Watts   Treas.
J. F. Engelhart   Adam Dilger
Ambrose Vandervort
Joseph A. Wilkin   Herman Krause

PUPILS

Anna Dunker   Lida Seymour
Leola Stearns
Edna Vandervort   John Curry
Mat. Curtis
Joseph Dilger   Ira McBride
Fred Engelhart
George B. Todd   Homer Quick
Dimmick Wilk in
Minnie Kesting   Ola M. Quick
Lizzie Furman
Edna Walker   Ruth Seybolt
Harriet Wilkin
Margaret Bell   Rena Prescott
Lottie Cottrell
Rachel Percival   J. D. Wilkin
James Welsh
Oran Quick   Leroy D. Hilferty
William Martin
Leon Corwin   Burton Crine
Albert Prey
F. Lee Nevin   Floyd Travis
Lamont Hornbeck   Archie Davis

INSTRUCTOR CO. DANSVILLE, N. Y

MATAMORAS STUDENTS 1901-1902

A souvenir school card from the turn of the century lists some familiar names of families still living in the area.

BANK OF MATAMORAS

On Monday, October 4, 1920, the Bank of Matamoras opened its doors to the public. In October of 1922, they erected their own building at 7 Pennsylvania Avenue. They offered their first dividend of 3% to stockholders in 1925. Citizens Bank presently occupies this building.

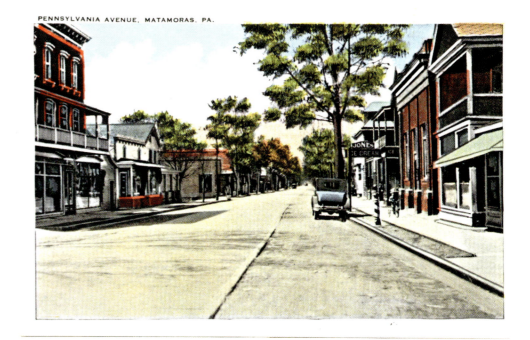

PENNSYLVANIA AVENUE, MATAMORAS, PA.

JONES' ICE CREAM

This card depicts a street scene of Pennsylvania Avenue facing south. William Henn tells us: "On the right, Decker's Barber Shop stands before the Bank of Matamoras. The sign projecting over the sidewalk was that of Jones' Ice Cream Parlor, owned by the Hamiltons who lived upstairs. 'Jones' was a favorite ice cream brand manufactured in Port Jervis. Across the street, Michael Uch's butcher shop was below the post office."

ELEPHANTS IN THE DELAWARE

Historically, rafts used to transport goods and people played an important role in the development of the Matamoras area. The raftsman's job was usually uneventful and he needed only to contend with the vagaries of the river but according to Frank Dale in his book Delaware Diary, Episodes in the Life of a River sometimes the unexpected happened. " In April 1869 timberman Frank Walker of Walton, New York was involved in one of the more humorous incidents on the river. Van Amburg's Circus was traveling by land from Port Jervis to Milford for a performance, but authorities feared that the old covered bridge over the river wouldn't hold the weight of the elephants. The elephants would have to ford the river, it was decided. Walker's raft, when it came upon the wading pachyderms, couldn't avoid them and smashed into one, badly cutting its ear. The wounded elephant, Tippoo Sahib, was a ferocious animal that had recently killed its trainer. Enraged, Tippoo Sahib attempted to climb onto the raft while at the same time blowing water over the crew. The animal's weight totally submerged the stern of the craft, but a timely jab or two with an oar discouraged the elephant from proceeding further. The traumatized crew escaped unscathed but not unshaken."

Destruction of the Matamoras R. R. Bridge by Ice, 1904

A View of the Delaware and Ruins of Matamoras R.R. Bridge

MATAMORAS RAILROAD BRIDGE

On June 9, 1897, a group of New York financiers chartered a railroad known as the Milford, Matamoras and New York Railroad Company. The firm of Terry and Tench of Steelton, PA were hired to build the railroad bridge. It was completed on July 30, 1898. Rails were laid and the first train ran across the bridge on September 3, 1898. A flood in 1903 weakened the abutments and an ice gorge in 1904 destroyed the bridge.

Avenue C, Matamoras, Pa.

LODER STREET, AVENUE C

Avenue C was originally named Loder Street in honor of the president of the Erie Railroad. Much of Matamoras' earliest development took place along Loder St. The present day Dew Drop Inn and adjacent Mance store were serving the community as a tavern and country store in the early 1880s. Several attempts throughout the latter part of the 19th century were made at establishing rail connections with the Erie Railroad along Loder Street. Rails were laid and the first train ran across the bridge on September 3, 1898. Tracks are visible in the foreground of this postcard. The track ran about one and one-half miles south of the bridge when construction was stopped for lack of funds. On the mountain near where the tracks stopped was a deposit of shale which, when crushed, made excellent roadbed ballast. A spur was built to the location and a large rock crushing plant was erected. Freight car shipments of crushed rock were hauled over the railroad bridge to Port Jervis. In 1902 11,283 tons of crushed shale were shipped. The operation ceased when the ice gorge of 1904 took out the bridge.

Delaware River Drive, Matamoras, Pa., near Port Jervis, N. Y.

DELAWARE DRIVE

Delaware Drive intersects with Pennsylvania Avenue at the Matamoras-Port Jervis Bridge. Delaware Drive follows along the Delaware River to the village of Mill Rift.

MATAMORAS SUNDAY SCHOOL

PENNSYLVANIA AVENUE, LOOKING NORTH, MATAMORAS, PA.

orrist McCaslin, former Matamoras historian, offers this information about the name of the town: "There are several explanations for how Matamoras acquired its name. Matamoros (note spelling) is a town in Mexico directly across the Rio Grande River from Brownsville, Texas, which had been named for Mariano Matamoros, a priest and hero of Mexico's war for independence. During the Mexican-American War (1846-1848) Matamoros was under attack by the forces led by General Zachary Taylor. At the same time, Mr. Parmenas B. Hulse and Mr. John Finkburg, energetic members of the Dutch Reformed Church of Port Jervis established a Sunday School in the growing community across the river. Seeing a similarity between their attempts to capture the youth of the village for the Sunday School and Taylor's efforts in Mexico they decided to call their project the Matamoras Sunday School.

Regardless of the origin, Dimmick, the planner and one-time owner of a large portion of the land that the borough now occupies, was so inspired by the name that he used it in his original plan of Matamoras. It is not known, however, when or why the spelling was changed."

STATE HIGHWAY ENTERING PORT JERVIS, N. Y., FROM MATAMORAS, PA.

PENNSYLVANIA AVENUE

hen Oliver S. Dimmick subdivided his farm and created Matamoras in the early 1850s, he sought help from John Biddis, son of the founder of Milford. Biddis' plat map followed the grid arrangement established by William Penn in Philadelphia and used by Biddis' father in Milford. Dimmick gave the streets proper names, such as Kidder, Loder, Biddis, Barker, Post, and Power. In 1905 when Matamoras was incorporated as a borough, the streets were renamed using letters and numbers. Loder Street was renamed Avenue C; Barker Street became Delaware Drive; Kidder Street, located north of Avenue C, was called Second Street; Biddis became First Street; Post was renamed Avenue D and Power was changed to Avenue A. Pennsylvania Avenue, the main street, was never renamed and is US Routes 6 and 209 to Port Jervis, NY.

MAYOR'S CORNER

Forrist McCaslin writes of this building: "Along Pennsylvania Avenue, there is an unaltered example of a turn-of-the-century, small town storefront. Constructed of concrete blocks that have the appearance of cut stone, the Schroeder building was originally a grocery, constructed and owned by Joseph A. Schroeder, who from 1912 to 1921 also operated the Matamoras Post Office at the store. His son, Jay Schroeder, who served as Pike County Commissioner from 1944 to 1969, took over the store in 1936, naming it 'Jay's Handy Corner'. As a news stand and a soda fountain it became well-known as a popular rendezvous for borough residents. More recently, Joseph W. Ricciardi, Mayor of Matamoras, operated the store which then became known as the 'Mayor's Corner.'"

Post Office, Matamoras, Pa.

Van Gordon Residence, Penn. Ave., Matamoras, Pa.

VAN GORDON HOUSE

The Van Gordon family kept a general store on Third Street, where they carried everything from nails to candy. This is their residence at 302 Pennsylvania Avenue.

MORTAR AND PESTLE

Grist mills and sawmills were very important to the development of any town. Sawmills provided the timber necessary to build homes and grist mills ground the farmer's grain into flour. William Henn tells us: "Until such time as a grist mill appeared on a local stream, the early settler was dependent on the primitive mortar and pestle. Sometimes a dumbbell shaped cast iron pestle was used to crush the grain. The mortar was constructed out of a stump closely cut to the root of a tree. The stump was inverted and the bowl hollowed out of the tough root end. Sassafras was preferred as the traces of its flavor were not bitter."

FALLS OF THE MILL DAM, MATAMORAS, PA.

MARFORD SILK MILL, MATAMORAS, PA.

MARFORD SILK MILL

The Marford Silk Mill, facing Fifth Street between Avenues F and G, was built in 1920. It was in operation for forty-five years. Their one hundred and twenty looms, with associated equipment, provided employment for fifty workers. The company was originally owned by Martin and Sanford and later by Welch and Son.

Old Indian Fort, - 1758 - Matamoras, Pa.

Would you please tell me Clendis' address & owe him a postal. Hope every one at Dingmans is prospering. L.E.Z.

SIMON WESTFAEL

According to Alfred Mathews in his book <u>History of Wayne, Pike and Monroe Counties, Pennsylvania</u>: "His marriage is kept in the records of the old Dutch Reformed Church, among those whose banns have been published, as follows: '1743, March 13. Simon Westfael, young man, born in Dutchess County, dwelling in Smithfield in Bucks County, to Jannetje Westbroeck, young woman, born at Mormel, dwelling at Menissinck, married the 17th day of April, by Peter Kuyckendal, justice of the peace.'"

OLD STONE HOUSE

Mathews also tells us that "Westfael" is the "old spelling of Westfall." Simon and Jannetje had five children. Their son, Simeon, married Sally Cole and built "the old stone house." Forrist McCaslin writes in the booklet "Matamoras Borough": "Legend has it that before fleeing one Indian attack, Sally buried her sewing basket in a cornfield. On her return she dug it up, elated because it contained a most valuable item–the only pair of scissors in the entire settlement."

HISTORIC HOUSE OVER A HUNDRED YEARS OLD.
MATAMORAS PENNSYLVANIA.

MEMORIAL

The back of this card reads: "World War II is not just a page in a history book. Memories are strong and will survive in the hearts of countless men and women. Thanks to our fearless warriors we live in freedom. On behalf of a grateful nation, allow us to salute every WW II Veteran. This monument was dedicated May 31, 2003." Veterans Memorial Park and Education Center is located at Airport Park, Matamoras. Photograph courtesy of Veterans Park Committee.

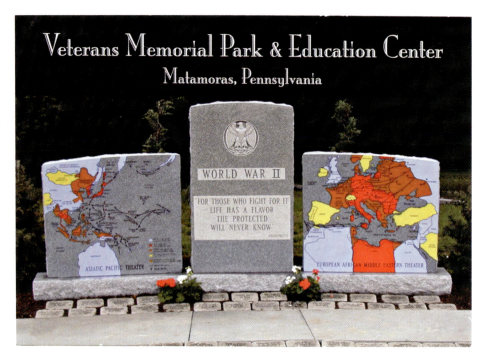

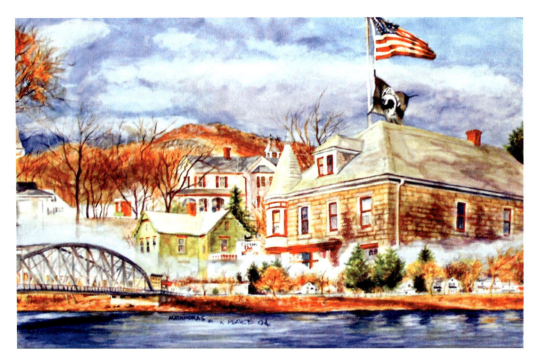

HAPPY BIRTHDAY

This Centennial painting was done by Mr. Kim Pearce in honor of the Matamoras Centennial Celebration in 2005. Happy Birthday Matamoras! Photo courtesy of Matamoras Centennial Committee.

BARRETT BRIDGE, CIRCA 1904

The iron Barrett Bridge was built on the foundations of the second Barrett Bridge that was destroyed by the flood of October 10, 1903.

Barrett Bridge, Matamoras, Pa.

BARRETT BRIDGE

This third Barrett Bridge was moved upriver while the fourth bridge was being constructed on the site.

Mid-Delaware River Bridge, Connecting Port Jervis, N. Y. and Matamoras, Pa.

BARRETT BRIDGE, CIRCA 1950

This is a postcard of the fourth Barrett Bridge built in 1939. It has survived several floods and continues in service today.

FLO-JEAN, CIRCA 1940

Part of the Flo-Jean Restaurant building just across the Barrett Bridge in Port Jervis, NY served as the toll house for the bridge until March 1922. According to a family story shared with us by Mary Ellen Theodore, niece of Florence Dalrymple, in the mid 1920s Harold Dalrymple of Middletown, NY was fishing in the Delaware near the abandoned tollhouse when he struck up a conversation with another fisherman. The fisherman was popular author Zane Grey. Grey extolled the beauties of the Delaware to Mr. Dalrymple who in turn told his wife Florence about the river and the tollhouse. The Dalrymples' Flo-Jean Restaurant opened in the spring of 1929. The restaurant was named for Florence and her sister Virginia, nicknamed Jean. The Flo-Jean became a local institution and popular destination for people from all parts of the area. After Mr. Dalrymple's death in 1952, Florence continued to operate the business until her death in November 1981. The Flo-Jean has survived several floods of the Delaware River and continues in operation.

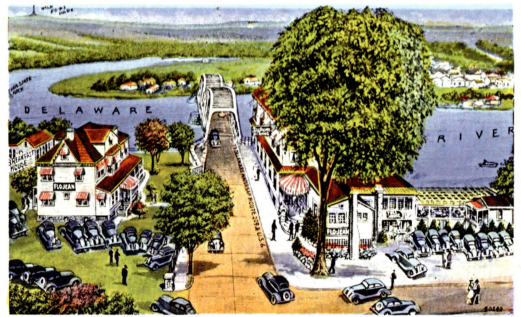

FLO-JEAN ON THE DELAWARE BY THE BRIDGE, PORT JERVIS, N. Y.

MATAMORAS AIRPORT

Mr. Henn tells us: "The Matamoras Airport owed its existence to the vision and concern of the members of the volunteer fire department in the Borough. The need for an area landing field had been accentuated by the fateful crash of a distressed airplane in the forbidding terrain of Pond Eddy. A bold step was taken in 1928 when the fire department purchased for $10,000, thirty-five acres of the Bell farm on the river flats within the borough limits. By solicitations among the populous, and a propitious loan of $8500 from the bank, the necessary funds were raised, with certain firemen vouching personal surety. The field was constructed on a do-it-yourself basis, among other things, involving the complete obliteration of an orchard, stumps and all. It was an amazing undertaking for a volunteer fire department and was destined to provide ample grist for the annals of Matamoras.

WPA

"During the depression, when the government was seeking programs for creating jobs, the up-grading of the airport became a prime prospect for the Works Progress Administration. (WPA) However, this government agency could not deal with a private entity, so, as a matter of expediency, ownership was transferred to the borough, on the basis that as revenues were derived, the fire department be reimbursed for its overall expenditures. Thus it was that after two years of WPA labor, with operations suspended during the winter, in 1938, the once modest local airport could boast of two paved runways, 1750 feet and 1425 feet long, with adequate field and flood lighting, including a beacon atop Taylor's Knob, and a sturdy hanger of 80 feet by 100 feet—all at no expense to the borough."

MATAMORAS AIRPORT

A PENNSYLVANIA-FEDERAL
WORKS PROGRESS ADMINISTRATION PROJECT
OFFICIAL PROJECT NO. 65 - 23 - 5036
SPONSORED BY
BOROUGH OF MATAMORAS
PIKE COUNTY

WORK BEGAN MARCH 1936   WORK COMPLETED JUNE 1938
CONSTRUCTION OPERATIONS SUSPENDED DURING WINTER MONTHS

In addition to servicing Matamoras and Port Jervis, this airport also provides an emergency landing field in an extremely rugged section of Pennsylvania.

771 BLUFF HOUSE, MILFORD, PA.

E.F.BRANNING'S
ARTINO CO. 3D.NY

BLUFF HOUSE

Henry Wells purchased the lots located at present-day 310 to 316 East Ann Street for the Bluff House in 1873. Mr. Wells later described them for Beers as "an unbroken wilderness" but Henry knew the location on the bluff overlooking the Delaware River was worth the struggle to clear the land. The first hotel he built contained ninety rooms. He enlarged it several times, first adding twenty-one rooms and then thirteen more. In 1896 when his business was established, he added another ninety rooms. The final structure was of such magnitude it covered the whole block from Ann Street to Catharine Street. It was advertised as Pike County's largest hotel and could accommodate 350 guests. According to Beers "the entire building cost something over fifty thousand dollars." The hotel was open only in the season, from June 15th to October 1st, and business was "conducted on strictly temperance lines."

MILFORD, PA., FROM THE KNOB.

STORY OF HENRY B. WELLS

Henry B. Wells was a lineal descendant of one of the earliest settlers in Pike County and was born in Milford on April 1, 1827. He was a son of Nathan, born in Milford in 1796, and Ann Wells, and a grandson of Israel. Israel was one of the three brothers, along with Jesse and James, who operated a grist mill and saw mill on the Sawkill. They also provided a ferry service across the Delaware River in pre-Revolutionary days and the area was briefly named Wells' Ferry in their honor.

BLUFF HOUSE FROM THE RIVER
MILFORD, PA.

HENRY THE CARPENTER

According to J.H. Beers, Henry assisted his father in his carpentry shop. By the age of twenty he was considered an accomplished carpenter. During the Civil War, when land was cheap, he would buy lots, build houses and sell them.

Bluff House, Milford, Pa.

HENRY THE BUILDER

As soon as a house sold he would buy more lots and build and sell more houses. He is credited with building about fifty houses in Milford and in Port Jervis, New York. In the Beers book, published in 1900, he mentions that Henry "owns considerable property at present" in Milford and Port Jervis.

PAUL BOURNIQUE

On June 6, 1853 Henry B. Wells married Phoebe Dewitt of Sussex County, New Jersey. They had six children. The youngest, daughter Kittie, married Paul Bournique. Paul was manager of the Bluff House in 1900. His father-in-law, Henry, was seventy-three at the time and according to Paul was "a silent force that helps to steer over the rough places."

Bluff House, Milford, Pa.

The Bluff House, Milford, Pa.

"DRY" ERA

In a 1900 Bluff House brochure, published by then proprietor P.N. Bournique, patrons were told "Having no license, we sell no liquors. Guests wishing them must furnish the same independent of us."

DANCING UNDER THE MOON

The brochure also says "It is impossible to give a fair idea of so lovely a village situated in this Switzerland of America." We are told there were hot and cold baths on every floor and gas lights in all the rooms. The main floor consisted of numerous drawing rooms, cozy corners, children's playrooms, a billiard room and a large ballroom. The hotel orchestra played dance music each evening in the ballroom and guests could dance there or outside under the moon on the pavilion. A bowling alley was also available and the brochure promises: "The bowling alley, a few steps away from the hotel proper, is so located as to cause no inconvenience to light sleepers."

OUTDOOR DANCING PAVILION   THE BLUFF HOUSE   MILFORD, PIKE COUNTY, PA.

Phone

BLUFF HOUSE
BEAUTY SHOPPE
Experts in all branches of Beauty Culture

BLUFF HOUSE   MILFORD, PA.

SCENERY

Local sightseeing was encouraged: "There are numerous interesting places to visit, among which are the various Falls of the Sawkill, Vandermark, Raymondskill and Dingmans, while the view from the Knob and Utter's Peak was scarcely overestimated by the little boy, who came running back to urge his momma to 'hurry up; I can see the whole world.'"

View up the Delaware, Milford, PA.

TRANSPORTATION AND TERMS

The back of the brochure tells potential guests:
"How to Reach Milford-Erie Railroad to Port Jervis,
87 miles from New York
Round Trip, New York to Port Jervis.....$3.60
Ten Trip Family Tickets, New York to Port Jervis.....$15.90
Saturday Afternoon Special:
Leaves New York at 2 O'Clock P.M.,
Arriving at Bluff House at 6 P.M.
Terms $10.00 to $18.00 per Week
Transient $2.50 per Day
Special Rates for Families Remaining for the Season for Children
and Servants-when writing state age and requirements"

GLIDDEN AUTO TOUR

On July 15, 1907 the Bluff House was one of the stops on a Glidden Tour of the American Automobile Association. The tour started in Buffalo, New York and ended in Saratoga Springs. On July 15 the first car to arrive, a Rapid, pulled up to the Bluff House at 12:20 PM. In all, fifty seven cars arrived at the resort where they were greeted by the Erie Band. The cars parked between the Bluff House and Harford Street and attracted much attention but were closely guarded.

The next day they departed en route to Albany leaving at one minute intervals. At that time Matamoras Borough had gained a reputation as a "speed trap," but borough officials agreed to suspend enforcement of speeding laws on July 16th to accommodate the Glidden Tour participants!

BATHING BEACH AND BATH HOUSES, MILFORD, PA.

BATHING BEACH

The Bluff House bathing and boating beach on the Delaware River was a popular rendezvous. An attractive pavilion with wide porches was erected to provide comfort for those who enjoyed participating in or watching water sports. Professor N. B. Coykendall staged water exhibitions and taught swimming. Guests were encouraged to participate in swimming races and prizes were awarded.

BATHING BEACH, MILFORD, PA.

BATHING BEACH AND BLUFF HOUSE, MILFORD, PA.

"WET" ERA

On June 21, 1935 when the Bluff House opened for the season it contained a "cocktail lounge" which reflected a new approach in the selling of liquor. Ladies were encouraged to imbibe and a new type of cocktail was sold each day for twenty cents. They also offered a "happy hour" with a 10% reduction in the cost of drinks between the hours of 1:00 PM and 7:00 PM.

Aerial View of Bluff House and Beach, Milford, Pa.

WAR RELIEF EFFORT

On Sunday, August 19, 1945 the Bluff House, now owned by Michael Conroy, was the site of a war relief benefit dinner. Among those speaking was David Malhame, Sr., a businessman who had been a prisoner of the Japanese. He would soon establish a vestment company in Milford.

The Bluff House was destroyed by fire March 26, 1947. Attorney Sidney Krawitz and his wife Lydia purchased the property and built their home.

SUMMER HOUSE

Norman Lehde tells us in the Heritage: 250 book that the Village Improvement Association erected a summer house on the "Bluff" overlooking the river, circa 1908.

Summer House on the Bluff, Milford Pa.

208560 J.K.

BOATING ON THE DELAWARE

The Bluff House proclaimed: "A flotilla of round-bottom steel rowboats and canoes is kept for the convenience of the public. Among anglers, the Delaware has long been known for its superior black bass fishing. Other varieties are also plentiful. Guides who know the fishing grounds and the best bait to use are always available."

VIEW DOWN THE DELAWARE FROM THE BLUFF, MILFORD, PA.

Delaware River from Bluff House   Milford, Pa.

"If all the world were postal cards,
And all the seas were ink,
And postage stamps were gratis,
Would you write me, do you think?"

MILFORD BEND

This circa 1940 view shows the river at the Milford bend, below the Bluff House, looking toward Montague, New Jersey.

Looking up Ann Street, Milford, Pa.   12460

BELOVED DR. KLAER

Pictured above, in this view of 306 East Ann Street, is the home that belonged to Dr. Harvey and Mildred Bournique Klaer. On October 17, 1976 Commissioners James R. Duffy, Jr., Warner Depuy, H. James Crellin and Milford Mayor Russell Roberts unveiled a plaque dedicated to Dr. Klaer. A proclamation thanked him for his years of service to the people of Pike County.

NORTHWEST CORNER OF ANN AND THIRD

The Westbrook house was owned by John C. Westbrook, Jr. and his wife, Josephine Crissman Westbrook, in the early 1900s. Mr. Westbrook was Pike County Prothonotary from 1875 to 1908. The house, as seen in this photo, had a large veranda which followed the line of the circular bay and extended on the side to form a porte-cochere. The home is presently being restored by Brian and Ingrid Pimley.

MILFORD METHODIST CHURCH

According to the history of the Milford Methodist Church, its origin can be traced back to blacksmith Bartholomew Weed. In 1813 Mr. Weed lived south of the Pike County Court House (present Sheriff's Office), on the opposite side of the street in a two room house. He established a family altar and held services on Sunday, preaching to anyone who wanted to attend. Circa 1817 he moved to Philadelphia, became an ordained Methodist minister and continued in his profession for sixty-two years.

In 1825 Reverend John K. Shaw was invited to preach at the Court House. He came to Milford and organized the first Methodist congregation composed of Mrs. Eliza Mott, Mrs. Louisa Broadhead, Mrs. Mary Olmstead, Mrs. Sophia Suiter and Mr. and Mrs. David Hand.

ORIGINAL CHURCH

On December 14, 1826 Judge John Brink, a trustee of the Methodist congregation, and Mrs. Brink deeded a piece of land on the Delaware River to the church. The church members built their church on the site of the present-day Milford Beach. The congregation was pleased to have their church in such a beautiful location but dismayed when every spring flood waters from the Delaware caused damage to the building. Circa 1835 they decided it was time to move to higher ground. They dismantled the church and reassembled it at their new location on 210 East Ann Street. This town lot was also given to the church by the Brink family.

METHODIST CHURCH, MILFORD, PA.

Published By C. O. Armstrong   METHODIST EPISCOPAL CHURCH, MILFORD, PA.   6207 M

M. E. CHURCH, MILFORD, PA.

NEW METHODIST CHURCH

The new church was erected at 206 East Ann Street during the Civil War and was dedicated on July 10, 1864. A parsonage was added in 1879.

THE WALTER RIDLEY FAMILY

In this postcard, depicting part of East Ann Street, it is possible to see the new Methodist Church, the parsonage and the original church. After the new church was built, the original church building was used for other purposes. At one point it was a seminary and later a boarding house. Ultimately it became a two-family home. The last family to live in half of the dwelling was that of Walter and Helen Ridley and their ten children. Arthur, one of their sons and an attorney in Milford, became an active member of the Milford Methodist Church. Perhaps partially because he was literally raised in the church, he felt a strong desire to serve his fellow congregates. To that end on December 4, 1958 the District Commission on Ministerial Qualifications voted unanimously in favor of granting Arthur Ridley a license to preach. He has been a popular guest preacher at many local Methodist Churches.

In 1963 the church razed the building and created a parking lot for its members.

ANN STREET, SHOWING M. E. CHURCH, MILFORD, PA.

— 202 —

A CAPPELLA

Prior to 1861 the Milford Methodist Church congregation sang hymns pitched by a tuning fork for their services. There was no choir. In 1861 a hand-pumped organ was purchased and the first choir established. Members of the choir were: Mrs. C.W. Armstrong, who also served as first organist; Mary E. Day, second organist; J. Halstead Wells, choir leader; and choir members Mary Wells, Henrietta Slack, Adelia Brown, and John Slack.

RALLY DAY

On November 11, 1910 the Ladies Aid Society decided a pipe organ was needed. They started the fund to buy the organ with ten dollars. In 1922 the fund was augmented by a bequeathment of one thousand dollars from the estate of William H. Schmitt. In 1925 a committee was established to secure the rest of the funds needed to buy an organ. Vera Myer was selected as Secretary and Paul N. Bournique was named Treasurer. It should be noted that, as the congregation struggled to find the funds for an organ, in 1913 the steeple on the church was struck by lightning and had to be removed. In 1926 a new, shorter steeple was built in time for the celebration of the church's 100th anniversary.

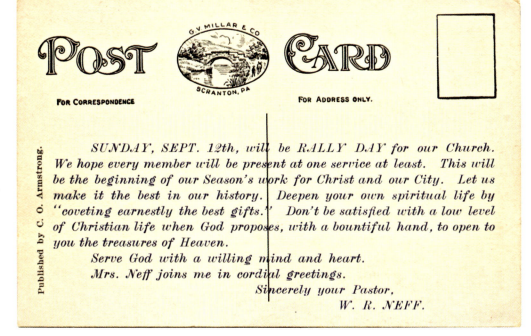

CHURCH IMPROVEMENTS

Throughout the years the congregations of the Methodist Church made numerous improvements to help preserve the historical and architectural integrity of the building. In 1890 the walls were frescoed and steam heat was added in 1892. In 1898 the oil lamps were replaced by acetylene gas fixtures. The period of 1903 through 1906 saw the installation and dedication of stained-glass memorial windows. In 1921 the church was wired for electricity. A church school education wing was built in 1962 that now houses the Ann Street Preschool Program.

On the evening of October 29, 1989 an arsonist's fire caused more than $500,000 worth of damage to the church. During the five month reconstruction period the congregation was invited to worship services at the Matamoras Methodist Church.

Methodist Episcopal Church, Milford, Pa.   13602

The Methodist Church, Milford, Pennsylvania   16698

THE UNITED METHODIST CHURCH

The Milford Methodist Church which had been chartered as the Methodist Episcopal Church became the Methodist Church in 1939 when it joined with the Methodist Protestant Church. In 1968 the Methodist Church united with the Evangelical United Brethren Church to create the United Methodist Church.

Historically the Milford Methodist Church was served by part-time or student pastors but in 1964 Reverend H. Wayne Cramsey assumed a full-time position. On December 22, 1967 Reverend Cramsey officiated at the wedding of Lorraine and Skip Gregory.

CHURCH ORGAN

On January 26, 1926, the organ committee established by the Ladies Aid Society met with Louis C. Odell, of the Odell Organ Company. The committee voted to recommend to the trustees the purchase of a "two manual electric magnetic organ with nine stops." This was accomplished, the organ ordered and installed and on June 22, 1926. Mrs. Lila [Howard] Kyte played the new organ for the morning service. Lila served as organist until 1931. Temporary volunteer organists followed until 1934 when Miss Ruth Maines of Matamoras was hired at a rate of $2.50 per week. While serving as organist Ruth met James Myer who was Superintendent of the Sunday School. They married in 1938. Ruth continued as organist for fifty-three years before retiring at the age of eighty. Jim served as the Superintendent of Sunday School for thirty-eight years.

HERRICK HOME

This was the residence of W.C. Herrick at 115 East Ann Street. It was razed to make way for a new home.

Herrick Residence, Milford, Pa.

Christmas '88 Milford Methodist Church

View up Ann Street. Milford, Pa.

No. 5   Moore & Gibson Co., New York.   Germany

ANNUAL TREE BEE

Please note in these photographs the similarity in the size and, therefore, presumably, the age of the trees. Norman Lehde wrote a newspaper column for many years entitled "Along Milford's Shady Streets." And, indeed, they were and are "shady" but not by accident. Tree bees in Milford date back to the 1830s.

NEIGHBORS

Circa 1840, according to a publication by the Milford Shade Tree Commission compiled under the auspices of chairwoman Valerie Meyer and given to us by Mary Jane Seidenstricker, Mrs. Emanuel Quick lived with her husband and children in a house on Ann Street. They also owned a large barn on another lot. Each spring Mr. Quick and his neighbors would hitch their horses to lumber-box wagons and go into the swampy areas surrounding the village and gather maple saplings.

Ann Street, Milford, Pa.

CHICKEN POT PIE

They would return in the evening with their wagons filled with young trees, put the horses in the barn and park their wagons. Then the foragers would gather in Mrs. Quick's kitchen and enjoy the chicken pot pie dinner that she and her friends, Mrs. Oscar Mott and Mrs. Emily Buchanan, had prepared. The next day they would pick one street, such as Ann, and plant the trees from one end of the street to the other. A different street was selected each year until all were "tree lined."

PALATIAL RESIDENCE, 116 EAST ANN STREET

Thanks to persistent and thorough research of county records, we are able to provide a concise and accurate account of the evolution of the building that would become the Milford Inn. In 1862 Dr. Edward Haliday, a broker from Brooklyn, relocated to Milford and bought four town lots from Elizabeth Cornelius, widow of Lewis, late proprietor of the Sawkill House. The lots comprised nearly an acre and were located at 110-116 East Ann Street. Dr. Haliday commissioned the construction of a palatial home, barns, office and shop and in 1864 records tell us he paid $1935 in taxes. In 1867 after adding cows, a cow stable, horses and ponies his tax was $2,887, one of the highest rates in the borough. We are told his home was one of the showplaces of the area and the furniture and fixtures in the house were imported from Europe. He lavished as much attention and money on landscaping the property as he did on furnishing the house. An ornamental wrought iron fence with intricately designed gates surrounded the beautifully landscaped grounds consisting of flowers gardens, elaborate pathways and gurgling fountains.

The Milford Inn, Milford, Pa.

A LETTER FROM EDWARD HALIDAY

Apparently Dr. Haliday was a bit of a wit as evidenced by an invitation he wrote to a friend regarding a party at his house on December 31st, 1866. The document is owned by the Pike County Historical Society, reprinted here with their permission and was found by their conservator Charlie Quilici.

"My dear Jim-
I would be pleased to see you at my house, this evening, to join with a few 'congenial spirits' in seeing the 'old year out & the New Year in.' The party will be purely a 'Stag' affair, consequently kid gloves will not be necessary-Trusting to the favor of your company-

I am truly fraternally yours,
E. Haliday"

LINCOLN PRESIDENTIAL ELECTOR

But Dr. Haliday did not relocate to Milford to merely entertain. He had a goal. According to Mathews: "Dr. Haliday was that year [1864] Presidential elector for Mr. Lincoln for this Congressional district." He was a staunch supporter of Abraham Lincoln and on February 6, 1864 Haliday printed the first issue of his newspaper, "The Northern Eagle." He wanted to spare no expense in converting the Milford/Pike County stronghold of Democracy to Republicanism. He strongly agreed with Horace Greeley's view of Pike County: "That it was a land of Democrats and the home of the rattlesnake, and that it contained ten gallons of whiskey to every Webster's Spelling Book." He sent a copy of his paper to every voter in Pike County and inaugurated a Republican meeting in Milford with Horace Greeley as speaker. Ultimately he was not successful in his attempts to convert the people of Pike to the Republican Party and "The Northern Eagle" ceased publication after the Civil War. Edward Haliday died in 1869 or 1870 and his estate was sold to the highest bidder, Emma Louise Hubbard, by Pike County Sheriff John Cornelius on August 25, 1871 for $19,000.

MILFORD INN, MID-WINTER VIEW.
OPEN ALL THE YEAR, PERCY LYMAN, PROP.

MILFORD INN

After a succession of owners who continued to maintain the property as a private residence, circa 1906 Mr. and Mrs. Percy Lyman bought the property and operated it as the "Milford Inn." Mrs. Lyman was a granddaughter of Louis Fauchere. She and her husband added rooms to the house to accommodate guests.

MILFORD INN, MILFORD, PIKE COUNTY, PA.

Milford Inn, Milford, Pa.

GRAND OPENING DANCE

Circa 1917 Mr. and Mrs. Fulvia Piergiorgi, of Hot Springs, Georgia, bought the Inn. On April 18, 1918 they placed this advertisement in the local paper: "Everybody is Invited to the Grand Opening Dance at the Milford Inn Saturday, April 20 commencing 8 P.M. Music by the Milford Orchestra."

1926

This postcard is dated "1926." An advertisement from that year tells us the Milford Inn was: "The Most Modern Hotel in Pike County. One square block of private garden with rare trees, flowers and shrubs. Three minutes walk from Delaware River, on Milford's most beautiful residential street. All rooms have private bath or running water. En suite or single. Open fireplaces and steam heat. Balconies and spacious piazza. Open air dining room. French cuisine."

ENTRANCE TO MILFORD INN   MILFORD, PA.

VEGETABLE GARDEN

The Milford Inn and several of the larger boarding houses or hotels in Milford had their own vegetable gardens. This enabled the chefs of these establishments to provide the freshest of produce throughout the "season."

FLOWER GARDEN

While vegetable gardens were commonplace, flower gardens were not. Few establishments had the property to indulge in such displays. However, the property, when owned by Dr. Haliday, was described as having "flowers outlining the curving flagstone walks through the gardens." This is a surviving flower garden as seen from the grill room.

GRILL ROOM, MILFORD, PA.

GRILL ROOM

The advertisement for the Milford Inn promised "French cuisine," but it also mentions an "open air dining room." Apparently the "Grill Room" is the open air dining room in which diners could enjoy a lighter meal such as grilled lamb chops.

FORMAL DINING ROOM

Guests at the Milford Inn often stayed for several weeks or for the season. Meals were served in the dining room as well as the grillroom and food preparation was an ongoing activity. The kitchen was located in the basement and staff members worked in shifts to prepare breakfast, lunch and dinner meals.

In the 1920s the Piergiogi family prepared and served French cuisine. In the 1930s when the Julius Calestini family operated the Inn, the menu offered many Italian-American selections. The Calestini family is credited with introducing pizza to local residents.

DINING ROOM, MILFORD INN, MILFORD, PIKE COUNTY, PA.

PARLOR

The interior design of decorative molding, French doors and multiple fireplaces provided comfortable space for patrons.

PARLOR, MILFORD INN, MILFORD, PIKE COUNTY, PA.

CONCEALED ICE HOUSE

On a quiet day guests could enjoy the melodic sound of water splashing from a two-tiered fountain into a large pool as they sat in any of the three gazebos on the property. These ornamental "summer houses" were an attractive addition to the landscape but one of them also had a practical use. It was an ice house! Ice blocks were cut from local ponds in the winter and stored in a cellar under the structure. Access was from a trap door in the floor of the gazebo.

Milford Inn, Milford, Pa.

MILFORD INN, CIRCA 1947

In 1933 Jules and Ernestine Calestini purchased the property. Cynthia VanLierde tells us in "Historic Sites in Milford": "They operated the Inn for many years until fire destroyed a large rear section of the building. After it was rebuilt, the Calestinis converted the building into apartments, leaving just the bar operating in the rear of the building. A casualty of the fire was the decorative cupola on the original part of the building. This was not replaced." In 2000 the Calestini family gifted the historic wrought iron fence to the Borough of Milford in memory of their father.

In 2000 Newton Memorial Hospital purchased the property and had the inn torn down. The Newton Memorial Hospital's Health and Wellness Center opened in December 2002.

ARMSTRONG HOUSE

View on Ann Street, Milford, Pa.

Designed by T.I. Lindsey, an architect based in Middletown, New York, this house at 206 West Ann Street was built in 1901 by Henry Canne for Clinton O. Armstrong, a prosperous Milford pharmacist. One of the contractors hired to help with the construction of the house was a "bell hanger." This was a mechanic whose trade was to install door bells in the house as well as "buzzers" throughout the house that would summon the servants.

REVIVED TREE BEES

The brochure published by the Milford Shade Tree Commission in honor of Arbor Day, April 29, 2005 tells us: "In 1949, after the lapse of nearly a century, David Malhame, Sr. revived the Tree Bee. In 1952, the Milford Garden Club, under the direction of Georgiana Kiger, continued the spring event to replace decaying trees along the borough streets. At the sounding of one blast on the fire alarm at one o'clock, all able bodied men gathered at the Firehouse. A short time prior to that, William E. Palmer arrived on the scene from his home in Westfall Township with the first load of ten swamp trees drawn by the beautifully matched team of Clydes, Nancy and Betsy."

HOME OF EDGAR PINCHOT

Edgar Pinchot, son of Cyrille and Eliza Dimmick Pinchot, worked in New York City for the wholesale drug firm of Pinchot and Bruen for twenty-five years. In 1875 he retired and returned to Milford where, according to Mathews, he " built an elegant brick residence on the corner of Fifth and Ann Streets, which he now occupies." This home was located at 203 West Ann Street where the basketball court is now, near the Milford Playground. By all accounts it was a beautiful home and was locally called "Inwall" because of a concrete block wall which surrounded it.

QUICK HOMESTEAD

The Milford Architectural Study Committee's research tells us this house at 214 West Ann Street "was a simple farmhouse which was the homestead of the Quick family in the early 1800's, possibly the late 1700's. In 1905 James Bull and his bride, Mary Wakeman purchased the three room house. In their renovations of the house the kitchen was literally picked up and moved so that a large room could be added to the center of the house. The two towering spruce trees framing the doorway of the home were planted by James and Mary when they were newlyweds. According to the local custom of the time the young trees were planted to symbolize the growing affection of the bride and groom." The 102-year old trees are still there. The home is presently owned by Ernest and Lynn Bush.

Mr. and Mrs. Josiah Foster Terwilliger
request the pleasure of your company at the celebration of their
Tenth Wedding Anniversary
Tuesday Evening, October the Thirty-first
Nineteen Hundred and Eleven
at eight o'clock
at their residence corner Ann and Sixth Streets
Milford, Pennsylvania.

JOSIAH FOSTER TERWILLIGER

Josiah Foster Terwilliger was the son of Almer Terwilliger and namesake of his grandfather Josiah Foster Terwilliger. The first Josiah was a popular political figure in Pike County and Milford and was a contemporary of Chauncy W. Dimmick and Charles R. Biddis. Almer worked in the watch case factory for twenty-five years but also served as constable and a member of the board of health for Milford.

Josiah Foster Terwilliger the second, author of this invitation, started as an assistant editor of the Milford Dispatch. In 1911 when this invitation was issued, he was editor of the newspaper and Milford borough auditor.

MILFORD BIBLE CHURCH

Reverend Marshall Weatherby in the Heritage:250 book relates, "The Milford Bible Protestant Church had its roots in a small Bible Study Group which began meeting on Sunday afternoons in April 1961, at the home of Mr. and Mrs. Karl Fischer, 400 Seventh Street, Milford." Meetings soon shifted to Pinchot Grange Hall at 303 West Ann Street. Originally this building was at 209 West Ann Street where it was operated for a number of years as a funeral chapel by Colin Black. On August 28, 1961 the application of the Milford Church was voted into membership by The Bible Protestant Church, Inc. In July 1975 the membership initiated a large building plan. The former funeral chapel was torn down and a new building with a stone exterior was built. This doubled the size of the sanctuary. A name change occurred in October, 1977 when the congregation became known as the Milford Bible Church. In 2002 the continued increase in church membership fueled the need for a larger building. The new Milford Bible Church is located off Route 2001 at 110 Foxcroft Drive. The West Ann Street building will revert to residences.

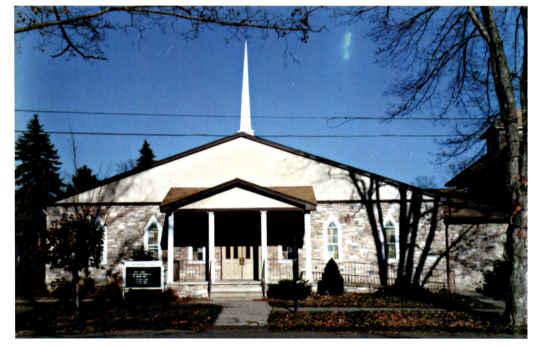

Field Club, Milford, Pa.

FIELD CLUB

The Milford Field Club was located at 300-306 West Catharine Street, the present site of the Edith Gregory and Gwen Crellin homes. The Club was organized in 1909 and its primary purpose was to promote the sport of tennis. Four clay courts and a modern clubhouse, with locker rooms and showers, were constructed. Many of the tennis "greats" of the day, Bill Tilden, Don Budge, Frances Hunter, Percy Keniston and Cecil Donaldson, came to Milford to play in the Delaware Valley Championship Games held every August. In 1922 Amos Pinchot, Gifford's brother, won the men's singles contest in the tournament. He defeated Emil Schields, a former Fordham athlete, in the finals.

BOROUGH BUILDING

The Milford Borough Building at 109 West Catharine Street was built in 1899 to serve as a meeting hall and fire house. The fire equipment was housed on the ground floor and the entrance tower gave access to the second floor meeting rooms. The first fire company in Milford was the Pioneer Hose Company, organized in the 1860s. It wasn't until the 1880s, when hydrants became available, that the Milford Volunteer Fire Company became better able to fight fires.

Milford Fire Department, Milford, Pa.

VOLUNTEER FIRE COMPANY

The people of the Borough of Milford have historically relied on volunteer fire fighters. The volunteers maintain state of the art firefighting equipment as well as provide rescue and ambulance services. Many volunteers have accepted leadership roles including Milford Volunteer Fire Department Company members pictured here: (L-R) Leith Hoffman, President; Red Helms, Chief 1985-88 and 1998-2000; Scott Fean, Chief 1983- 85 and Skip Gregory, Past President. In 1962 during Skip's tenure as president, the present firehouse at 107 West Catharine Street was built on the site of the former Milford Steam Laundry.

MERRITT B. QUINN

Merritt Quinn was born to Merritt and Pauline Boileau Quinn on the Quinn Farm at 217 Sawkill Road, Dingman Township on October 24, 1919. When he was a young man he helped with chores on the farm. One of his chores was to assist his father when he delivered milk to the families in Milford. Merritt says, "he knew who lived in every house."

Merritt first threw his hat into the political ring in 1961 when encouraged by Edith Gregory to run for a seat on the Milford Borough Council. He was elected and continued to serve on the council for twenty-six distinguished years. In 1968 Merritt became a Milford businessman when he purchased the Pike Beverage store. He had a building constructed in 1972 at 204 West Harford Street to house his business which he renamed Milford Beverage. Merritt, a dedicated thirty-eight year member of the Milford Lions Club, has assisted that organization with all its community projects from placing American flags on Harford and Broad streets to erecting a star on the Knob at Christmas.

In 2005 he was successful in his bid for re-election as Mayor of Milford.

EPISCOPAL CHURCH, MILFORD, PA.

Violet Terwilliger wishes the pleasure of your Company Monday August 12th from 3 to 5 P. M.

EPISCOPAL CHURCH

The Episcopal Church in Milford began in 1849 when a visiting New York City clergyman held the first Episcopal service in the Pike County Court House. Regular services began in July 1886 when an Episcopal service was held in the Presbyterian Church.

CHURCH BUILT

The Church of the Good Shepherd was formally organized on April 3, 1871. The cornerstone of the first Episcopal Church building at the corner of Fifth and Catharine Streets was laid in June, 1871. The first services in this building were held in June, 1872. The church was consecrated on September 14, 1877.

Published By C. O. Armstrong   CHURCH OF THE GOOD SHEPHERD, MILFORD, PA.   6208 M

EDGAR PINCHOT

The church was organized with the election of Edgar Pinchot as Senior Warden and Edgar Brodhead as Junior Warden. John C. Mott, D.M. Van Auken, W.C. Broome, C. W. Dimmick, Sidney A. Hanes and M.M. Dimmick were all selected to serve as Vestrymen.

RECTORS

Those men serving as rectors for the church from 1871 to 1886 are listed by Alfred Mathews as "Rev. W.B. Hooper, Rev. A. H. Gersner, Rev. Samuel Edwards and Rev. D'Estang Jennings."

Church of Good Shepherd, (Episcopal), Milford, Pa.

Protestant Episcopal Church, Milford, Pa.

CHURCH FIRE

EPISCOPAL CHURCH, MILFORD, PA.

After the forty-three year-old wooden building burned on September 28, 1913, the resilient Episcopalians planned a new building. The replacement stone structure was completed in 1914. The stone work was accomplished by members of the Snyder family. Andrew, Leonard Snyder's grandfather; Joe, Frank Snyder's father; George, Carl Snyder's grandfather; Josh C., Lillian Musselwhite's grandfather; and John L. and Charles, two of Andrew's sons, all served as masons.

BUILDING THE CHURCH

The new church was built on the old foundation lines but the width of the stone walls was much greater than those of the wooden structure. This caused the interior of the church to be about two feet narrower on every side than was the original church. The stone came from the Pinchot property.

Masons Leonard Snyder and his father John L. were awarded the contract to build an addition to the church in 1964.

PUBL. BY C. O. ARMSTRONG

Episcopal Church. Milford, Pa.

THE CHURCH OF THE GOOD SHEPHERD – ST. JOHN THE EVANGELIST

Sandy Beecher in the Heritage:250 book tells us: "The Milford parish of Good Shepherd and St. John's parish in Dingmans Ferry were served by Reverend Richard Aselford who would 'ride circuit' on Sundays to preach at both churches. In 1971 the Dingmans Ferry Church property was acquired by the U.S. Army Corps of Engineers for the Tocks Island Project. Following an invitation by Good Shepherd to join its congregation en masse, it was decided by the respective vestries to merge the two churches. The present day Episcopal Church in Milford became the Church of Good Shepherd –St. John the Evangelist on July 16, 1972."

K 1039

Church of The Good Shepherd, Milford, Pa.

CROSS

The interior is laid out, as are the cathedrals in Europe, in the form of a cross with nave and transept.

— 222 —

GASSMAN HOME

This home was at 305 West High Street. It was owned by Frank Gassman. Frank's nephew, Richard Gassman, is the present Mayor of Matamoras.

COUNTRY ESTATE

This magnificent home at 501 Seventh Street was built for Elias Mallouk. Mr. Mallouk was an importer of cotton and linen fabrics who had vacationed at the Winsor on High Street before building his summer home on Seventh Street. Mr. Mallouk was born in Egypt but immigrated to New York where he spent his winters in his Long Island home. Summers were spent at his Milford residence. The home is presently owned by Michael J. Beno.

A COUNTRY ESTATE, MILFORD, PA.

PHILLIPS HOME

Robert Reid built the home at 702 Sixth Street. Robert Warner Reid was the grandson of Ebenezer Warner, the founder of the First National Bank of Milford. Robert served on the bank's first board of directors. The present owner of the home is Pat Phillips.

MISENHELDER HOUSE, CIRCA 1930

The Misenhelder House was located at 201 West John Street. Originally this building was located on the west side of Broad and John Streets. Phillip Misenhelder bought the building from the McLaughlin Family in 1912. The one-story structure was moved to its present site on John Street in two parts. Phillip added a second story. Cynthia Van Lierde tells us the Misenhelder House was a boarding house famous for the food and hospitality provided by Phillip and Bridget Misenhelder from 1919 to 1953. State Police assigned to the Milford area stayed at the house and stabled their horses in a large barn to the rear of the house. After Phillip's death, Mrs. Misenhelder provided lodging for guests until her passing in 1959. From 1962 to 1980 the building was used as a nursing home. Today it is maintained as an apartment house known as Milford Manor.

WILLIAM ARMSTRONG HOUSE

It is believed that this building at 110 East High Street was completed in 1898. William Armstrong, a highly successful builder in New York City credited with building the Washington Market and an addition to the Museum of Natural History, could afford to build his summer home as lavishly as he desired.

The Winsor.   Milford, Pa.

THE WINSOR

In 1926 the Armstrong family heirs, no longer interested in keeping the house, sold it to Harold M. Winsor. Mr. Winsor was an excellent chef who ran the big establishment as a first-class hotel, the Winsor. For a brief time it was the most fashionable place to stay in Milford.

ARMSTRONG FAMILY

In 1930 Mr. Winsor relinquished the house to the Armstrong family as he was unable to keep up with the mortgage.

THE WINSOR, MILFORD, PA. "THE HIGHEST PRICED HOUSE IN MILFORD."

MARGARET DUER JUDGE SCHOOL FOR EXCEPTIONAL CHILDREN, MILFORD, PIKE CO., PA.

JUDGE SCHOOL

Circa 1940 the Armstrong family had had enough and sold the house to Margaret Duer Judge for five thousand dollars. She ran a successful home for mentally challenged children for twenty-five years. Edith Gregory bought the property in 1967. The present owners are Lee and Greta Palmer who maintain six apartments in the building.

ST. PATRICK'S CHURCH, 1957

A ground-breaking ceremony was held for the new Saint Patrick's Church on July 1, 1956 on the northeast corner of Fourth and East High Streets. The ceremony was conducted by the Rev. Vincent J. Mahon. The cornerstone was laid in October, 1956 by Msgr. Connell McHugh VF of Mt. Pocono, PA. The church cost $115,000 to build and was dedicated on June 30, 1957.

The belfry contains a carillon of electronic bells which plays for services, weddings and funerals. Photograph courtesy of Jim Levell.

ST. PATRICK'S CHURCH, 2006

Cynthia Van Lierde in "Historic Sites in Milford" tells us about the building at the southwest corner of East High and Fourth Streets. "The convent building was constructed by A.D. Brown, for the Swepenhiser family, around 1870. George Swepenhiser, a Civil War veteran, served for many years as Commissioner's Clerk in the Court House. Next occupants were Mrs. Buchan and her son, Lloyd. They sold to Chester A. Dissinger, former Superintendent of Schools." The Dissinger family lived there until the Diocese of Scranton bought the property which then became part of Saint Patrick's Parish. A Catechetical Center, Nursery School, Kindergarten and Convent were established in 1946 and staffed by Sisters, the Servants of the Immaculate Heart of Mary. The Center was closed in 1981. The building was remodeled in 1994 to serve as a residence for the pastor. In 2005 the building was moved to 209 East High Street to make room for the construction of a new Catholic Church. The first service in the new Catholic Church was October 15, 2006.

Photograph courtesy of Jim Levell.

UPPER MILFORD, PA. 6209 M

VIEW FROM FOSTER HILL

The next four postcards offer the reader wonderful views of the Borough of Milford from Foster Hill. The original Catholic Church, located on the northwest corner of 8th and James Streets, is pictured in this card on the right. Promotional rhetoric espoused by the Milford Chamber of Commerce in the 1920s tells us:

WOODCRAFT

"The Milford Chamber of Commerce is pledged in faith and fixed in purpose to develop to the utmost the natural advantages of this region as a summer recreational and residential section; and its wild lands as a preserve for those who enjoy hunting, fishing and woodcraft at any season of the year.

C. O. Armstrong. MILFORD, PA., FROM FOSTER HILL. 6433 M

BUILDING SITES AVAILABLE

"While Milford and its environing hills and valleys are famous chiefly for the rest, health and happiness they afford summer vacationists, we wish to impress on all who might be interested that there are many rugged, magnificent building sites commanding beautiful views, and choice lots in and about our villages suitable for cottages or year around homes.

Milford from Foster Hill, Milford, Pa.

MILFORD, PA., FROM FOSTER HILL.

HAND OF WELCOME

"For information regarding Milford and other sections of Pike County, inquiries should be sent to the secretary of this organization. While desiring to foster the Elysian character of this land of heart's desire, we are glad to invite others here to enjoy it with us."

Please note the magnitude of the Bluff House overlooking the Delaware River.

MILFORD, PA.   The Orchard

THE ORCHARD

Anthony Stumpf was a successful New York City banker. He bought property at the top of Foster Hill Road (Seventh Street) in the 1880s and built a home for his family. The large family farmhouse was later operated by his wife and his daughter, Amelia, as a boarding house. It was called "The Orchard" in recognition of the many fruit trees growing on the property. The high elevation of the property made it an ideal place to grow apples, pears and peaches.

FOSTER HILL DAIRY FARM · J. SANTOS

FOSTER HILL DAIRY FARM

Amelia married Julio C. Santos, a house painter. Their son, Julio A. Santos was born on February 24, 1906 in Bronx, NY. He was six months old when his father and mother returned to Orchard House. Julio began helping his father with farm chores when he was twelve. In 1923 when he was seventeen, he began his dairy farm with one cow. He added to the herd and sold milk to the public under the auspices of the Foster Hill Dairy Farm. About the same time he began a long courtship with Marion Herbst, Pike County's first woman pharmacist. They were married in 1933 and lived in a home on Foster Hill until 1941 when they bought the Tuscano Farm on Routes 6 and 209. Presently the Orchard House/Foster Hill Dairy Farm property is home to Richard L. Snyder and his llama farm.

LEE THURSBY

In the late 1930s Lee Thursby designed and constructed the Malibu Dude Ranch at 351 Foster Hill Road. It was built as a guest ranch with a western design. The main ranch house contained a living room, game room, dining room and several bedrooms. The guest cabins were grouped near the ranch house. All accommodations included private bathrooms.

MALIBU DUDE RANCH

In his advertisements Mr. Thursby stated: "One desiring the social activities and formality found at a beach or mountain resort will find these lacking at Malibu." He goes on to say that "discriminating people seeking a quiet, restful vacation, with plenty of horse activity, will find Malibu an ideal place."

"All that's best of the West at MALIBU RANCH in the Poconos"

Aerial View of Malibu Dude Ranch, Milford, Pa.

VIEW OF MALIBU RANCH HOUSE, MILFORD, PA.

SPRING-FED POND

The ranch provided a fresh water spring-fed pond for swimming and fishing for those guests who preferred less horseback riding and more typical summer vacation pursuits. There were also areas for hiking, target-shooting and pitching horseshoes. Deer, bear and small game hunting was encouraged when in season.

CORRAL SCENE, MALIBU DUDE RANCH, MILFORD, PA.

RODEO

Each guest at the ranch was assigned to a specific horse whose temperament reflected the ability of the rider. Rodeo activities took place in the main arena. Some guests became expert ropers.

COWBOYS

Trail rides were everyday occurrences. Cowboys employed by the ranch served as guides. The rides were through picturesque wooded terrains or over scenic country roadways. The eight-hundred acre ranch allowed guests to experience different scenery on each daily ride.

MALIBU DUDE RANCH, MILFORD, PA.

"All that's best of the West at MALIBU RANCH in the Poconos"

Malibu Dude Ranch, Milford, Pa.

CHUCK WAGON

According to Mr. Thursby: "Once or twice a week the chuck wagon is sent on ahead into the beautiful pine-covered mountains to waterfalls and other scenic points, where we ride to meet it. We cook our lunch under the pines, spend a couple of hours resting and return to the Ranch in the late afternoon. We vary this occasionally with a breakfast ride."

CHOW HALL

LIVING ROOM AT THE RANCH HOUSE—MALIBU RANCH—MILFORD, PA.   102

The living room at the ranch house was a congenial meeting place for rainy day activities. Wholesome meals with home-made bread and pastries were served in the dining room, or chow hall, of the house.

STEVE EMANUEL

On March 12, 1966 Steve Emanuel purchased Malibu Dude Ranch. He had been a visitor to the ranch in the 1950s when he used it as a place to escape from his work in New York City.

WRANGLER

Today the term "wrangler" is used more frequently than "cowboy," but horseback riding and rodeo weekend events are still the main activities at the ranch. Mr. Emanuel tells us it is "the longest continuously running ranch in the East" and he allows his guests to "ride all day" if they so choose.

Malibu Ranch, Milford, Pa.

We are celebrating the completion of our 20th year at Malibu Ranch. On March 12, 1986 at 6:30 p.m. we are having a cocktail party and buffet to mark this occasion. It would be our pleasure to have you come and join us.

Steve & Peggy Emmanual

R.S.V.P. 296-7281

SPRING, 2006

Today the ranch encompasses eight-hundred acres, allowing its guests continued diversified trail rides. The ranch comprises seventeen buildings, has eighteen employees and stables seventy horses. The Emanuel family continue as hosts.

CHILDS PARK CAMPGROUNDS

The story of Moon Valley Ranch, as told by Viola Canouse, Milford Township Secretary and Tax Collector, actually begins in 1925 in Childs Park, Dingmans Ferry, PA. Francis Kern, her father, was a guard at Childs Park Campgrounds when he met and married Ethel Hoover in 1931. Childs Park has three waterfalls, Factory, Fulmer, and Deer Leap. Viola was born in 1933. Her baptismal ceremony was held under the Deer Leap Waterfall.

RAINBOW VILLAGE

In 1941 Francis and Ethel Kern bought property on Silver Lake Road opposite Shepherd's Corner. Francis built their home, as well as a group of tourist cabins, which they called Rainbow Village. Viola says: "He loved to do fancy, storybook-like buildings and some remain to this day." Pictured is the main entrance to Moon Valley Park.

CHARLES (DOC) STROH

In 1949 Francis and Ethel purchased nine-hundred and seventy-six acres on the outskirts of Milford from Charles (Doc) Stroh. There was a small hunting shack on the property as well as a barn where Doc Stroh kept horses and goats. Violas tells us that her parents "when visiting the property, while negotiating the purchase, happened to be there as a full moon came over the mountain, and they decided to name their new home 'Moon Valley.'"

MOON VALLEY RANCH

The Kern family lived in the small hunting cabin while their home was being built. Mr. Kern built summer housekeeping cottages on the property. In the beginning the business was called Moon Valley Ranch and a western theme was used in decorating.

MOON VALLEY GAME FARM

The family cleared a trail that led to the waterfalls on Laurel Swamp Brook. They decided to name the falls "Rainbow Falls" in memory of their former home. While at that home they had adopted two deer and these animals became the nucleus of their "Moon Valley Game Farm."

STAGECOACH

In 1953 Mr. Kern decided to make the game farm into a storybook land with structures on which children could play! He built a stagecoach, jail, whale, and shoe. Pony rides were offered and accommodations for picnics were provided.

FOXES

Individual structures, such as this "Lollypops' House," served as cages for some of the animals. Foxes lived in this attractive house in the Story Book Land area of Moon Valley Park.

PETTING ZOO

The animal population available for the children to see, and in some cases pet, was extensive. The collection included a lynx, bobcat, pygmy donkey, Shetland ponies, racoons, llamas, porcupines and rabbits.

SHOE

"There was an old woman who lived in a shoe"...you know the rest. But many young children learned and experienced this and other nursery rhymes at Moon Valley Park.

UNIQUE EXHIBITS

The park was advertised as: "One of the most enchanting and unique exhibits in the East, where the young at heart can relive the experiences of their storybook friends."

PINOCCHIO

Children are invited to walk inside the whale and relive the adventures of Pinocchio.

GRANDDAUGHTERS

The children pictured in these cards are Lorelei and Jacki Canouse, daughters of Richard and Viola Canouse and granddaughters of Mr. and Mrs. Kern.

BOOT HILL

WESTERN PIONEER TOWN
MOON VALLEY PARK

The Western Pioneer Town built by Mr. Kern featured a barber shop, Wells Fargo office and sheriff's office. Boot Hill Cemetery was adjacent to the town.

MOON VALLEY PARK

In 1965 Richard and Viola Kern Canouse purchased the property. Over the next few years they remodeled the cottages, built several year-round homes to rent and expanded and updated the summer attraction. They renamed the business Moon Valley Park.

PIONEER TOWN

Viola tells us that the cottages were also often renamed. Her parents had used western names, like Rawhide, in keeping with the western pioneer theme.

BO-PEEP

The cottage pictured here is called Oriole because the Canouses favored bird names. Somewhere along the way they were also named for fairytale characters and guests could stay in the "Bo-Peep" or "Goldilocks" cottage.

HANSEL AND GRETEL

Three of the cottages could accommodate two to four people and included one bedroom, living room, kitchen and a bath. Others were larger and the "Hansel and Gretel" had four deluxe, modern bedrooms, spacious living room, kitchen and bath and could be rented throughout the year.

DIORAMA

The Canouses added more species of animals and amassed a collection of exotic birds. The gift shop was sited in a diorama of stuffed animals and birds in natural settings.

PRIVATE COLLECTION

On display was a large private collection of ornamental birds. They had seventeen varieties of ornamental pheasants, five kinds of quail, three types of peacocks, fourteen varieties of pigeons, four different kinds of doves and twenty-four varieties of fancy chickens.

BONAFIDE BEAGLES

Families came to Moon Valley Park in order for their children to experience the magic of the fairy-tale theme of the park. Ornithologists also came to see the wonderful array of birds. But Beagle dog afficionados came because the Canouse family was well-known in the tri-state area for raising registered members of the breed.

LAUREL SWAMP BROOK

The property purchased by the Kerns from "Doc" Stroh included land that fronted Laurel Swamp Brook. According to the Canouse family, the waterfall on the brook, which they called Rainbow Falls, was "a lovely, delicate wonder of nature."

RELAXED VACATION

In other advertising literature, the Canouse family promised: "If a relaxed vacation in a country atmosphere is what you're looking for, Moon Valley Park is the answer. Only a half mile from town for convenience, our small group of cottages can satisfy the nature lover's yearning for the slower pace of yesteryear. Picture yourself in a cozy efficiency cottage, surrounded by majestic evergreens, beside soothing brooks. Our farm and woodland setting can be your answer to 'getting back to nature.' We even have our own waterfalls and you can fish in our trout streams or small lake. Each cottage has a private picnic table and lawn furniture. TV cable hookups are available in cottages.

SWIMMING POOL ADDED

"Our guests have free access to Moon Valley Park Animal Farm & Storybook Land, the oldest privately owned attraction of its type in the Poconos. Quick snacks are available at our refreshment stand. A Recreation Room with ping-pong, pool table and games is open evenings-playground facilities, shuffleboard, volley ball, and other games are on premises. A commercial pool, public river beach, golf courses, horseback riding, shopping, laundry, movies and all churches nearby. WE HAVE OUR OWN POOL NOW!"

MOON VALLEY FALLS

Viola tells us: "One of the new additions was a large museum for horse drawn vehicles and farm implements. It was built especially to house the old Hiawatha stagecoach, which had been stored for years in an old barn in the area. The Hiawatha stayed at Moon Valley Park until the Pike County Historical Society raised enough funds to have it restored and a new home built for it at the Columns." The Canouse family operated the business for another 22 years. Their daughters, Lorelei and Jacki, worked in the business with their parents for a number of those years. In 1987, the business section of the property (around 68 acres) was sold to Robert and Janet Miller. Over the years since then, they built a housing development on the hillside where the old deer pens had been located and named it Moon Valley Falls. The Canouses relocated to an adjacent area called Sunset Trail off of Moon Valley Road and on an adjacent hillside.

Bird's Eye View, Milford, Pa., showing the Delaware River and Mountains in New York, New Jersey and Penn.

BIRD'S EYE VIEW

The first post card in this book was "Birdseye View of Milford, Pa. from New Jersey." This time the photograph has been taken from the Knob rather than from New Jersey or from Foster Hill. In order to caption the Foster Hill cards we quoted from a promotional brochure published by the Milford Chamber of Commerce in 1923. We'd like to share more of that with you here. No credit is given, nor name mentioned, as to who wrote the following words. That is unfortunate, as the Delaware Valley we see here is beautifully portrayed in the unknown author's words.

Milford, Pa., from the Knobb

PICTURESQUE VILLAGE

"The picturesque village rests on an elevation about six-hundred feet above sea level. Below it, to the east, courses the swift flowing Delaware. The famously beautiful valley which takes its name from the river extends north and south as far as the eye can reach. With its interwoven colors of golden grain, green pastures and woodland stretches; with its peaceful homesteads and herds of cattle; with its lowlands rising gently in the distance till they terminate at the base of eastern hills; with its river banks bright and lush with foliage, the valley is a tapestry of nature's fairest weaving, the river a winding silver ribbon spun through it.

GATEWAY OF THE CLIFFS

"To the north, the village is bounded by the Vandermark Creek, famous for its mountain trout, while at the south flows the Sawkill which courses through a glen of cedars, pines and rhododendron. Back of this sylvan dell rises majestically the Knob-the Gateway of the towering Cliffs. Forest hills of shade and sunlit spaces are but little changed since the days of the Lenni Lenapes. Gorges and gaps, lakes and streams, waterfalls of great height and beauty, silent pools, wild ferns, and flowers, and the song of birds, delight the tourist in this land in which nature has so artfully blended the charms of hill and vale."

Milford, Pa., from the Knob.

We're all O. K. at this end of the line
And hope that you report the same.
Isn't a Postal Letter fine?
There's nothing to do but write your name.

BIRD'S-EYE VIEW OF MILFORD, PA.

EDMUND CLARENCE STEDMAN

While the author of the preceding verse is unknown, we know that one of America's great poets, Edmond Clarence Stedman, wrote as follows of Milford and its surrounding country: "But here there is no swooning of the languid air, and no seeming always afternoon. It is a morning land with every cliff facing the rising sun. The mist and languor are in the grain fields far below, the hills themselves are of the richest, darkest green, the skies are blue and fiery; the air crisp, oxygenated, American. It is no place for lotus eating, but for drinking the water of the fountain of youth, till one feels the zest and thrill of a new life that is not unrestful, yet as far as maybe from the lethargy of mere repose."

THE MARGUERITE

The Marguerite, located at 119-121 Sawkill Avenue, was another of Milford's well known boarding houses. Richard E. and Mabel Struthers Humbert began construction of the building in the 1880s on land given to them by Mrs. Humbert's family, the Struthers. Richard and Mabel had four children, Mabel, Robert, Lucy, who died in infancy, and Marguerite, for whom the hotel was named. Marguerite (Peg) married Hugh Astlett, and the family continued the expansion of the hotel.

Published by C. O. Armstrong   THE MARGUERITE, MILFORD, PA.   7572

SAWKILL AVENUE

The Marguerite was originally a two story building with a large attic and vine-covered front porch. It soon proved too small for the boarders who clamored to come to the house along the Sawkill to enjoy food from the garden and rustic country living. In 1906 the house could accommodate seventy guests. Each guest paid ten to sixteen dollars per week with children being charged according to their age!

The Marguerite, Milford, Pa.   11993.

TWIN TURRETS ADDED

In 1910 half the boarding house was destroyed by fire. It was rebuilt and the owners added a third story and a large wing with twin turrets. The added conveniences, represented by the large dining room and bathrooms, provided comfort for the guests. The wide portico and large wrap-around veranda afforded guests a favored relaxation; a place to sit and rock and enjoy the brook in rustic surroundings.

THE COLONIAL HOTEL, MILFORD, POCONO MTS., PA.

THE COLONIAL

After 1925 the business was sold to Harry Dranow who installed a handball court and a swimming pool. The hotel was later purchased by the Pleshette family who changed the name of the hotel to the The Colonial. The Colonial closed in the 1940s and was in a severe state of deterioration when it burned to the ground on a blustery cold night in the winter of 1967.

On the Sawkill, Milford, Pa.

THE GLEN

"Glen" is defined in Webster's Dictionary as "a secluded narrow valley" and that paints a fairly accurate picture of the Sawkill Glen, or as it was most often called, the Glen. It was located on private property near the home now owned by the McGaughey family at 100 Sawkill Avenue.

WELLS' DAM

The McGaughey family traces their ancestry back to the Wells brothers. The mill pond just before the Glen was created by these ancestors who erected a dam in the Sawkill. The mill pond insured a constant source of water for the mills in times of drought. The dam on the Sawkill was called Wells' Dam.

THE MILL IN THE GLEN, MILFORD, PA.

SUMMER HOUSE

This summer house was probably built by the Sawyers, Mrs. McGaughey's family. It was located behind the McGaughey home near the entrance to the Glen.

VIEW OF THE DAM

This postcard shows the dam, the proximity of the McGaughey house and the summer house.

FOOT BRIDGE TO THE GLEN

Foot Bridge in the Glen, Milford, Pa.

The Village Improvement Association paid for erecting a bridge across the Sawkill leading into the Glen which allowed easier access to the area. People living in the Milford area held picnics and celebrations in the Glen. Many African-American families from the Port Jervis area used it as a camp meeting place in the 1880s and 1890s. Every boarding house and hotel within walking distance promoted it as a part of their attractions. The Glen was also used extensively as a backdrop for scenes in movies made in Milford in the early 1900s.

BRIDGE AT THE GLEN, MILFORD, PA.

FOURTH OF JULY CELEBRATION

On Saturday, July 4, 1896, the people of Milford came together to celebrate the holiday. There was a gala parade in which three Milford fire companies marched to the music of the Erie Band of Port Jervis. The fire companies were the Vandermark Hose #1, led by Foreman William J. Beck; Sawkill Hose #2, with Warren Chol as Foreman and Hook and Ladder #1, headed by Foreman Paul Bournique. There were horse-drawn floats and brightly costumed marchers. Sam Truax, a Civil War veteran who played Uncle Sam in every July 4th parade for many years, also marched. After the parade everyone met in the Glen for a picnic and a variety of contests.

TWO DOLLAR PRIZE

According to a newspaper account of the day, Arthur McCarty beat Roswell Palmer for a prize of two dollars in a sack race. Charles Degen won a one dollar prize in the greased-pole contest. Other events included a wheelbarrow race in which the contestants wore blindfolds.

View from Bridge in the Glen- Milford, Pa.

No. 2551. Published by the Bazaar. (Printed in Germany).

223099

WELL'S DAM, MILFORD, PA.

WELLS' DAM, CIRCA 1918

Olive Wright tells us the house at 106 Wyckoff Lane pictured here was owned by Ora Durham. In the 1930s Ora rented the house during the summer months to the Dranow family who owned The Colonial. Later she rented it to the Mac McCollum family. In the 1940s she sold the house to George and Nellie Wyckoff. They named it Overbrook and raised their four children George, Olive, Betty and Mildred in the home. The Wykoff's daughter Olive and her husband William Wright subsequently acquired the property.

UPPER GLEN

The Glen served as a favorite location for photographers and cinematographers. When movies were made in Milford in the 1900s, movie stars were frequent visitors to the town and the Glen. Norman Lehde tells us about some of these stars : "Milford, the popular resort, attracted many stars of the theatre. In the 1870s Joseph Jefferson, who made a career out of playing 'Rip Van Winkle,' paid several visits to Milford, staying at the Sawkill House. He liked the town so well he made efforts to buy property but without success. He then bought land in Monroe County.

SARAH BERNHARDT

"Sarah Bernhardt spent some time in Milford and her son, Maurice, rented a cottage from his friends, the Reviere family. Another former actress who retired to Milford was Jeannie Gourlay Struthers, who had been a member of the cast of 'Our American Cousin' in Washington's Ford Theatre, the night of Lincoln's assassination. The presence in Milford of the Struthers family led to the acquisition, by the Pike County Historical Society, of the 'Lincoln Flag' which was used to cushion the wounded president's head."

In the Upper Glen, Milford, Pa.

The Glen was also a popular locale for courting couples and this is how one unknown author describes that use of the Glen: "The ever-singing Sawkill is a constant and most dear companion. It is especially dear to the ladies, who with one accord, delight in walking by its side, in sitting in its cool recesses, in sewing, reading, dreaming, or conversing to the music of its silver song. The Glen, which is quite within the village limits, and through which the streamlet makes its way, has been a trysting place for generations; for how many lovers, who shall say?"

BIOGRAPH PLAYERS

Norman continues: "In 1912 a new group of performers arrived in Milford; pioneers in a new medium, the motion picture. Unlike the stage stars who had previously visited Milford, they were not just visiting, sitting on hotel verandas or walking leisurely through the Glen. They would be in Milford, working at their profession under the direction of David Wark Griffith. Griffith came to Milford with his Biograph players and with the speed of production, for which he was noted, filmed two pictures: 'The Informer,' a Civil War story, and 'A Feud in the Kentucky Hills.'

Yes or No. In the Glen, Milford, Pa.

K. 2668. In the Glen, MILFORD, Pa.   (Germany)

KISSING TREES IN THE GLEN, MILFORD, PA.

10799

EARLY CINEMA STARS

"Griffith's players stayed at the Sawkill House with some players being lodged in nearby homes. Griffith himself stayed at the Milford Inn. Some years ago, both Frank Crissman (son of the hotel owner) and his sister, Milicent Switzer, recalled for this writer some of the excitement generated by the Griffith visit and the sight of seeing 'movies' being taken in town. Mrs. Switzer recalled that Griffith was a hard taskmaster who had his actors out early in the morning to start the day's work and that he often improvised scenes on a sudden inspiration and might call any of his players who were idle at the time into action to play in these added scenes. She recalled a team of oxen belonging to a local farmer being used by Griffith in several scenes and that the Delaware River and the Glen were used extensively for set locations.

LILLIAN AND DOROTHY

"Frank Crissman, who wrote from California, recalled the thrill of being an 18-year old and playing a soldier as an 'extra' in Civil War battle scenes and having his picture taken by the famed cameraman, Billie Bitzer, while eating lunch with actress Gertrude Bombeck; and driving a carriage to the Dietrich Farm on the Dingman Road every afternoon for milk, sometimes accompanied by the Gish sisters if they were not working. George Pollion wrote us a few years ago that the Gish girls, Lillian and Dorothy, stayed at the home of his parents across from the Sawkill."

Lover's Walk in Lower Glen, Milford Pa.

No. 32629. Pub. by C. O. Armstrong, Milford, Pa. (Printed in Germany).

THE RACEWAY

The raceway carried water from the pond by the Mott Street Bridge through the lower glen to the flume which supplied the water power for the Metz Ice Plant.

THE RACE IN THE GLEN. MILFORD, PA.

1792 ENTRANCE TO LOWER GLEN, MILFORD, PA.

E.F.BRANNING'S
ARTINO CARD, N.Y. CITY (GERMANY)

ENTRANCE TO LOWER GLEN

Pictured here is the bottom entrance to the lower glen which shows the water from the raceway leading to Metz's Ice Plant.

FARMERS' HOTEL

John C. Beck built the Vantine Hotel, circa 1875, on the corner of Harford and Sixth Streets at 300 West Harford Street. He built large bedrooms with a bathroom on each floor and a dining hall and barroom on the ground floor. The kitchen was located in the basement and food was brought to the dining hall by use of a dumb-waiter. Mr. Beck called his establishment "Farmers' Hotel" because many farmers, especially those living in Dingman Township who would pass by his establishment on their way into town, stayed at his hotel.

VANTINE HOTEL

Advertisements tell us the grounds of the Farmers' Hotel were very attractive. There were large mowed lawns and black cherry, pear and apple trees. A grape arbor stretched from the back of the hotel to the rear of the property. There was a large barn, in part of which carriages of the guests were parked. It also housed pigs, chickens and horses.

The name was changed to the Vantine Hotel when Henry and Mary Lohmann bought the property. Later owners Bill and Christine Richards operated the hotel for many years. They sold the business to Ray Eckert. He changed the name to Dutch Oven and ran the business as a discotheque. In 1974 he sold to Albert Luhrs who tore down the hotel to build his new Luhrs hardware store. The building is now occupied by Eckerd Drugstore.

ROWE BROTHERS

The original mill built circa 1830 was destroyed by fire in 1882. Owner Jervis Gordon built a new mill with enhanced mechanisms that allowed him to establish his very successful business of converting buckwheat into flour. The mill was located on the upper portion of the Sawkill at 150 Water Street and used water power provided by the Sawkill and Vantine Brooks to operate. Civil Engineer Bob Fish explains that one cubic foot of water falling from a height of eleven feet equals one horse power. In 1904 John and Chance Rowe purchased the property from Jervis Gordon. The Rowe brothers built an addition for their extensive machine and wood-working shop.

THE UPPER MILL

Circa 1968 Chandler Saint owned the ninety-seven year-old mill property and kept an antique shop and clothing boutique in the building. In 1984 Mr. Saint sold the property to The Water Wheel Group who restored parts of the water wheel milling system to provide educational information to the public. Under the auspices of The Water Wheel Group, the property became officially known as the Jervis Gordon Grist Mill Historic District and is on the National Registry of Historic Places. The property is commonly known as The Upper Mill. Photograph courtesy of Kristen Olson Murtaugh.

Dam at Arlington and Humbert Cottage   Milford, Pa.

HUMBERT COTTAGE

The Humbert Cottage, located across Sawkill Avenue from the present day American Legion Hall at 102 Route 2001, was run by Mrs. Paul Humbert. The cottage was not as elaborate as surrounding hotels and Mrs. Humbert was therefore able to offer less expensive rates. Folks could stay for eight to ten dollars a week. Children, as at the Humbert family's Marguerite House, were charged "according to age." Transients could spend the night for $1.75.

TREASURE HILL

The Humbert Cottage became City Folks Country Inn and later, when purchased by John and Alice Muir in the 1950s, Treasure Hill. The late Frances Gatzke told us she "was more familiar with the place when Harry and Alice Armstrong owned it. That was in the 1930s. She (Alice) was an artist who painted some designs in the rooms. At that time, there were two small cottages in the back. There was also a swimming hole in the brook. There was a cabin up on the hill that had been used by a T.B. patient many years before."

Treasure Hill
Milford, Pa.   Myer Photo

MUIR HOUSE INN AND RESTAURANT

In 2000 Sean Strub purchased the property. After extensive renovations, Mr. Strub opened The Muir House Inn and Restaurant on the Sawkill Brook. He named The Muir House in honor of John Muir, naturalist, writer and founder of the Sierra Club. Photograph courtesy of Jim Levell.

THE ARLINGTON, MILFORD, PA.

THE ARLINGTON

The Arlington was located at 200 Route 2001 at the intersection of Christian Hill Road and Route 2001. Ross Kleinstuber, late Dingman Township Historian, tells us about the selection of the name for the steep and winding road: "Anyone who has driven Christian Hill Road will appreciate the origin of the name. The old timers in the area said that anyone who could drive a team and loaded wagon either up or down it without cussing was a true Christian."

The original Arlington was built circa 1890 by Frank Seitz for his parents. It was a three story building with the general appearance of other hotels in the area. Additions, such as the cupola and extensions to create more rooms, were added in later years by other owners.

LOST IN A POKER BET

The Seitzs operated the business until 1901 when Frank lost the hotel in a card game to Harold Thornton whose family owned the Dimmick Inn. The Thorntons sold the hotel to Mr. and Mrs. Edward Boyd who ran it as a summer boarding house. Ed Boyd was also a butcher who had a shop on Broad Street.

HOME-LIKE

Mrs. Boyd placed an advertisement in the 1923 Chamber brochure that read: "On the main road about ten minutes walk from Milford Village. Nicely furnished, well ventilated rooms. Bathrooms on each floor. Finest of spring water. Electric lights. Table supplied from our own farm. Sawkill Creek is just across road from house, and guests enjoy boating and bathing, also fishing in season. Dirt tennis court on premises. The Arlington is particularly noted for its select patronage, home-like appointments, and picturesque surroundings and is desirable for those who dislike a public hotel."

THE ARNDT FAMILY

In the 1940s Felix and Rosa Arndt and their young daughters, Jeanette and Audrey, assumed ownership of the Arlington. In the off season the Arndt's provided the first hot lunch program for the children who attended the Dingman Township School on Fisher Lane. They prepared the meals at the hotel and delivered and served them at the school.

Mrs. Arndt was a 4-H leader from 1949 to 1952. She taught an after-school "Fun to Cook" class at the hotel.

The Arndts added improvements to the Arlington Hotel. They built a motel on the property and installed an in-ground pool after the 1955 flood destroyed the natural pool in the Sawkill that had been used by their guests.

AMERICAN LEGION

Mr. and Mrs. Maun, with their nine children, were the next owners of the hotel/motel establishment. They refurbished the dining room, added a bar and opened the subsequent restaurant to the public. In April, 1978 the Mauns sold the property to Richard Meserole and his family. The Meseroles advertised "traditional service and comfort in the old fashion way." They began hosting a steer or pig roast every Friday night during the summer.

The Arlington was heavily damaged in a fire on February 24, 1981. The remains of the building were razed. In 1983 the American Legion Post 139 bought the property and erected their building.

12414

Cliff Park House, Milford, Pa.

CLIFF PARK HOUSE

Cynthia Van Lierde tells us in "Historic Sites in Milford," published in 1980: "Cliff Park Inn and Golf Course is a heritage created by five generations of Buchanans. The land was acquired by George Buchanan in 1803. It is unique in the fact that ownership has been in the Buchanan family since that time. The original farm house, built in 1820, is the heart of the present Inn. The two rooms now serving as dining rooms were originally the kitchen and dining room. The fireplace (still operable) was a 'cooking' fireplace. With its crane, copper and iron pots, it is now the focal point of interest in the larger dining room. Guests are intrigued with the high fireplace mantle; the antique sideboard; and other family heirlooms. Lace covered round oak tables add a touch of Victorian elegance and Old World charm to an Early American setting."

CLIFF PARK INN AND GOLF LINKS

In 1906 Annie Felt Buchanan enlarged the original farmhouse to accommodate summer boarders. She also converted the farm fields into a golf course. Cynthia writes: "It took many years to clear more land and plan the course. The prolonged illness of her husband, Harry Buchanan, Sr., slowed construction and the responsibility of going forward with this ambitious project was hers. Unfortunately, Mr. Buchanan passed away in 1912, a year before the course was completed (1913) and opened to the public.

Cliff Park Inn and Golf Links   Milford, Pike Co., Pa.

SAND TEES

"Frank Hyatt, a sportsman and daily golfer, was a friend of the Buchanans. He shared their enthusiasm for the construction of a golf course and acted as advisor and architect during the construction of the nine hole course. These were located where the first five are now, right in front of the Inn, where guests could sit on the spacious 'wrap around' porch, and watch the golfers. It is interesting to note that two of the first greens that were planted with South German Bent Grass are still in use. Cliff Park was the first golf course to import this as an experiment that proved very successful. Early golfers had to form their own sand tees. Their golf balls were formed of gutta percha and larger than today's regulation golf ball. A set of clubs consisted of a driver, a spoon; brassie; and niblick; in addition to the various mashies and the putter. Golf, as it is played today, is in sharp contrast to that played on the Cliff Park Course in the early 1900s."

CLIFF PARK INN GOLF LINKS, MILFORD, PA.

HAWAIIAN BAND

In 1927 the Buchanans built a fashionable clubhouse which included locker rooms, card rooms and a dining hall with a six-foot high fireplace. The dining room could comfortably accommodate one hundred guests. Cynthia tells us about one function held in the new clubhouse: " On one occasion, with their flair for the unusual, the Buchanans brought an Hawaiian band from New York. This was one of 'THE' social gatherings of the year, and caused a stir in hotel circles in Milford." The golf course was extended in 1936 and again in 1970. In 1947 most of the greens were rebuilt.

The Inn was transferred to the National Park Service in 2003 and is now part of the Delaware Water Gap National Recreation Area. Jamie and Yvonne Klausmann, who lease the facility from the National Park Service, remodeled and reopened Cliff Park Inn on Labor Day, 2004.

Gousset Falls, Milford, Pa.

HACKER'S FALLS

Just past Cliff Park off of Route 2001 on the left-hand side of the road is a rugged path one may take to reach "Gousset" or "Hacker's" Falls. An old deed, found for us by James Leiser, mentions a forgotten road in the area of the falls called Gousset Mill Road. It is assumed a man named Gousset operated some type of mill there prior to Arthur H. and Emily P. Hacker's purchase of the property in 1924. Bruce, Marion and June Steele as well as Phillip and Thelma McCarty, who live in the area of the falls, remember as children calling them "Goosey" Falls.

June Steele tells us she has a pair of old andirons in the shape of owls in her fireplace. Mr. Hacker's mother was from England and had furnished the Hacker house with many imported antiques. Mr. Hacker gave the andirons to June's father in gratitude for his performance as caretaker of the house prior to the sale of the property to the Park Service.

THE SCHANNO FAMILY

Emil Paul Schanno, his wife and six children immigrated to the United States from France in 1876. They settled first in New York City but later moved to the Milford area as had many of their countrymen. In 1893 their son Joe Schanno purchased ninety-five acres of land from George Quinn in the area that now encompasses Foxcroft Drive. He built a barn and twelve-room farmhouse on his property. He married Lizzie Olmstead, a Pike County native, and they operated the farmhouse as the Chestnut Grove House for summer boarders. In 1904 Joe and Lizzie built a three-story addition onto the farmhouse and renamed their enlarged structure the Schanno House.

The Schannos offered their boarders simple country meals. Orchards and gardens on their property allowed them to provide their guests with fresh fruits and vegetables. The cows and chickens they kept ensured fresh milk, butter and eggs would be used in their recipes. Lizzie started baking each day at 4 AM in order to offer their clientele freshly baked bread with breakfast.

Schanno House, Milford, Pa.

SCHANNO HOUSE

Joe Schanno died in January, 1933 and Lizzie continued to operate the Schanno House until 1939 when she sold it to the Geohring family of Hillside, New Jersey. George and Grace Geohring and their three children Betty, George and Carol lived in the house and continued to operate it as a summer boarding house. They also opened the house to hunters in the fall during deer season. They could accommodate up to forty boarders in their eighteen guest rooms.

The Geohring children helped with the business. George was in charge of a large vegetable garden and the care of farm animals on the property. Carol served as a chambermaid and waitress as did her sister Betty.

In the 1940s the family added a bar. In 1959 they sold the business to Phillip Axt who opted to only operate the bar portion of the business.

SCHANNO HOUSE, Milford, Pike Co., Pa.

SCHANNO HOUSE, MILFORD, PIKE CO., PA.

RED FOX INN

Alan and Ronnie Lieb bought the Schanno House and renamed it the "Red Fox Inn." They did extensive renovations to the building and grounds. The porch was removed and shutters added to the windows. The appearance of the building after the exterior renovations were completed caused Cynthia Van Lierde to praise it as an "American Gothic Farmhouse."

When the dining room was renovated large notched beams were uncovered and left exposed. The furnishings Alan and Ronnie used in the room had belonged to his grandmother who had brought them from England. Everything combined to create an atmosphere of old-world charm which transported dinner guests back in time. Complementing the ambiance were superb culinary presentations created by the Liebs.

MILFORD BIBLE CHURCH

The Liebs sold the Red Fox Inn building and opened Le Gorille Restaurant on Twin Lakes Road in Shohola Township. The Red Fox Inn building was renamed by the new owners who attempted to continue in the restaurant business. They failed and closed the business. In 1996 the Milford Bible Church purchased the property on which they planned to build a church large enough to meet the needs of their growing congregation. The building that had begun life as the Chestnut Grove House in the late 1800s was razed. In 2001 the project of building a church was started. On March 1, 2003 the congregation of the Milford Bible Church held their first service in the new church. Photograph courtesy of Jim Levell.

THE PASTORAL STAFF

Senior Pastor Rodney Ryle began serving the congregation of the Milford Bible Church in December, 1986. Pastor Neal Wintermute began serving as Associate Pastor in July, 2003. He also assumed the duties of the Christian Education and Outreach programs. In August, 2004 Pastor Brian Garver joined the staff as Pastor of Youth Ministries. Photograph courtesy of Jim Levell.

DALLOZ HOMESTEAD

Louis Dalloz came from Besancon, France in 1870. He purchased a large tract of farmland in Dingman Township on Raymondskill Road. He married Leotine Rigny of Milford. Her family also had a large farm in the township adjoining the Dalloz property. Mr. Dalloz sold his property and he and Loetine established a summer boarding house on the one-hundred thirty acre Rigny estate.

Published by C. O. Armstrong   DALLOZ HOUSE, NEAR MILFORD, PA   7576

DALLOZ HOUSE

The bulk of the estate was heavily forested and provided a bucolic serenity to the ambiance of the Dalloz House. The adjacent pristine Raymondskill Creek provided opportunities for swimming and excellent fishing experiences.

Merritt Quinn tells us his grandmother Katie Gebhardt Boileau worked summers at the Dalloz House. When she was a young lady she walked from her family's farm, the Gebhardt farm, to the adjoining Dalloz property. She served as a waitress and chambermaid and earned two dollars and fifty cents per week plus room and board. She was allowed to keep the fifty cents but was required to add the two dollars to the family coffer.

12412   Dalloz House, Milford, Pa.

DALLOZ RESORT

The Dalloz House was actually two houses and contained thirty-eight guest rooms. Not surprisingly, most of the clientele were French residents of New York City. Mr. Dalloz died on January 5, 1899. Funeral services were conducted at the Dalloz House by Reverend W.R. Neff, Pastor of the Milford Methodist Church. Mr. Dalloz was buried in the cemetery located at the northeast corner of Raymondskill Road and Route 2001. This cemetery, originally called the French Cemetery, has in recent years become known as the Old Union Schoolhouse Cemetery.

CAMP NETIMUS

Camp Netimus, at 708 Raymondskill Road, is a summer equestrian camp for girls ages seven through sixteen. It is located on property once owned by the Rigny/Dalloz families. The camp is comprised of four hundred eight acres. It was established in 1930 as a place "for girls to grow, learn new things, make friends...all while having fun."

UNION SCHOOL HOUSE

The Union School, one of seven one-room schoolhouses with eight grades used to educate the children of Dingman Township, was located near the southwest corner of Raymondskill Road and Route 2001. Milford Mayor Merritt Quinn tells us he and his sister Katherine completed all eight grades at the Union School. Merritt finished in May, 1934 and Katherine in May, 1935. Both went on to graduate from Milford High School in 1938 and 1939 respectively. Merritt remembers walking to school for first grade from Camp Netimus, a distance of 2.1 miles. Later when he and his sister were living at Quinn's Farm on Sawkill Road, they were bussed to the school. Bus drivers included Frank and Margaret Castle, Charles Travis, Floyd Quick and Floyd Travis. The Union School closed in 1936 when the new school opened at 961 Fisher Lane.

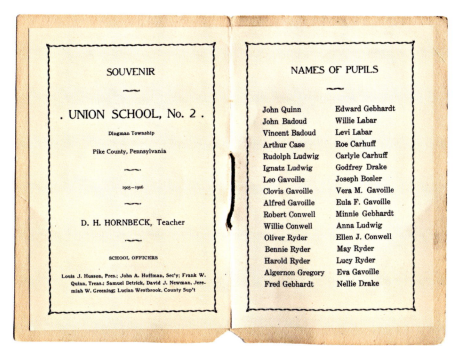

SOUVENIR

. UNION SCHOOL, No. 2 .

Dingman Township

Pike County, Pennsylvania

1905–1906

D. H. HORNBECK, Teacher

SCHOOL OFFICERS

Louis J. Husson, Pres.; John A. Hoffman, Sec'y; Frank W. Quinn, Treas.; Samuel Detrick, David J. Newman, Jeremiah W. Greening; Lucian Westbrook, County Sup't

NAMES OF PUPILS

John Quinn	Edward Gebhardt
John Badoud	Willie Labar
Vincent Badoud	Levi Labar
Arthur Case	Roe Carhuff
Rudolph Ludwig	Carlyle Carhuff
Ignatz Ludwig	Godfrey Drake
Leo Gavoille	Joseph Bosler
Clovis Gavoille	Vera M. Gavoille
Alfred Gavoille	Eula F. Gavoille
Robert Conwell	Minnie Gebhardt
Willie Conwell	Anna Ludwig
Oliver Ryder	Ellen J. Conwell
Bennie Ryder	May Ryder
Harold Ryder	Lucy Ryder
Algernon Gregory	Eva Gavoille
Fred Gebhardt	Nellie Drake

UNION SCHOOL PUPILS, 1905-1906

This souvenir program contains names of families still residing in our area.

Road to Silver Spring House, Milford, Pa.

STAR ROUTE 2001

The man pictured here with his two bloodhounds is standing on Route 2001. This is the road, the Milford end of which was recently repaired, that takes many people from Milford to their homes in Pocono Woodland Lakes, Gold Key Estates, Country Club Woods and other areas in Dingman Township.

REMY LOREAUX

According to an article in the Pike County Dispatch, and reprinted here with her permission, T.A. Crerand tells us: "Frenchman Desire Loreaux (1800-1875), more commonly known as Remy Loreaux, was the founder and operator of a brewery in Pike County that produced one of America's first bottled beers for home consumption. Loreaux's brewery was built in Pike County about three miles from Milford in Dingman Township on the creek where Raymondskill approaches the old Milford Road, now Route 2001.

Silver Spring House, Milford, Pa.

OLDEST OF ELEVEN

"According to records provided by Lori Strelecki, curator of the Pike County Historical Society at The Columns in Milford, Loreaux was one of Milford's early settlers. He came from France with scarcely a dollar in his possession shortly after the arrival of the Pinchot family from France and was employed in Milford for about a year by the mother of Cyril C.D. Pinchot. He was the oldest of eleven children and at the age of fifteen had accompanied his father and uncle in the campaign under Napoleon Bonaparte.

-DISTANT VIEW SILVER SPRING HOUSE, MILFORD, PA, 2T.

Lake Juliette, Silver Spring House, Milford, Pa.

EXCEPTIONAL SPRING WATER

"Loreaux was a successful businessman in New York importing baskets and then invented a machine for cutting out letter envelopes. He manufactured them but failed to have the invention patented. In 1833, he purchased 160 wilderness acres in Pike County from the McCarty tract that included an exceptional spring. He constructed a primitive log cabin and then brought his relatives from France to live on his farm. He made additional improvements to the farm at a cost of over $40,000.

OLD SILVER SPRING HOUSE (BREWERY), MILFORD, PA.

120473

STONE BREWERY

"Loreaux was a respected citizen, married and a father of eleven children. He built a stone brewery structure in 1840 to begin his successful business and enlarged it in 1852. In 1864, Loreaux petitioned for a license to operate a tavern and kept a public house mainly patronized by Milford residents and surrounding neighbors. It was a favored place to hold supper parties up until his death in 1875 on his birth date, January 13. According to a news recollection of the brewery that appeared in the Milford Dispatch on Sept. 17, 1896:

FIRST BOTTLED BEER

"Mr. Loreaux's beer became famed far and wide. At first his market was limited to Milford and vicinity; but before long he supplied large quantities to New York customers. He was adept in the brewer's art and originated a patent process in which corn was, for the first time, used with barley malt in the manufacture of beer. The Loreaux brewery also claims the distinction of sending out the first bottled beer for family use in the United States. The liquor was put up in quart claret bottles, and the corks were forced in by hand and tied down with strong twine. But, notwithstanding the primitive methods employed, the beer, according to old timers, was of the richest quality, having more of the characteristics of ale than of modern lager.' Up until then, beer for home consumption was purchased in taverns and carried home in pails.

Silver Springs House, Milford, Pa.

12718

SHERIFF'S SALE

"Sadly, in Loreaux's declining years, his real estate holdings were sold at a sheriff's sale in 1873. The public notice listed a large frame dwelling, one large brewery with a dwelling attached, large frame building near the brewery, two large barns, blacksmith shop, other out-buildings, a fine spring of never-failing water, and a large stream of water running through the premises referred to as the Raymondskill. Even after Loreaux's death, his brewery remained a memorable place to visit on moonlit nights to those who enjoyed the romantic scenery surrounding the old stone brewery.

SILVER SPRING HOUSE. NEAR MILFORD, PA.

SILVER SPRING HOUSE

"The news account continues, 'Miriam Coles Harris makes it the scene of a tea party in one of her novels, entitled, "A Perfect Adonis." The Brewery is such a queer old place, she says, and the teas there used to be quite famous.' Eugene O. Boillotat and his wife, granddaughter of Loreaux, acquired the property and by the mid 1890s, removed the deteriorated brewery structure. The Boillotats built and operated a 40-room summer resort near the old brewery site named Silver Spring House with facilities ranging from a tennis court to a pig pen."

RUSTIC BARONIAL HOME

Harman Residence, Raymondskill Falls, Pa.   12467

Sue Kopczynski, Historian for the National Park Service, tells us on May 13, 1909 Archer and Mary Harmon of New York City bought property located between Raymondskill Road and Bridle Vail Creek in Dingman Township. They built a large, two-story rustic baronial style house. Archer Harmon was an entrepreneur and the promoter, builder and President of the Guayaquil and Quito Railroad in Ecuador.

GOLDEN SPRING HOUSE

Mr. Harmon died in Virginia on October 11, 1911 in a horseback riding accident. Mary Harmon inherited the property and later married Leo W. Wertheimer. Mrs. Wertheimer became socially active in the local community. She liked to produce plays and give parties. They called their home Golden Spring.

Golden Spring, Milford, Pa.   13258

TITANIA AND PRINCE CHARMING

In 1913 she wrote and copyrighted an operetta called "A Tempest in a Teapot." This card shows a scene from the production of that on the steps of the Wertheimer home.

ARCHITECT HENRY NICHOLS WRIGHT

On May 3, 1943 Leo Wertheimer sold the house to Gustavo Ramirez. Mr. Ramirez hired architect Henry Nichols Wright to design the alterations of the existing house to incorporate solar technology. Later owners were the Blitzer and Nadler families. The property is now owned by the National Park Service. Local attempts are being made to have it designated as part of the National Trust.

Titania and Prince Charming.

Entrance of Golden Spring, Milford, Pa.

CHATILLON HOUSE

67 Lake View House (Chatillon's), Milford, Pa.

Mathew Chatillon was born in France, immigrated to New York City and ran a hotel on Leonard Street near Broadway. In 1836 he bought land in Dingman Township near present-day Mt. Haven. In 1860 he retired from the hotel business in New York and built a thirty-five room hotel on his property. In 1875 he bought more land until his property constituted three-hundred acres. His son, Louis Chatillon, was born in the hotel on October 20, 1865.

Lake View, Milford, Pa.

LAKE VIEW

Louis Chatillon started working in the hotel with his father when he was fifteen years old. In 1888 father and son built a twelve acre lake and stocked it with trout. This added to the summertime appeal of the hotel. Louis was a Pike County Jury Commissioner from 1895 to 1898. He ran for the office of Pike County Sheriff in 1897 but lost to E. Vandermark.

MT. HAVEN

According to information provided by the Filone family, Tony Filone and his twin brothers Andrew and John left a luncheonette business in Queens in 1966 to join their uncle at Mt. Haven. With the help of their families, the Filone brothers transformed a four hundred acre former New York State Senator's estate into a unique vacation resort.

GRACIOUS HOSTS

The family expanded the resort to include deluxe family cottages, colonial style apartments and comfortable suites. The glass enclosed Garden Room and Skylight Room complete with hanging plants, trees and lead crystal art offer a memorable dining experience. The former senator's mansion and a recently constructed outdoor pavilion enable many local organizations to hold parties, weddings, barbecues and banquets at Mt. Haven throughout the year.

DINING HALL, CAMP LOG TAVERN, MILFORD, PA.

CAMP LOG TAVERN

According to Mathews' <u>History of Wayne, Pike and Monroe Counties, Pennsylvania</u> "Joshua Drake had a log tavern near the centre of Dingman Township, about one mile from what afterwards became known as the Log Tavern Ponds." US Geological Survey maps called Log Tavern Lake "Little Log Tavern Pond." Its larger neighbor, now Gold Key Lake, was "Big Log Tavern Pond."

Honey Raider tells us that in the 1930s her uncle Ben Fassler and his partner Max Shoenberg wanted to buy a camp located near the Log Tavern Ponds called Camp Log Tavern. Their goal was to create a resort similar to Unity House, a summer retreat near Bushkill, PA established in 1918 by New York City Locals 22 and 25 of the International Ladies' Garment Workers Union. Sam Fassler, Honey's father, was asked to help fund the Camp Log Tavern purchase. He complied because he was an avid horseman and knew he could stable his horses on the property.

CAMP LOG TAVERN LAKE

Log Tavern Lake is a 90-acre spring-fed lake of glacial origin. It is two and one-half miles in circumference and one mile wide. Beginning in 1958 an American Red Cross Aquatics School was held at the camp, then known as Camp Indian Trails. During one summer school session, scuba divers attempted to find the depth of the lake. They went down ninety feet before the water became too murky for further exploration.

The lake allowed summer campers to enjoy swimming, boating, canoeing and fishing. Anglers could catch pickerel, bass, sunfish, perch, and catfish. In the 1960s a drift of DDT from aerial gypsy moth spraying decimated the fish population. It slowly recovered and was later augmented by private stocking of lake trout.

In addition to providing recreational opportunities, the lake water was used for summer refrigeration. Ice blocks were harvested from the lake in winter, packed in sawdust and stored in an ice house behind the camp's kitchen.

Scene at the Lake Front, Camp Log Tavern, Milford, Pa.

SOCIAL HALL

The Social Hall was the center of evening activities. The second floor had a large stage and dressing rooms. Those and a sophisticated stage lighting system allowed the campers to enjoy professional weekend variety shows staged by well-known entertainers and plays performed by eminent touring companies. In 1953, a "social staff" that included dancers, singers, and a comedian were hired to provide additional entertainment. The camp had a band that played each evening for dancing and movies were shown weekly.

The ground floor of the Social Hall housed the Canteen which served ice cream, soft drinks and light snacks. There was also a room containing ping-pong tables.

In later years the more intimate Lounge, with a fireplace and bar, was built on the hillside between the Social Hall and dining room.

SOCIAL HALL, CAMP LOG TAVERN, MILFORD, PA.

TYPICAL GUEST CABIN

In the early days the rustic cabins, like all the camp buildings, were log-sided. Cabins contained sinks and toilets but no showers. Instead there were separate shower houses. The one for the women campers was on the west side of camp. The one for the men was on the east side. The shower houses were not roofed which proved to be an unpleasant feature on rainy, chilly days. Water was pumped from the lake to a reservoir above the camp where it was chlorinated and then distributed by gravity. A central boiler provided hot water. By the 1950s the camp had built its own laundry to handle the enormous volume of towels and linens generated by the campers.

In 1947 when Lew Miller bought the camp, he and his wife, Eve, and their children, Bob and Judy, moved from Willow Grove, Pennsylvania to live at the camp year-round. Eve's sister Gussie Duhovitch supervised the housekeeping department and her husband Joe was head of maintenance.

TYPICAL GUEST CABIN AT CAMP LOG TAVERN, MILFORD, PA.

AERIAL VIEW OF LAKEFRONT

In this picture the swimming area can be seen directly in front of the Social Hall. The enclosed area was a swimming crib of shallow water designed by the camp management for inexperienced swimmers. Because slippery rocks covered most of the lake bottom, the camp sunk a wooden floor in this area to further insure the safety of the swimmers. The swimming area was later moved further east, but some parts of a sunken dock and the wooden floor of the crib remained. In September 1958 Red Cross Aquatics School divers attached cables to the submerged pieces, pulled them from the lake and disposed of them.

Most of the camp was built on a hillside that rose rather steeply from the lake. The elevation of the lake is 1,300 feet and the dining hall was located at the top of the highest point of the camp at 1,400 feet. Guests who had to walk from waterfront cabins to the dining hall three times a day joked about walking up "Cardiac Hill."

GAY! EXCITING! CAMP LOG TAVERN

Honey Raider's father, Sam, opted out of the camping business in the early 1940s. He bought property, which the family still owns, across the lake from the camp. Honey tells us her Aunt Molly Shiner teamed with her Uncle Ben who continued to run Camp Log Tavern. When Ben retired, Molly found a new partner, Lewis E. Miller. In 1947 Lew Miller became the sole owner. Mr. Miller realized that the previously used word-of-mouth campaign was not an efficient method of promoting the camp. He elected to run advertisements in major New York and Philadelphia newspapers. Additionally brochures such as a 1954 Vacation Bulletin were mailed in response to inquiries as well as to guests from previous years. The 1954 season ran from June 13 through September 12. Weekly rates per person ranged from $49 to $90 depending on time of year and type of accommodation. Three meals daily and most activities were included. Those guests wishing to go horseback riding or play golf were charged extra.

SOCIAL HALL, BASKETBALL AND VOLLEYBALL COURTS

This picture was taken in 1953. The log siding on the Social Hall, as shown in previous pictures, has been replaced with painted boards.

Basketball was a popular sport at the camp and many camp employees played on their college basketball teams. The management arranged exhibition games between Camp Log Tavern staff members and staff from area resorts such as Tamiment and Unity House. The court was lighted for these night games.

Camp Log Tavern's programs were designed to appeal to adult couples and singles. Weekend entertainment was often of an adult nature. Although families were welcome during some weeks at the beginning and end of the season, there were no programs or facilities for children at the camp.

Lew Miller promoted the camp's relaxed, informal atmosphere. Some women still chose to dress for Saturday dinner, but men seen wearing neckties were traditionally thrown into the lake! That practice ended after a near-tragic occurrence when a victim hit his head on the dock.

LAKEFRONT SWIMMING AREA

Because the lake shore was wooded and extremely rocky, lawns around the camp were created by importing topsoil. One guest, not accustomed to Pike County's rocky terrain, when participating in a hike around the lake, asked, "Who planted all the rocks?"

This picture shows another swimming crib in shallow water created when the swimming area was moved. An area of deep water, safe for diving, was roped off. Rafts were provided for those who wanted to rest or sunbathe on the lake. The camp had fifty canoes and rowboats and lessons in paddling and rowing were offered. Water safety was a top priority. American Red Cross-certified lifeguards were on duty all day, and unsupervised swimming at any time was strongly discouraged. "Swimming the lake," though, was a camp tradition. Guests and staff members with sufficient skill and stamina were permitted to swim across or around the lake. They were accompanied by staff members in a rowboat that contained life-saving devices.

TENNIS COURTS

Camp Log Tavern was established in 1922 as a tennis camp. The original owners entered into the costly project of building the courts on what was then swampland next to the lake's outlet. The ten clay courts were as carefully tended as a golf course and the caretaker who laboriously rolled the surfaces every day imperiously denied access to anyone without proper tennis footwear. Tennis professionals such as Bobby Riggs and Jack Kramer played exhibition matches. On one occasion, as a joke, Miller and Riggs exchanged serves using boiled potatoes.

Weekly men's and women's tournaments were held throughout the summer. Winners of the weekly tournaments were invited back for a free weekend at the end of the summer and a chance to compete in the "Tournament of Champions" for the Camp Log Tavern Trophy.

Adjacent to the tennis courts was a four-wall handball court, one of the first in the Poconos.

CABINS, A NEW LOOK

By the early 1950s the old log-sided cabins had been refurbished. The shower houses were gone and each cabin had a bathroom with shower. The one hundred cabins at Camp Log Tavern could accommodate 360 guests. In peak season it was often necessary to find off-site housing for additional campers. They came daily to the camp grounds for meals and activities. Judy Miller Feller, daughter of Lew Miller, provided the information on Camp Log Tavern from 1947 to 1961.

CORRAL AND SOFTBALL FIELD

The camp's original stable was demolished in the mid-1940s. The barn and corral that replaced it were located farther from the center of camp. The barn contained ten horse stalls and space for feed and equipment. Riding lessons were confined to the corral but, as Camp Log Tavern was surrounded by 2,200 acres of woodlands, there were miles of trails that could be used by more advanced riders. Camp Log Tavern did not own horses. Horseback riding was offered by horsemen who brought in their stock for the summer. This arrangement continued until 1952 when the popularity of riding waned.

The camp had little natural open space. The softball field pictured here was one of two created by loads of fill and topsoil trucked to the site. Deer were rarely seen in the campgrounds during the summer but, after the campers left, large herds grazed the lawns and ball fields.

DINING ROOM

Lew Miller took great pride in the quality of the food he served and the smooth operation of his kitchen. Providing meals for as many as 500 guests during the peak season was a formidable task. There were extensive menu choices for all meals, and, with a few exceptions, unlimited seconds. The head chef and many of his assistants employed by Mr. Miller worked on cruise ships during the winter and returned to the camp each summer. Mr. Miller hired college students for his all-male wait-staff. Many future doctors, lawyers, and other professionals earned their tuition at Camp Log Tavern.

Adult vacation destinations and expectations began to change in the 1950s. People wanted to stay at resorts with amenities that included swimming pools and golf courses. In response to a diminished adult clientele, Mr. Miller closed Camp Log Tavern at the end of the 1955 season. He adjusted some of the camp's facilities and programs and re-opened the grounds in 1956 as Camp Indian Trails for children. Mr. Miller sold Camp Indian Trails in 1961.

BIG POND

The information provided with the next four postcards was written by Carol Walter Ramagosa. "In the beginning...the lake was quiet; probably formed when a glacier receded, leaving a depression filled with icy, cold water. Many years later, it most likely was fished by the local Delaware and Leni Lenape Indians, who surely hunted the bountiful forest of Oaks, Pines, and Chestnuts. After the arrival of Pennsylvania's first developer, William Penn, and after the end of the American Revolution, the lake was part of land granted in the late 1790s to John Brodhead, Sr., Nicholas Neleigh, Jr., and Mordecai Roberts. Each tract consisted of about 400 acres, and the lake, present-day 'Gold Key Lake,' was named 'Big Pond' and later became known as 'Big Log Tavern Pond.'

SUNNYLANDS

One 'Brooklynite,' John Hilliard, associated with the Shohola Falls Corporation, a lumbering company, in 1899, began accumulating land adjoining Big Log Tavern Lake. Over the next several years, he purchased more tracts, which are today's Gold Key and Sunrise Lake developments. John Hilliard made many improvements on a site fronting the lake. He built a main house, a gate house, a boat house; barns, numerous other smaller structures; (smoke house, vegetable cellar, ice house and blacksmith shop). He landscaped the property, adding stone walls and a maple and oak tree-lined driveway. The 'Hilliard place,' as it was known locally, was self-sufficient. John and Eleanor owned the property until 1929." Walter Annenberg, a former Ambassador to the Court of St. James, had purchased the land from John Hilliard and named his property "Sunnylands." Photograph courtesy of Carol Walter Ramagosa.

CLUBHOUSE AT GOLD KEY LAKE

"The next Sunnylands owners, Sebastian Ramagosa and sons, James, William and Gilbert were seeking a place for recreation and relaxation from their amusement business at the New Jersey shore in Wildwood. For a short time they, like previous owners, resided there only part-time, but eventually Bill Ramagosa and his wife Billie Ann became the first permanent, year-round residents of Sunnylands. Determining that the Milford area was an ideal place to raise their three children, they maintained a small farm, raised turkeys, made charcoal, and participated in community life. In the 1960s, Ramagosa, with others, subdivided the property at Big Log Tavern Lake, renaming it Gold Key Lake, and began the second-home communities Gold Key and Sunrise Lake.

GOLD KEY ESTATES

"The legacy of providing a respite from a more hectic pace and sharing the natural beauty of the area with neighbors from across the Delaware has persevered. Many summer residents have become year-round residents. Today, Gold Key is enjoyed by many who, like early owners John and Eleanor Hilliard, ventured 'west' to pursue a piece of the American dream—owning a home surrounded not by a white picket fence, but a fence of spruce, oak, birch, and enjoying a refreshing quality of life." Photograph courtesy of Jerry Goldberg.

Mott Street Bridge Milford Pa.

MOTT STREET BRIDGE

In 1903 a modern iron bridge was erected over the Sawkill in the Upper Glen. Passage over this bridge from Milford put the traveler on Old Bridge Road which connected to the River Road. From there it was possible to travel south to Dingmans Ferry, Bushkill and Monroe County or to the Delaware River and across the bridge into New Jersey. The bridge survived the floods of 1903 and 1955. After the 1955 flood the Mott Street Bridge was once again used to access Route 209 as the roadway to the concrete bridge on East Harford Street was washed away. The Mott Street Bridge was closed to vehicular traffic in 1990 and to pedestrians in 2007.

HARVEY HOTALEN'S HOUSE

This is a view of the bridge, circa 1908, as seen from Old Bridge Road looking across the bridge to Mott Street. There is no house immediately across the bridge on the left hand side. Harvey Hotalen, who owns the house now on that site at 118 Mott Street, received a picture of his house and a letter from Charles Metz, Jr in 1991. In the letter Mr. Metz explains that Harvey's house was built on property the Metz family owned near the Delaware River on the south side of the Sawkill Creek. He goes on to tell Harvey that his father, Charles Metz, Sr., was born in the home which was later moved to Mott Street. Mr. Metz doesn't offer any explanation as to when or how this relocation took place. Luckily, at a later date when Harvey was making repairs to his home, he found faded documents that answer the "when" part of the puzzle. A George Smith, Jr. left a message on a piece of cardboard that declares himself as the "house-mover on December 1, 1910."

Mott St., Bridge, Milford, Pa.

A COLD DECEMBER

While Harvey was thrilled to get that piece of information, it doesn't explain "how" or, more specifically, what route was taken when the house was moved. Harvey and his family and friends have long speculated about this and have various theories. Because of the original location of the house it must be assumed the house had to have been taken across the Sawkill to get to Mott Street. The Mott Street Bridge has high sides so Harvey doesn't believe George could have gotten the house over that bridge.

One theory has to do with the date on which George moved the house. According to the Penn State Daily Weather Summary web site, it was very cold in Milford in late November and early December of 1910. The average temperature toward the end of November was twenty degrees. This cold snap continued into December when a low of two degrees was registered for December 10. It can therefore be presumed the Sawkill Creek was frozen enough to allow George to move the house across it on a sled-like conveyance. Photograph courtesy of Harvey Hotalen.

Road Entering Milford at Glen

13593

BRIDGE BY THE ICE HOUSE

Mr. Hotalen has looked at old maps and documents and has speculated that a permit may have been needed to move the house since it was located in Dingman Township but no record of a permit has been found. An old map shows the bridge by the ice house was in place in 1910. It appears to have had no side or height constraints at that time, so another theory suggests this bridge was used. Susan Metz, Skip, and others believe this to be the case. Harvey is undecided as he believes the bridge may have been too narrow to accommodate the house. He remains open to suggestions as to how his house crossed the Sawkill.

NEFF HOUSE

Reverend Warren R. Neff served as pastor of the Milford Methodist Church from 1895 to 1899. During his tenure Doctor Neff compiled a document detailing the first seventy-five years of the church's history. Much of his information came from interviews he conducted with twenty former pastors of the church.

He and his wife Harriet lived in the Milford Methodist Church parsonage when their son Herbert was born. After the Neffs relocated, they returned to Milford often and in 1911 purchased property and built a summer home, pictured here at 108 Old Bridge Road. Although Reverend Neff no longer served as pastor of the Milford Methodist Church, he and his family spent as much time as possible in their Milford house. Herbert married a Milford native, James Van Etten's daughter, Anna Louise. Herbert and Anna Louise lived and worked in New Jersey but, as had his parents, enjoyed spending time in the house. When they retired the house became their permanent residence. In 1977 Terry and Pamela Zeigler purchased the house from the Neff Estate.

PINE GABLES

In 1957 Robert and Janet Schields purchased this home near Old Bridge Road, now 194 Glen Crest Road, from Harry Frees. Bob and Janet and their two sons Craig and Lee, lived in the home for thirty years until selling it to Jimmy Luhrs. In 1989 John, Marie, and Patricia Dudzinski purchased the home. This is one of a series of cottages built in this area by the Sawyer family. All were named. This one is called "Pine Gables." This is also one of the few roads, one of the few enclaves of houses on the edge of Milford, untouched by the Tocks Island Dam Project.

ROAD OUT OF THE GLEN CIRCA 1908

This is a picture of Old Bridge Road leading from the Mott Street Bridge to River Road, Route 209.

Road out of the Glen, Milford, Pa.

No. 32556. Published by J. A. Myer. (Printed in Germany).

The Road to Dingmans, Milford, Pa.

Z12323

RIVER ROAD, ROUTE 209 SOUTH

In the 1960s there was some question on the national level about future availability of drinking water for the New York City and Philadelphia areas. In order to address this problem, the Federal Government decided to dam the Delaware River about six miles upstream from the Delaware Water Gap, near Tocks Island thus creating a reservoir. This process would cost about $1.2 billion. It would also mean the river corridor, as we know it, would be under the waters of the huge new reservoir. On September 1, 1965 President Johnson signed PL 80-158 authorizing the establishment of the Delaware Water Gap National Recreation Area and the purchase of forty-six thousand acres around the dam and reservoir project. The Federal Government subsequently bought, razed, or allowed to fall into ruins, most of the buildings you will see in these last pages. The Tocks Island Project was officially de-authorized in 1992.

GRAND VIEW HOUSE

GRAND VIEW HOUSE

William Metz was the proprietor of the lovely Grand View House located across from the Milford Cemetery entrance. Apparently Mr. Metz was correct in asserting in a brochure advertising his House: "The view is unsurpassed, overlooking town, river and valley." He could also boast that it was within walking distance of "post office, stores, and churches." This brochure also tells us there were forty rooms "commodious" with new furniture. There were "closets and lavatories" on all floors with "sanitary" plumbing throughout.

DANCING PAVILION

Continuing the advertisement is: "A Word About Milford. It seems hardly necessary to describe Milford and its surroundings. Poets have sung their praises, and the shaded glens, beautiful falls, magnificent shale roads for driving and wheeling, mountain prospects, towering cliffs, and charming valley scenery have all been described in enthusiastic prose by visitors. The fishing and hunting are good in season. Fine trout streams are within easy access, and the Delaware River, which furnishes abundant sport and opportunity for bathing and boating, is very near. Outdoor recreation is afforded by the golf grounds, race track, ball grounds, etc., near by, and a new dancing pavilion connected with the house."

DANCING PAVILION

SPACIOUS DINING

Henn describes the Grand View Hotel as "a countryfied place," perhaps in part because of the unelaborate dining room. It's probable that Mr. Metz did not want draperies to obscure the beautiful scenery visible from each of the many windows. Terms to stay at the Grand View Hotel were: "$7.00 per week and up; children $5.00. Transients $2.00 a day. The proprietor would give special rates for the season on application." Mr. Metz also advised patrons to take the train from the "foot of Chambers Street, New York, to Port Jervis, New York." A newspaper report of December 10, 1908 tells us the hotel was completely destroyed by fire.

DINING ROOM

VIEW FROM THE GRAND HOTEL

The journey in the remaining pages of this book begins at the Old Bridge Road and continues South on the River Road to Dingmans Ferry. Most of the buildings, houses and businesses you will see in these pages are gone. Families were scattered and ancestral homes destroyed by the government for the Tock's Island Dam project. The displacement of Lorraine Helms Gregory's childhood home and ultimately the destruction of it sets the tone for the bittersweet end of this book.

LORRAINE'S STORY

Lorraine's parents, Edison and Myrtle Hoffman Helms, and her eldest brother Edison, Jr. "Sonny," moved into their new home in Dingman Township in 1927 when Sonny was three years old. Both her father, the son of Peter W. and Jane Swezy Helms, and her mother, the daughter of Ira and Lena Shadler Hoffman, had extensive ancestral ties to Dingman Township.

The house was located approximately one mile south of the intersection of Broad and Harford Streets in Milford and was on the east, left, side of Route 209.

Her father worked for the Erie Railroad in Port Jervis but also kept a small farm on the property where he raised cows, pigs and chickens. The farm animals, as well as vegetables from the large garden he maintained, provided the family with plentiful, healthy food.

This picture shows Sonny with Uncle Richard "Judd" Hoffman's mules. Lorraine is astride one of the mules.

THE HELMS CHILDREN

Lorraine's mother and father opted to have their children born at home. Lorraine's older brother Norman, nicknamed Red, was born in 1929. Lorraine followed in 1939. She became an older sister to Lee when he was born in 1941. Baby Shirley arrived in 1948 with the aid of Dr. Daniel Schultz and Nurse Sonia Gatzke.

Sonny graduated from Milford High School in 1942. He worked for the Erie Railroad as a fireman until he enlisted in the United States Army. During World War II, he served as a Staff Sergeant in the Phillipines, where he died on February 25, 1945.

Four years later Lorraine's family would be devastated by the unexpected death of her father. While still recovering, the family received notice from the Delaware River Joint Toll Bridge Commission [DRJTBC] that their property would be seized under the provisions of eminent domain to be used for the entrance to a new Delaware River Bridge.

Pictured here are Myrtle and Shirley Helms and their neighbor, Amelia Meader whose home was also taken by the DRJTBC.

Lorraine's mother, now a widowed parent of three young children, decided to buy a house adjacent to her sister Edna Lauer's home on the Upper Raymondskill Road. The house was adequate but could not replace the family homestead of thirty years. Myrtle decided on a bold approach. She met with representatives of the DRJTBC and asked if she might be allowed to salvage her home if she moved it to a new location. They agreed and Myrtle began the arduous task of moving the house, garage and barn across Route 209 to the site she had selected near the entrance to the Milford Cemetery. After securing numerous permits, Litts Construction Company moved the house and buildings.

This picture shows moving day with Litts' truck.

THE HELMS HOMESTEAD

In August, 1954 Lorraine, her mother, Lee and Shirley moved into their newly renovated homestead. Shirley was about to start first grade and the future looked bright.

On May 25, 1961 Lorraine's mother died suddenly of a heart attack. Lorraine, now a registered nurse, returned home to raise Shirley. She took a job with the Pennsylvania Department of Health. Lorraine married Skip in 1967. They lived in the home until 1971 when Lorraine received notice that the Federal Government would use their power of eminent domain to secure the property for the Tocks Island Dam Project. This time the home could not be saved.

The Cliffs from Model Farm, Milford, Pa.

No. 82550. Published by the Bazaar. (Printed in Germany).

THE COLE FAMILY

During the Revolutionary War the extensive bottom-land between the Raymondskill and the Sawkill Creeks was owned by Cornelius "Case" Cole. His homestead was on the lower part of the tract under the mountain near the Raymondskill. At a time when the Indians were in an unfriendly mood, the Coles had a unnerving experience which had a fortunate ending. Thanks to Laura Brink, a granddaughter of the pioneer settler, a colorful description of this episode is related in Mathews History:

DUTCH ROSE BLANKETS

"An old squaw camped on the land every summer and fished in the streams. She claimed the land and told Mr. Cole he must pay her for it. He replied that he had already paid for his land. Mrs. Cole advised her husband to settle with her and he finally concluded to do so. She demanded two Dutch rose blankets, five gallons of whiskey and one sheep. These (rose) blankets were woven of a long nape-like wool, with roses interwoven. One day, after he had procured the things, she appeared with about thirty Indians and secured all that she had demanded, being very particular not to have the sheep killed until she had received the blankets and whiskey. The sheep was killed, the whiskey distributed and a noisy pow-wow was held all night. Mr. Cole, expecting the Indians to become drunk and attack him, said to his wife:

Model Farm from the Cliff, Milford, Pa.

PICTURE OF A HORSE

'Now, Maria, you see what trouble we have got into.' The old squaw, however, left with her friends and returned to her home in Wyoming Valley and never troubled him more. They made a rude picture of a horse in Mr. Cole's cellar, which other Indians seemed to understand, and during all the Indian wars that followed, his property remained untouched, although the battle of Conashaugh was fought within half a mile of his place, nothing was disturbed that belonged to Case Cole, because the Indians said he had paid for his land."

MODEL FARM

In 1850 Ebenezer Warner purchased a portion of the Cole tract which was opposite Minisink Island. Ebenezer was very successful in the operation of his farm and it was called a "model" farm. He also grew crops on the upper part of Minisink Island, using a scow to transport teams, equipment and crops across the passage known as Brink's Rift. Rafts had foundered there and the boards left behind became a convenient source of lumber for Ebenezer. During the Civil War he was a Deputy Federal Marshal and, on horseback with his saber, searched out draft evaders. He was a founder and large stockholder of the First National Bank of Milford, a pioneer institution of its kind in Pike County.

MODEL FARM NEAR MILFORD, PA.

View down the Delaware Valley from the Cliffs, Milford Pa.

Squire Brink, when 14 years old, fell off the Cliffs, 169½ ft. high and rolled 63 ft., Milford, Pa.

JOHN BRINK

According to an article printed in Milford Magazine: "It was a hot day in August, 1869 and fourteen-year-old John Brink was bored. He had finished his morning chores at the family farm three miles south of Milford. He was torn between going for a cool dip in the Delaware River or climbing up to Utter's Cliffs for the soft summer breezes and panoramic view. Brink chose the Cliffs, a decision that would change his life. After a twenty-minute hike to the top of the Cliffs, he could see his entire world; the one-room school he attended, his family's farm and the Utter farm. He could see the large, two-story frame building that was one of the best shad fisheries on the river. He and his friends spent many May evenings catching shad to sell to their neighbors. Across the river, he could see New Jersey.

UTTER'S CLIFFS

"Suddenly distracted by a noise behind him, he turned, lost his footing and slipped. In just a few seconds, which probably seemed like an eternity to him, John Brink plummeted off the Cliffs and into the history books. According to the Milford Herald of August 7, 1869, Brink fell one-hundred sixty-three feet before being snagged in the branch of a tree. Then he fell another twenty feet down the mountain to the spot from where he was eventually rescued. The distances noted on the post card are slightly different. Either distance is a very long way to fall, and an even longer distance from which to survive such a fall. Brink's most serious injury was a skull fracture, which a local doctor repaired by setting a silver dollar in his skull.

VIEW NORTH FROM UTTERS CLIFFS, NEAR MILFORD, PA.   13

LIVED TO TELL THE TALE

"John Brink lived to tell the tale and become the stuff from which local legends are made. An article from <u>Rafting on the Delaware</u> notes that 'old timers recount that a barrel of red paint was poured over the precipice to mark the unfortunate man's descent-which drew comment from river men as they passed on their way to market, many of them doubting that a man could fall down the cliff and live to tell the tale.' The traces of red paint spilling down the side of the Cliffs are long since gone, but John Brink lived to tell the story of his miraculous survival many, many times. He went on to become a Justice of the Peace in Milford, which earned him the title Squire Brink. Few could ever come to his court without thinking of the piece of silver holding his skull together.

LOOKING UP THE DELAWARE RIVER FROM CLIFFS, MILFORD, PA.

120469

ARTIST GEORGE BENSEL

"The picture of Brink on the postcard is from a portrait of Brink painted by noted Philadelphia artist George Bensel. Bensel was a frequent summer guest at the Sawkill House, where the portrait hung in the barroom for many years. Utter's Cliffs are still as prominent and proud as ever, raising high above the Delaware River Valley, welcoming the few visitors who venture to their treacherous edge. Those who make it, however, still can enjoy the spectacular views, little changed from the days when John Brink relaxed, dreamt and slipped into the sky."

— 301 —

BATTLE OF THE RAYMONDSKILL

The Shady Drive to Raymondskill Falls, Near Milford, Pa.

These postcards, circa 1920, show idyllic images of the Raymondskill Falls and surrounding area. But one-hundred-forty years earlier, things weren't so peaceful. In the mid-1700s, James Philip McCarty established a farm in New Jersey near present day Montague. According to Mathews: "He started a clearing on the Pennsylvania side, up the Raymondskill, and had stock over there. One rainy day in April, 1780, McCarty crossed the Delaware and went up to his clearing...He was riding his horse when it started and gave a snort. McCarty looked and saw an Indian. He rode on, however, as if he did not see him...but when he got out of sight, he slipped from the horse and ran across the creek and down near its mouth, where he crossed it again on a foot log and followed down the Delaware under cover of the bank to the usual place of crossing, opposite the stone fort in New Jersey. He hid in the brush, and waited for someone to come across for him, for he concluded that his people would become alarmed on account of his absence, and look for him.

CAPTAIN PETER WESTBROOK

"His brother, John, became anxious about him towards night fall, and, in company with Sam Helm, started accross the river from the fort, to look for him. As McCarty saw them coming, he stood up, and Sam Helm, mistaking him for an Indian, immediately drew up his rifle and fired. The ball hit McCarty in the shoulder; then they saw what they had done and carried him across to the fort. He told them about seeing the Indian, and Captain Peter Westbrook immediately began to make preparations to reconnoiter the Pennsylvania side in force next day. He received reinforcements from the Pennsylvania side, Lieut. Ennis along with Capt. VanEtten. They crossed from the fort next morning-thought they would find the Indians on PowWow Hill, an elevated plateau, at the mouth of Raymondskill. Part of the men went up over the hill and the rest went up the Raymondskill. Those that crossed PowWow Hill found two Indians, and Sam Helm shot and wounded one of them badly. (Years afterward they found a skeleton of an Indian in a cleft in the rocks not far away.)

Entrance to Raymondskill Falls, PowWow Hill, Near Milford, Pa.

BASTIAN SPRING

"They worked their way up the mountain and came together, and followed the Indian trail single file. When they reached Bastian Spring, where there is a bluff at the right, they were fired upon by the Indians, who were in ambush. The Captain and about one-third of his men in front stood their ground, while those in the rear broke and fled. The men who fought dropped behind trees and returned the fire of the Indians. Abram Westbrook, who was a young man, kept close to his uncle, the Captain, and fired away with his gun, but he noticed the Indian he had selected did not fall. The Captain looked around and saw they were alone and that the Indians were trying to surround them. He told his nephew to load his gun and then they started to retreat. They had not run far, when they came to a thicket and there they parted, Abram taking one side and the Captain the other. Abram reached the Delaware and crossed with the other fugitives who had rendezvoused there.

The Park, Raymondskill Falls, Near Milford, Pa.   12474

The Falls at Low Water, Raymondskill Falls, Near Milford, Pa.   12469

SAM HELM

"Sam Helm was shot through the fleshy part of both thighs, but waded down the Conashaugh, supported by two men, who carried a stick that he leaned on. Lieut. Ennis was killed and twelve others, and a number were wounded. The place to which they retreated is below Cave Bank, and is called Death Eddy to this day. They went up in force the next day and found Capt. Westbrook killed and scalped near the thicket where he separated from young Abram Westbrook. The dead were taken up and buried in the Old Minisink burying ground (in New Jersey), and cedar posts were placed at their heads...If the forces under Westbrook had stood their ground, they might have defeated the Indians, but they were under no discipline...The gun which he (Abram)? used was a borrowed one, and afterward found that the barrel was crooked, which accounted for his poor shots."

LOWER RAYMONDSKILL FALLS AND BRIDAL VEIL FALLS 10

RAYMONDSKILL FALLS

Literature from the National Park Service tells us: "The real gem of the area is Raymondskill Falls, which is about five miles north of Dingmans Falls. This falls is the highest in the area and falls in three beautiful sections.

SECOND SECTION HIGHEST

"The second section of the falls is the highest of the three, falling about seventy feet down a steep rock wall in several cascades that change direction.

LOWER RAYMONDSKILL AND BRIDAL VEIL, NEAR MILFORD, PA.

"Below this pool is the third section of falls which is by far the most beautiful of the three. Adding to the beauty of its steep staircase-like cascades and its 180-degree curved rock cliff is a cascade from a smaller seasonal stream that appears more in wetter months."

Raymonds Kill Falls, Near MILFORD, Pa.

STONE RESTROOM

Gary Letcher tells us in his book <u>Waterfalls of the Mid-Atlantic States</u>: "The stone restroom at the Raymondskill Falls parking area is infamously known as the 'million-dollar outhouse.' Constructed by the National Park Service in 1994 for about $350,000, the privy was widely criticized as an example of government spending gone wild. Featuring composting toilets, a slate roof, high-tech paint, and beautiful stone facing, the restroom should last many decades."

VIEW DOWN THE DELAWARE FROM THE CLIFFS, SHOWING HOTEL SCHANNO AND INDIAN POINT HOUSE,

MILFORD, PA.

VIEW FROM THE CLIFFS

Pictured in the foreground of the card is the Hotel Schanno. The Indian Point House can be seen in the center of the card. Both the Indian Point House and Hotel Schanno were located on River Road, present day Route 209 South, approximately three miles below Milford. The Hotel Schanno was located near the intersection of Raymondskill Road and Route 209.

BRIDGE AT HOTEL SCHANNO

This card depicts a portion of the River Road near the Hotel Schanno and the bridge over the Raymondskill Creek. One fork in the road lead to the hotel while the other continued to Dingmans Ferry. As with present day Route 6 which roughly followed the Owego Turnpike, the new Route 209 roughly followed the River Road. The relocation and reconfiguration of the road included a new bridge over the Raymonskill Creek but the Schanno family continued to use the old bridge as one of the entrances to their hotel. This bridge survived the 1955 flood and served as the only access to Dingmans Ferry from Milford until the Route 209 bridge was repaired.

Milford Road at Hotel Schanno   13685

EMILE SCHANNO FAMILY

Emile Schanno was born on July 22, 1827 at Turckheim in the Province of Alsace. He was Mayor of Turckheim and owned a flour mill and extensive vineyards. He lost his property and standing in 1870 when Germany invaded France. The German occupation continued and Emile was afraid his sons, Joseph, Paul, Charles and Leon would be conscripted into the German Army.

In 1876 he was able to secure passage for his family to America. They arrived in New York City but quickly made their way to the Milford area where a large number of their countrymen resided.

Hotel Schanno, Milford, Pa.

HOTEL SCHANNO

In 1892 three of Emile and Caroline's children, Anna, Charles and Paul, built the Hotel Schanno on a site surrounded by thirty-seven wooded acres. The Raymondskill Hotel owned by Henry Depue had previously occupied the site at the bottom of a deep gorge carved by the Raymondskill Falls. Cynthia Van Lierde tells us: "Built close to the ground and only two stories high, the 19 room hotel was more graceful in appearance than most of its 19th century contemporaries, which were usually 3 stories in height, with high roofs making possible additional quarters, for help or management. Another attraction was the wide 'wraparound' porch for guests who came to relax and enjoy the rural scene."

FAVORITE STOP ON RIVER ROAD

The location the Schanno children selected for their hotel was beneficial to their business. The hotel was well-known for its French cuisine and was a favorite meal stop for carriage parties traveling on the River Road between Milford and Dingmans Ferry. The surrounding forest with the Raymondskill Creek running through it made the hotel a popular destination of hunters and fishermen.

Raymondskill Creek at Hotel Schanno, Milford, Pa.

THE GOLDEISENS

In the early 1900s Leon Scahnno joined his brothers and sister in the operation of the hotel. After Paul died in 1909, Anna in 1912 and Charles in 1917, Leon assumed full responsibility for the management of the thriving business. Leon died in the late 1930s. His will stipulated the business and property would go to his brother Paul's three daughters; Madeline Goldeisen, Margurite Edmundson and Pauline Hendershott. Madeline and her husband Charles assumed management of the hotel. The Goldeisens continued the family tradition of catering to fisherman and offering fine dining. In the 1950s Lorraine's mother worked as a waitress in the dining room. She also played Santa Claus for Christmas parties. Madeline and Charles often asked their friend Edith Gregory for her expertise when decorating the dining room for weddings and other special events.

Hotel Schanno, Milford, Pa.

FLOOD OF 1955

In August of 1955 flood waters reached nearly to the ceilings of the first floor of the Hotel Schanno. The Goldeisens repaired the damage and in the fall of that year sold the property to the Vincent Manna family. The Mannas operated the hotel until 1965 when they sold it to Larry and John Hoey. The Hoeys leased the building to Joe and Virginia Splendora. The Splendoras changed the name to the Shanna House and offered an Italian menu. Joe, a locally esteemed artist, used a large first-floor room for his studio. In June 1972 the property was purchased by the Army Corps of Engineers. They continued the Splendoras' lease. When Joe retired the hotel closed permanently and eventually was destroyed by fire.

HOTEL SCHANNO, MILFORD, PA.

Dr. Hughe's Summer Home. Raymondskill Falls. Pa.

DR. HUGHE'S SUMMER HOME

Merritt Quinn remembers two houses that were located between Raymondskill Falls and Silver Spring Road. One belonged to the Hughes and one to the Hawthornes. He tells us that Leon Boileau, his grandfather's brother, was caretaker for both families. Dr. Willis Weeden and his wife Alice were the homeowners when it was confiscated for the Tocks Island Dam project.

INDIAN POINT HOUSE, CIRCA 1909

20 Indian Point House, Milford, Pa.

Data recorded in early history books about the Milford area tells us the first members of the McCarty family to arrive in America came penniless from Ireland but became, "through diligent work, wealthy farmers, having vast amounts of land in Dingman Township extending from the mouth of the Raymondskill for a considerable distance up-stream."

Judy Brink McCarty provided information about the family from which we learned that William Penn's sons were having a terrible time hanging onto the property in our area bequeathed to them by their father. Founding fathers of what would become the state of Connecticut believed the territory belonged to them and came to claim it. In November of 1770 information provided by Judy tells us: "The Hon'ble Thomas Penn and Richard Penn, Esq'res, Proprietaries of the Province of Pennsylvania paid expenses of the Sheriff, Justices and Posse on a Journey up Delaware to oppose the Connecticut Intruders." One of the stops made by this group on their journey was at an inn near the mouth of the Raymondskill owned by "Vanacka's. M'Carty's & Rosecrantz" where it cost them one pound, ten shillings and three pennies for food and lodging.

INDIAN POINT HOUSE, CIRCA 1930

While the Inn at which the Penn group stayed was in the valley, after the Civil War John H. McCarty built a home and boarding house on one of the hills above it. Indian Point and PowWow Hill were names given to this plateau that was used by the Leni Lenape Indians as a watch tower. It was from these heights signal fires could be employed to communicate with the tribes up and down the river.

McCarty called his establishment Raymondskill Falls House as it was close to the falls "near a large picnic grounds." He rented rooms for one dollar a day.

INDIAN POINT HOUSE, MILFORD, PA.   **PHONE 5-F-3**

VIEW FROM INDIAN POINT HOUSE

Around the turn of the century, Beraldi McCarty, a great-grandson, built Indian Point House on the majestic peak. He advertised: "Modern conveniences, all amusements, tennis, boating, bathing, fishing, hunting and mountain hiking on our grounds of over 200 acres." The guests could also enjoy "Spring Water" and an "Excellent Table." The rates were nineteen to twenty-five dollars per week and four to six dollars per day.

Aerial View, Indian Point House, Milford, Pa.

INDIAN POINT HOUSE, MILFORD, PA.

INDIAN POINT HOUSE, CIRCA 1935

Management of the Indian Point House passed to the fifth generation of the McCarty family when Philip, Sr. and his wife Christina (Tina) assumed ownership. Carolyn Purdue, retired District Magistrate, recalls Indian Point House as a great place to work. She worked at the House for three summers as a waitress and kitchen assistant and she, as well as other employees, were treated as members of the family.

The McCartys sponsored a team in the Milford's Women's Softball League. Carolyn and three other employees, Terri, Betty and Evelyn, played each Tuesday night at the Milford Baseball Field. Guests staying at Indian Point House attended the games, waved banners and cheered to show their support.

Tina was an active member of the congregation of the First Presbyterian Church of Milford. She belonged to the Women's Association and, in January 1973, accepted a position on the church's planning committee to formulate events in celebration of 150th Anniversary of the church.

The McCarty property was taken by the government for the Tocks Island Dam project.

Road View between Dingman's Ferry and Milford, Pa.

THE VAN ETTENS OF CONASHAUGH

William Henn writes about the Van Etten family in his The Story of the River Road. "The VanEttens [sic] are one of the eminent pre-revolutionary families along the River Road, who for four generations have occupied the family farm just below Conashaugh Creek, opposite Mamanock Island. It was in 1745, that Jacobus VanEtten [sic] of New Jersey bought, from William Allen, a tract at the mouth of the Conashaugh. His son, Johannes (1732-1815), who married Maria Gonsalus in 1750, built in that year, what was probably the first house in that area. He erected a stockade around his house, for it was a time when the Indians were in an ugly mood, having been ousted from their cherished land by the infamous Walking Purchase. Johannes became a renowned Indian fighter as well as the foremost soldier of the Revolution in what is today Pike County. At the time of the French and Indian War he organized the local militia and for a time was in command of Fort Hynshaw in Bushkill. In the Battle of Conashaugh (1780), he commanded a company of militia and was then commissioned a captain of Volunteers.

VAN ETTEN FAMILY

"Three of his sons and a son-in-law were heavily involved in the fight, to wit: James (wounded), John, Manuel and Benjamin Ennis (killed in action). After the demise of his first wife, Johannes married the widow of Daniel Decker, whose maiden name was Rachel Williams. Johannes and Rachel were buried on the VanEtten [sic] farm in the family plot, and years later their remains were removed to the cemetery at Milford. The location of the grave of Maria Gonsalus VanEtten [sic] is unknown. As future generations of the VanEttens [sic] arrived on the scene, some of the progeny built their homes on the family farm, and the sprawling tract became subdivided. By the mid-1800s, a VanEtten [sic] schoolhouse had been erected for their offspring. Indicative of the life style of an earlier day is the following item from the Milford Dispatch of 1881: 'Uncle Sam VanEtten, [sic] the old time proprietor of the raftsmen's hotel on the banks of the Delaware, is the most successful muskrat trapper in this vicinity. During the year 1880, he caught 104 of the animals in box traps, and in 1879, trapped 106.'"

90 Conashaugh Spring House and Annex, Conashaugh, Pa.

The cross marks the meeting place. Remember? Florence went home to-day. Call me up around seven and I will in the vicinity of 'phone. J.P.S.

DANIEL ENNIS VAN ETTEN

Mrs. Elizabeth Walters, Curator of the Monroe County Historical Society, and a fifth generation Van Etten, tells us her grandfather, Daniel Ennis Van Etten, sold much of the Van Etten farm to John Zimmermann in 1882. An old dwelling at the southern end of the farm had been the home of John Van Gorden and his wife Mary, the parents of Lucinda Van Gorden, wife of Daniel Ennis Van Etten. The Zimmermann family allowed a local Brownie troop to use the home for their activities and it became known as the Brownie Holiday House.

Conashaugh Spring House, Conashaugh, Pa.

CONASHAUGH SPRING HOUSE

Some of the property owned by the Van Etten family was in an area near the River Road that the Indians called conashaugh; their word meaning "elegant land." In 1837 Robert K. Van Etten and his brother Solomon built a one-and-one-half story boarding house that catered to raftsmen in conashaugh near an artesian well. In 1873 the Van Etten brothers decided to enlarge their house to accommodate summer guests. They named their enlarged establishment the Conashaugh Spring House. In 1884 Robert and his sons John and James formed the R. K. Van Etten and Sons company. The company built an addition on the existing structure consisting of 100 rooms which could accommodate 175 guests. The Conashaugh Spring House became one of the elite resorts along the River Road. Their brochure claimed "select patronage with references available as far South as Savannah, Georgia." The hotel was destroyed in a fire in 1915.

ZIMMERMANN FARM

The Van Etten farm was located five miles south of Milford and three miles north of Dingmans Ferry. John Zimmermann was a successful hat manufacturer in Brooklyn when he decided to buy the farm and continue its operation. Most of the property consisted of fields in the valley along the Delaware River but the high point on the estate became known as Zimmermann's Peak.

ZIMMERMAN'S PEAK, DINGMANS FERRY, PA.

MARIE ZIMMERMANN

Marie Zimmermann was born in Brooklyn in 1879. According to a profile in "Spanning the Gap," a newsletter published by the DWGNRA, she was three years old when her father purchased the Van Etten farm. She became very familiar with the family's summer home and at the age of thirteen camped alone on the property, caught her dinner in a nearby brook and cooked it over an open fire. When Marie was 18 she took a course in metalworking at Pratt Institute. She also joined the Arts Student League in Manhattan where she studied drawing, painting and sculpture.

Her metal art works incorporated gold, silver, iron, copper and bronze combined with precious and semi-precious stones. She also developed a unique style of combining wood, wrought iron, enamel and semi-precious jewels in her industrial art designs.

Marie maintained a studio and residence in the National Arts Club Building in Gramercy Park, New York.

Cedar Road between Milford and Dingmans Ferry, Pa.

NATIONAL HISTORIC PLACE

In 1910 Marie helped design a new home for her family on the property. She combined architectural elements of Dutch, Colonial Revival, Norman Cottage and English Arts and Craft in an eccentric, but attractive way to create the distinguished residence. She retired in 1944 and moved to the farm where she pursued her interests in gardening, hunting, fishing and farming. Marie spent summers at the farm, but wintered in Punta Gorda, Florida. In 1969 she made Florida her permanent home.

The Zimmermann property was purchased by the federal government in 1974. On November 1, 1979 the Zimmermann farm was listed on the National Register of Historic Places. In 1997, under the leadership of Bill Kiger and later, ably assisted by JoAnn Parsell, local residents formed a committee called Friends of Marie Zimmermann. They have spearheaded efforts to re-establish Marie's national reputation, restore her farm and recognize her as an artist with determination and creativity.

Road between Milford and Dingmans Ferry, Pa.

Cedar Drive near Dingmans Ferry, Pa.

THE CEDAR DRIVE

Merritt Quinn tells us this picture of the "Cedar Drive" shows both sides of the Zimmermann property which was dissected by the River Road. The trees may have been planted by Gifford Pinchot and John Zimmermann as research shows this allee, tree-lined lane, leading to the Zimmermann house is similar to the one leading to Grey Towers.

Merritt also mentioned that his father told him "when nothing else will grow, a cedar tree will grow" and he recited a jingle about a local character, Barney Kane. Apparently Barney was a nice fellow and a handyman fond of strong drink who very often spent the night in a hay mow in any farmer's barn along the River Road. The jingle goes: "A rich man rides a taxi and a poor man rides a train. But Barney Kane walks the Dingman Road and he gets there just the same."

ADAMS BROOK

Adams Brook Bridge near Dingman's Ferry, Pa.

Adams Brook is located on Route 209 South and traverses land owned by the National Park Service. John Leiser tells us it is a nice area for hiking. While walking along the stream, the hiker will first encounter a small waterfall and, farther up the stream, a larger waterfall about three hundred feet in height. The larger falls were once known as Adams Creek Falls but are now known as Liberty Falls. Beyond Liberty Falls is the remains of what may have been a dam on the brook where, in 1881, Garret B. Brown had a sawmill.

Published by Geo. B. Van Auken   Adams Brook Farm, Dingman's Ferry, Pa.   7863.

LAFAYETTE QUICK

Peter A.L. Quick was the grandson of Peter Quick, a brother of Thomas Quick, who was the first non-native to settle in what became Milford. His father, John B. Quick, had operated the Half Way House on the old Milford to Port Jervis road. Peter A.L. Quick was born on February 1, 1819 in Milford. On April 19, 1858 he married Catherine Angle of Milford. They had five children, one of whom was LaFayette W. Quick.

ADAMS BROOK FARM

Peter A.L. Quick owned a five-hundred acre property which included Adams Brook. In 1891 he gave his son, LaFayette, two-hundred acres. LaFayette Quick built the Adams Brook Inn which was sited close to Adams Brook and the Delaware River on River Road. The Inn could accommodate fifty guests. The rates charged by Mr. Quick were seven to eight dollars per week for adults, four dollars for children and seven dollars for servants.

Adams Brook Farm, Dingman's Ferry, Pa.

ADAMS BROOK INN, DINGMANS, PA.   H. R. RYDER, Prop. and Owner

ADAMS BROOK INN

When H.R. Ryder purchased the property in the late 1920s he installed electric lights in all of the rooms. He also built a garage to house guests' automobiles. In this picture the sign in front of the Adams Brook Inn promises "Special Cooked Dinners." He opened the Inn's dining room to motorists traveling on the River Road.

REFORMED CHURCH

The Dutch Reformed Church was organized in four places in the Minisink Valley in 1737. Some of the first members of the Church in the Dingmans Ferry area were Cornelius VanAken, William Ennis, Lambart Brinck, Andries Dingenman, Jan Van Etten, Benjamin Depuy and Dirck VanVlidt. Early services were held in people's homes. There was no properly ordained Dutch minister.

REFORMED CHURCH, DINGMAN'S FERRY, PA.

DUTCH REFORMED CHURCH

Casparus Fryenmoet was a sixteen-year-old who had recently come to the area from Switzerland. He had received a partial education for the ministry while in his homeland. The congregants of the four Dutch churches were so eager for a minister of their own, they paid for Fryenmoet to go to Holland where he was to complete his studies and receive ordination from the Classis of Amsterdam. He did this and on his return he was hired by the Dutch Reformed Church congregations to conduct their worship services. He was paid seventy pounds in "New York" money and one hundred schepels (a schepel is three pecks!) of oats for his horse.

The building is owned by the National Park Service who lease it to Doug Cosh and Terry Talent. They operate the Phoenix Gift Shop from an out-building on the property.

595. Dutch Reformed Church, Dingmans Ferry, Pa.

THE HOBBY SHOP

The Hobby Shop, built by Charles Cron and operated by the Hibbs family, was an antique store located north of the Dutch Reformed Church on Route 209. In later years the Rossbachs ran the business.

ADAMS' GENERAL STORE

Adams' General Store was on the southwest corner of Routes 209 and 739. It was built by William Dusenberry who was born in Dingmans Ferry on April 17, 1859. According to Beers in his Commemorative Biographical Record of Northeastern Pennsylvania, William Dusenberry graduated from Coleman's Business College in Newark, NJ in February of 1884. He subsequently "was a partner in the mercantile establishment of Smith & Dusenberry at Layton N. J., until October, 1891, when they opened a branch store at Dingmans Ferry." In the 1920s the building was sold to H. W. Adams. He opened a grocery store and called it Adam's General Store. After the death of Mr. Adams, the store closed. In 1973 James Richardson purchased the property and conducted multiple businesses including an antique shop he called Richardson's Rarities. On January 2, 1979 the driver of a tanker truck loaded with gasoline was unable to avoid hitting a barrel lying in the road. The tanker crashed into the building and exploded. James Richardson perished in the fire.

ADAM'S GENERAL STORE, DINGMAN'S FERRY, PENNA.

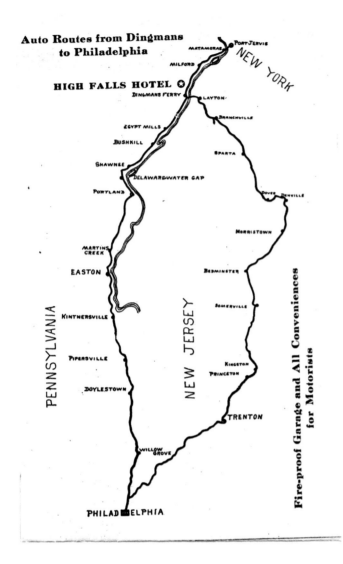

DINGMANS FERRY TO PHILADELPHIA

Prior to the automobile the High Falls Hotel, as did most hotels in the Dingmans Ferry area, relied on the ability of their patrons to travel by railroad, disembarking in Port Jervis, New York or Bushkill, Pennsylvania. There they would be met by horse-drawn carriages provided by the hotels to complete their journey. The advent of the automobile enabled guests to drive directly to their destinations. Therefore road maps were often included in advertising literature provided by the hotels.

DINGMANS FERRY TO NEW YORK CITY

Patrons were invited to drive to the High Falls Hotel on the River Road, present day Route 209. As stated on this map: "High Falls Hotel is located on the celebrated natural shale road and in the midst of those scenic beauties and grandeurs which have long made this section famous." Paving of Route 209 began in the 1930s.

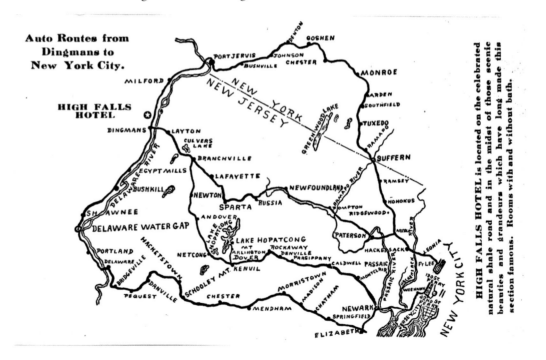

FODDY

A ndreas Dingenman, Andries Dingenman or Andrew Dingman was born in Kinderhook, New York in 1711. Mathews uses all three spellings but refers to the founder of Dingmans Choice, later Dingmans Ferry, as Andrew Dingman, the Americanized version of the Dutch name. Andrew Dingman chose the site of what became the town in 1735. He cleared the land and built a house and barn. He got along well with the Native Americans and seemed to live a fairly peaceful, prosperous life. He had two sons, Isaac and Andrew Dingman, Jr. Andrew, Jr. was called Foddy. Foddy married Jane Westbrook and their son, Daniel Westbrook Dingman, was born on April 14, 1775.

HIGH FALLS HOTEL, OLD WING, DINGMANS FERRY, PA.

A CORNER OF THE PORCH AND DRIVE, HIGH FALLS HOTEL, DINGMANS FERRY, PA.

PEOPLE'S CHOICE HOTEL

C irca 1810 Judge Daniel Westbrook Dingman built a fourteen room hotel, the first in Dingmans Ferry, on Main Street. He named it "People's Choice Hotel." Judge Dingman and his son, Martin, maintained ownership of the hotel until 1866 but were not proprietors. They rented the hotel, first to Solomon Westbrook then to William Brodhead and later to R.D. Wilson.

HIGH FALLS HOTEL

DINGMAN'S FERRY   **PIKE CO., PENNA.**

R. D. WILSON

R.D. Wilson apparently wanted to continue the popularity the hotel had enjoyed under the management of William Brodhead, so he placed an ad in the April 1, 1852 edition of the Milford Herald. "People's Choice Hotel...The subscriber having taken the well-known stand at Dingmans Choice–known as the People's Choice Hotel–formerly occupied by Wm. F. Brodhead; would be happy to receive the former customers of this house, and all others who may please to call."

BRANDIES AND SEGARS

William Henn tells us the rest of the story of the High Falls Hotel: "In a subsequent advertisement Wilson invited 'a continuation of the Traveling and Raftsmen custom...(stating) his BAR will be furnished with the choicest Wines, Brandies, and Segars...etc.' The inn became known as the Dingman Hotel in the 1860s when Daniel Decker was the occupant. There were '14 bedrooms and 14 beds.' Martin W. Dingman and his son S.H. (Solie) went surety for the liquor license.

HIGH FALLS HOTEL, DINGMAN'S FERRY, PA.

1906.

HIGH FALLS HOTEL

"The bucolic character of the hotel, as well as the village, were transformed in 1865, when Dr. Philip Fulmer, having sold the tannery, bought the hotel and changed its name to the HIGH FALLS HOTEL. By 1879, the Milford Dispatch wrote 'This hotel, with the single exception of the Bluff House, is the largest in the county with accommodations for 200...Clear spring water, bathing houses and Boats in the Delaware. A garden of five acres, ice houses, and dairy connected with the house. Grove of maples for children's playground...The proprietor is a practicing physician.'

High Falls Hotel, Dingmans, Pa.

13666

High Falls Hotel, Dingman's Ferry, Pa.

ELITE PATRONAGE

"The appeal was to an elite patronage, and its gracious style and excellent cuisine attracted a choice clientele from the metropolitan areas of New York and Philadelphia. The Rev. Dr. McCosh, President of Princeton, was a summer habitue, and in his day Bill Tilden frequented its tennis courts. After the passing of Dr. Fulmer in 1902, the MacDowell Brothers, who operated a chain of hotels, assumed the new management. During their years, a following of celebrated artists patronized the place, among whom appear the names of T. Addison Richards, Linsley, Simons, Briggs, Hart Whittredge, Moran, Sword and Beard. With changing times, a pattern of decline set in, and 'The Pearl of Sylvan Retreats' was ingloriously consumed by fire in 1946. Paul Snearley's gas station was destined to occupy this spot."

DINGMAN'S FERRY, PENNA.

THE DINGMAN HOUSE

A part of the Dingman House, located across Route 739 from the High Falls Hotel, was reportedly one of the original homes in the town. The old section was a three-room structure with an attic. It had a large fireplace that housed a swinging crane used for holding cooking pots. It was built by William Brodhead, the husband of Jane Dingman, Judge Daniel Dingman's daughter. William Brodhead sold the house to his wife's brother, Martin Westbrook Dingman. Martin enlarged the house and opened it as an inn that could accommodate twenty guests. When Martin died his daughter, Francis Dingman, continued to run the Dingman House. Unlike the larger hotels in the town, it was able to offer "an inexpensive vacation at a respectable place." Giles and Hazel Irvine owned and operated the hotel from 1932 until it was taken by the government in 1974.

IMPORTANT STEP FORWARD

The dam on Dingmans Creek was built by Judge Daniel Dingman to facilitate his establishment of a grist mill circa 1830. As has been noted before, these mills enabled area farmers to have their grain crops ground into flour.

Pub. for George B. Van Auken

OLD DAM AT DINGMANS, PA. 7115

OLD DINGMAN MILL

Dingman leased the mill to McCarty and Van Etten and, ultimately, in 1879 Thomas Darragh bought the mill. By then additions to the structure included a wheelwright shop and blacksmith shop operated by Joseph Lattimore. At one point the mill was also used to press apples to make cider. Circa 1903 the bridge over the Dingman Brook was relocated and the mill was torn down. Lumber salvaged from the mill was used to build the Gensel family home on Mill Street also called Johnny Bee Road.

ROUTE 209, CIRCA 1913

South of the bridge on the right is the home of Daniel Jagger. He was a raftsman who had the reputation of being the hardest working man in Delaware Township. On the left in the picture is Allen Albright's General Merchandise Store. In later years this was the site of the Dingmans Ferry Garage owned by Percy and Ted Dye. The last owner of the garage was Arnold Prehn.

THE OLD OAKEN BUCKET, CIRCA 1906

The Old Oaken Bucket, Dingmans, Pa.

The wooden bucket was used to draw water from a public well on Mill Street. In the background of this card you can see Allerton's photograph, souvenir and ice cream pavilion. Pictured in the older cards that follow is Darragh Mill before it was torn down.

FAREWELL TO MY VALLEY

We will share with you as captions for this and the next two postcards a poem written by Lydia Brodhead Nyce who lost her home to the Federal Government. She was eighty-five years old when she and her family were displaced by the Tocks Island Project. She had lived, as had many of her pioneer ancestors, in the river corridor her entire life. Her poem is as follows:

"The river runs so peacefully
Between the fields and hills,
Widening, as a quiet pond
Or through a deep rift spills-

Once, the birch canoes of Indians
Moved silently by day-
While in the night, their camp-fire light
Cast Shadows cross the way-

THE OLD OAKEN BUCKET, DINGMAN'S FERRY, PA.

" There white men came, with eager tread
To farm the fertile land,
And worked to earn a livelihood
By strength of their own hand-

In winter lumbering began;
They cut with axe and saw,
And dragged huge logs near river bank
To wait the first spring thaw.

As rafts of logs, went swiftly down,
The fields were turning green,
And farmers worked hard with their plows
to bring truth to their dreams.

The Old Oaken Bucket, Dingmans Ferry, Pa.

Old Oaken Bucket, Dingmans Ferry, Pa.

" The years passed by, and city folk
Came to spend the summer-
We made our home a boarding house
And welcomed each new-comer.

There highways and great bridges grew
O'er our peaceful valley,
And throngs of people came this way
Fleeing crowded alleys-

So engineers will build a dam
And we shall say farewell-
But in our hearts, there'll always be-
Fond dreams they cannot quell."

THE DELAWARE HOUSE

According to the Beers' book, John Lattimore was one of seven children born to Robert and Margaret Craig Lattimore who had settled in Dingmans Ferry in 1808. John married Dorothy VanAtten. His sister, Elizabeth, married Cooper Jagger. John Lattimore built the Delaware House south of Johnny Bee Road on the right side of Main Street. On November 21, 1866 he invited all to attend "Grand Opening Ball at the Delaware House, Dingmans Ferry, Thursday, Ev'g, Dec. 6. A general invitation is extended to all. Proper Music for the Occasion Will be in attendance. John Lattimore, Proprietor. Dingmans, Nov. 21, 1866."

DANCING BEARS

The Delaware House was popular with tourists and townspeople. Meetings of various social groups were held there. Dance classes were offered in the winter months. In 1877 Randall Van Gorden, known as "Ran," purchased the hotel. He was known as a "down-to-earth" innkeeper who dispensed amiable hospitality to "natives and wayfarers." In the 1890s he extended his hospitality to a traveling show complete with dancing bears. The bears were each charged five cents to cross the Dingman Bridge, the same amount human pedestrians had to pay!

The flagstone sidewalk on which one bear is standing was removed in the early 1930s when Route 209 was paved. It was moved next door and put in front of Mary, Aunt Mame, Brown's house.

CYCLING AND BASEBALL

Cycling clubs made the Delaware House a regular stop on their Port Jervis to Delaware Water Gap run. Some of those noted by William Henn are the Scranton Bicycle Club, Brooklyn Bicycle Club, Wissahickon Wheelmen of Germantown and the Hudson County Wheelmen, N.J. Baseball players also gravitated to the House. In the 1890s the Delaware House was the headquarters for the Dingmans Ferry baseball team that played on a diamond in the back of the House. The only access to and egress from the field, which was fenced in, was through the barroom. This arrangement guaranteed a brisk bar business on game days! The games, played with rival teams from the villages and towns of the area, were a source of much interest for vacationers as well as for villagers. Some team members were: William Richards, George Darragh, John Hornbeck, Royal Lakin, Anson Kintner, Warren Van Gorden, James Barry, Charles Middaugh, William Truax, Andrew Middaugh and Gus Middaugh.

THE DELAWARE HOUSE
DINGMANS FERRY, PA.

Delaware House   Dingman's Ferry, Pa.

FROESE FAMILY

Marie Froese Hoffman recalls moving with her parents to Dingmans Ferry when she was 12. Her parents, Karl and Therese Froese, purchased the Delaware House from William Napier in 1937. During the years the Froese family ran the business it was referred to as the "Old Reliable" Delaware House. Marie says among the signatures in the old hotel register was that of Teddy Roosevelt. It also contained a written record of the 1903 flood of the Delaware River. The register is now in the Pike County Historical Society's museum, The Columns.

After the death of her parents, Marie and her husband William continued to operate the business until it was purchased for the Tocks Island project.

METHODIST CHURCH

The first Methodist Episcopal Church in Dingmans Ferry was organized in 1830 by Bishop Asbury. He traveled the Delaware River valley on horseback from Wilmington, Delaware to Philadelphia, Pennsylvania and points north. His circuit enabled him to preach to congregations along the way some of whom were from Sandyston, New Jersey and Milford and Dingmans Ferry, Pennsylvania. Bishop Asbury offered services every day and twice on Sunday. He completed his circuit every four to five weeks and earned an annual salary of $64 to $100.

LOWER MAIN STREET, CIRCA 1906

This card shows us lower Main Street in Dingmans Ferry. The Methodist Church is situated on a small hill just south of Wilson Hill Road. The Church was dedicated on November 10, 1871. The first trustees were Jacob Hornbeck, John L. Rosencrance, Joseph Buckley, James H. Emery, Moses Shoemaker and Peter Humerfel.

Historically, as there were no other churches in Dingmans Ferry, families of all faiths attended services at the Methodist Church.

Methodist Church, Dingmans Ferry, Pa.

Published by George B. Van Auken. 069 D

LOWER MAIN STREET, DINGMAN'S, PA.

IRVING AND ELLEN SMITH

Irving Smith served as superintendent of the Dingmans Ferry Methodist Church Sunday School. Irving and his wife, Ellen, received special recognition from the members of the church in March 1960. They were presented with a scroll in appreciation of their thirty-six years of dedicated service to the Methodist Church School.

BELLEVUE HOTEL

The Bellevue Hotel stood on a small hill near the southern end of Main Street. Fred Cron Jr., son of the last owners of the hotel, Anna and Fred Cron Sr., tells us he understood that P.F. Mercier had built the hotel. In 1902 W.E. Kern and P.F. Mercier advertised in "The Delaware Valley Railroad Guide." Their ad tells us: "Tables supplied with fresh vegetables, milk, and fruit from our own gardens." They charged eight to ten dollars per week. In 1941 Russell and Anna Hilbert from Pinebrook, New Jersey purchased the hotel. Shortly thereafter, the Hilberts divorced and Anna assumed ownership of the hotel. Anna Hilbert was of Dutch descent and had a strong work ethic. She kept a clean hotel, catered to her guests' wishes and provided the best home-cooked food in the area. Her business flourished. In 1945 she married Dingman native Fred Cron.

Methodist Church, Dingman's Ferry, Pa.

Bellevue Hotel, Dingmans Ferry, Pa.

BELLEVUE HOTEL

• • • • •

DINGMAN'S FERRY

PIKE CO., PA.

E. M. Kern, } Proprietors.
P. F. Mercier,

PRICELESS TREASURES

In 1959 the Crons, while modernizing the plumbing in the basement, uncovered a most unlikely treasure. They found an old trunk cached away in a dark corner of the crawl space under part of the hotel. They pulled it free, opened it and were struck by the unusual nature of the papers it contained. Fortunately their intuition deterred them from burning the documents as they turned out to be priceless sketches and notebooks depicting the hardships endured by members of the celebrated Fremont Expedition of 1840. The Crons later learned three Kern brothers, Richard, Edward and Benjamin were among the 27 men led by John Charles Fremont and guided by Christopher "Kit" Carson sent west to chart the wilderness.

KERN BROTHERS

It was determined the Kern brothers were uncles of former Bellevue proprietor W. E. Kern. It is thought the documents were passed down to Mr. Kern after their deaths. Two brothers were killed by Indians and the third died at an early age.

The documents were entrusted by the Cron family to the Bank of Matamoras where they were safely stored. Later the Crons agreed to allow the artworks in their possession to be exhibited at the Amon Carter Museum, Fort Worth, Texas. Many of the items have recently been sold to Harvard University.

Bellevue Hotel, Dingmans, Pa.

BELLEVUE HOTEL
Fred and Anna Cron
"Serving Home Style Dinners"

HORS D'OEUVERES

Coleslaw – Sour Beets – Cucumbers in Sour Cream
Cottage Cheese – Date & Nut Bread – Potato Salad
Bread & Rolls
Lettuce & Tomato Salad

APPETIZERS

Home made Soup   Tomato Juice Cocktail
Fresh Fruit Cocktail
Fresh Shrimp Cocktail $1.00 extra

ENTREES

SATURDAYS & SUNDAYS, HOLIDAYS

Fresh Turkey, stuffing, cranberry sauce $4.50
Southern Fried Chicken, cranberry sauce $4.50
Fresh Roast Duck, stuffing, applesauce $4.75
Fried Pork Chop with applesauce................. $4.50
Roast Leg of Lamb with mint jelly.............. $4.75
Prime Ribs of Beef $5.75
Pot Roast of Beef................................ $4.75
Ham Steak..$4.50

WEEKDAYS

Southern Fried Chicken, cranberry sauce......... $4.50
Fried Pork Chops with applesauce............... $4.50
Prime Ribs of Beef $5.75
Pot Roast of Beef................................ $4.75

ALSO ON FIRDAY ONLY

Breaded Filet of Sole, tartar sauce............... $ 4.50

Children's Dinners $3.00 except Prime Rib which
are $4.00.

A large variety of vegetable are served with every dinner.

BELLEVUE HOTEL MENU, CIRCA 1968

The Bellevue was well-known for the family style dinners they served. Anna's bountiful table held a wide variety of hors d'oeuvres and appetizers guests could savor while waiting for the main course. Many of the side dishes offered were comprised of fresh vegetables from the Hotel's garden. The dessert table contained homemade pies, cakes and puddings. During Anna's tenure, summer boarders and those guests who came during hunting season paid six dollars per night with meals included. Menu courtesy of Fred and Helen Cron.

THE INVOCATION, SILVERTHREAD FALLS, DINGMANS FERRY, PA.

OA4724

VILLAGE STORE AND POST OFFICE, DINGMAN'S FERRY, PA.

GRACE DRAKE'S STORE

Grace Drake had this building constructed in the early 1950s to house her variety store. It was located on the southern corner of Johnny Bee Road and Route 209. Marie Hoffman remembers among the items for sale in the store were bolts of cotton material Grace kept primarily for the women in the area who liked to make quilts. Marie tells us her young son Billy could walk from the Delaware House to Grace's store to buy penny candy. Grace also sold balloons at two for a nickel, but Marie remembers when Billy only wanted one! He paid his nickel and took one balloon! Grace later delivered the second balloon to Marie.

THUNDERCLOUD

Thundercloud's mother was a Blackfoot Indian and his father a Frenchman. His French name was Dominick Plante. As an adult he was considered at that time to be the quintessential Native American and he frequently served as a model for works by Frederic Remington and John Singer. He came to Dingmans Ferry in the late 1890s to serve as a model for an artist, Henrietta Hashagen, who was staying at the High Falls Hotel. He later married Henrietta and they made their home on Mill Street in Dingmans Ferry. Their daughter, Wanita, lived in the home until her death in 1968.

He is pictured here at Silver Thread Falls, previously known as the Soap Trough.

THE ROAD LEADING TO HIGH FALLS, DINGMANS FERRY, PA. 7861

FARM CART

The lower sign reads "Ferry ½ mile Silver Lake." The upper sign gives the mileage from this point on the River Road to Stroudsburg, roughly south and to Port Jervis, roughly north. The house in the foreground is the home of General George VanAuken, a village blacksmith. The other house pictured belonged to Sarah Titman, a widow of Maurice Layton, who was a Civil War veteran.

DINGMAN FALLS

High Falls or Dingmans Falls are located off Route 209 in Dingmans Ferry and are, according to what photographer Allerton wrote on his glass negative, one-hundred thirty feet high. This makes them higher than Niagara Falls! The back of this promotional card calls them "a magnificent cascade of water tumbling over moss covered rocks and ending in a peaceful mountain pool."

Dingmans Falls

SOUVENIRS

This is a picture of the souvenir gift shop operated by the Ogden family of Milford when they owned Dingmans Falls.

BROOKSIDE FARM

This postcard tells us: "Brookside Farm, House and Grounds, Delaware, Pike Co., Pa." We believe, because this circa 1910 picture was printed as a post card, it is likely this home functioned as a summer boarding house. Shirley Estok tells us there was a cluster of buildings about three miles south of Dingmans Ferry on Route 209 near the intersection of Briscoe Mountain Road. We know this village was called Delaware as it had its own post office in 1828 where, according to William Henn, James D. Briscoe served as postmaster. However, we can find no specific data regarding this house and would welcome any information a reader may be able to provide.

Brookside Farm, House and Grounds, Delaware, Pike Co., Pa.

WALNUT GROVE FARM

WALNUT GROVE FARM HOUSE, Dingman's Ferry, Pike County, Pa.

Solomon H. Dingman, great-great grandson of Andrew Dingman, sold a tract of land on River Road, close to where it crossed Dingmans Creek, to Jacob Hornbeck in 1870. Jacob Hornbeck gave the property to his two sons, Isaiah and William. William built a home that had twenty rooms for boarders. He called it Walnut Grove Farm. He welcomed guests and charged them six to seven dollars per week. Children were accommodated for four dollars per week.

SHADY LAWN HOUSE, CIRCA 1906

The location of the Shady Lawn House on a hill in Dingmans Ferry enabled guests to enjoy fine views of the Delaware River and the Delaware River Valley. William Dusenberry and his wife, Estella, were proprietors of the Shady Lawn House in 1906 when they placed an advertisement in a brochure published by the Erie Railroad. They promoted their location and noted they could accommodate thirty-five guests at a rate of eight to ten dollars per week. Their ad mentioned their facility was one of only two boarding houses in the area that could provide golfing opportunities. A golf course had been created by Bryon Shoemaker at Pine Hill to the south of Shady Lawn. Mr. Shoemaker allowed patrons of Shady Lawn access to the course.

Published by Geo. B. Van Auken

"SHADY LAWN," DINGMANS FERRY, PA.   7860

THE DUSENBERRY FAMILY

William Dusenberry had relocated to his native Dingmans Ferry when he opened a branch store of Smith and Dusenberry in 1891. On September 23, 1896 he married Estella M. Bevans of Layton, New Jersey. The Dusenberrys made their home in Dingmans Ferry and in October of 1897 William was appointed postmaster. Members of his family living in the area included his sister, Susie, who was married to John P. Van Etten, proprietor of the Conashaugh Spring House and his mother. His mother, Mary J. Stoll Dusenberry De Pue, lived in Milford with her second husband, John S. De Pue.

Shady Lawn House, Dingmans, Pa.

SHADY LAWN HOUSE, CIRCA 1950

Promotional information on the back of this postcard states: "Shady Lawn House is a friendly resort in the Poconos at Dingmans Ferry, Pa, 75 miles from New York City. Fun and relaxation for honeymooners or vacationers. Families welcome. Boating on the Delaware River. Sports and a modern filtered swimming pool. Excellent accommodations, homestyle cooking. For reservations write or phone Dingmans Ferry, Pa 8405."

KINTER'S MARKET

```
              KINTNERS MARKET

                 SPECIALS
               April 15----17

Wonder White Bread                        .17¢
Red Jay Pink Salmon      1 lb. Can          47
Canned Solid Pack Chicken    1 lb. Jar    1.49
Norwegain Sardines                        2/43
White Eggs  Doz.                            53
C & B Orange Juice 8 oz. Can              2/29
Cranberries Whole & Jelly                 2/39
A-Treat Spda Qt. Bot. All Flavors
                  Inc. Deposit & Tax        21
Ritters Catsup                            2/37
Frozen Peas                               5.95
```

1954

Kintner's Market was located between the Delaware House and the Methodist Church on Main Street. Jay and Eva Kintner operated a grocery store and meat market. Both Jay and Eva waited on customers but Jay also served as butcher. When her services were not required, Eva was content to take note of daily activities in the village from her rocking chair by the front window.

The special items offered for sale from April 15 to April 17, 1954 are products with which most of us are familiar. A-Treat sodas, however, are a fairly Northeastern Pennsylvania product. The A-Treat Bottling Company was founded in 1918 by Joseph Egizia in Allentown, Pennsylvania. Mr. Egizia had owned a soda fountain and he decided he could re-create his soda fountain treats on a large scale and bottle and sell them. He did and his sodas are still available and can be ordered on-line. We are not certain if Ritter's Catsup is still available but we did learn it contained tabasco sauce!

ROAD TRIP, 1914

Mr. Allerton noted on his glass negative that he took this picture "Oct. 4 1914." At that time, car owners had to register their cars with the county prothonotary. An attempt was made to discover the name of the owner of X2068 to no avail. Mary Brown's house is located next to the Delaware House in the background.

DELAWARE RIVER FERRY

Mr. Henn, in his book <u>The Story of the River Road</u>, quotes an article from the Milford Herald of 1898. The editor of the Milford Herald got his information from Alfred S. Dingman, a great-great grandson of pioneer Andrew: "The old ferry across the Delaware River at Dingman's Ferry was started in 1735 by Andrew Dingman (1st) and continued its trips between Pennsylvania and New Jersey without interruption for 101 years, or until 1836, when the first bridge was built. The ferry remained in the Dingman family during the century, its operators being Andrew Dingman (1st), Andrew Dingman (2nd), Judge Daniel W. Dingman, and Andrew Dingman (3rd), the latter being the father of ex-County Commissioner Alfred S. Dingman, who is a resident of Milford. The flat is about 12x45 feet and is operated with a cable."

684   OLD DINGMANS FERRY, 1889 PIKE CO., Dingmans Ferry, Pa.

Published by Geo. B. Van Auken   Bridge Over Delaware River, at Dingman's Ferry, Pa.   7862.

DINGMANS FERRY BRIDGE, CIRCA 1906

The Perkins brothers, who owned Horsehead Bridge Company, bought the franchise that had been owned by the Dingmans Choice and Delaware River Bridge Company at a tax sale at the turn of the century. They erected an iron bridge partially constructed from the remains of a bridge that had spanned the Susquehanna River at Muncie, Pennsylvania. The bridge opened in November, 1900. The tolls charged on the bridge have changed little over the years. The company's 1834 charter stipulated the driver of a four-wheel horse drawn carriage had to pay fifty cents to cross the bridge. Today, commuters who purchase discounted tickets pay the same. The bridge is the only privately owned bridge spanning the Delaware River. The bridge owners continue to be the Perkins family one of whom is Jack Perkins of television fame.

Episcopal Chapel,
Dingmans Ferry, Pa.

EPISCOPAL CHURCH, CIRCA 1914

The Episcopal Church of St. John's the Evangelist was a uniquely beautiful Gothic style structure. It was built on a hill near the Bethany Turnpike, Route 739, just north of the Dingmans Choice Bridge and next to the Shady Lawn Hotel in 1887. Land for the church was donated by John Kilsby and lumber donated by Walter and Arthur Adams was used in the construction. The parish of St. John's was organized through the combined efforts of residents and summer guests of Dingmans Ferry. On October12, 1956 a Special Congregational Meeting was held and the church was reorganized to serve as a year-round church. Pastor Reverend Richard Aselford of the Church of the Good Shepherd of Milford served as pastor of the church for sixteen years. In 1971 when the church was purchased for the Tocks Island project, the parishioners voted to join with the Church of the Good Shepherd in Milford. During the razing of the building, light fixtures from the church were salvaged and installed at the Milford Community House.

Mountain View House, Dingmans, Pa.

MOUNTAIN VIEW HOUSE, CIRCA 1912

The Mountain View House was built by Samuel Snearly. It could accommodate twenty guests and charged seven to eight dollars weekly. It was destroyed by fire in the 1930s and never rebuilt.

OLD STONE HOUSE 1906

Matthew M. Osterberg provides this information in his *Images of America, Dingmans Ferry*: "Daniel Dingman, the grandson of Andrew, built the Dingman Ferry River House in 1804. Daniel exerted the most critical impact on the village's early development. He served 10 years as state representative and used his influence to construct the Bethany Turnpike (Route 739), connecting Dingmans Ferry to New Jersey and Wayne County. His foresight resulted in the establishment of the first Dingman School. For 25 years, as an associate judge for this region, he rendered decisions in a legendary style. In local history, Daniel Dingman is remembered as a strong individual and a witty character not easily forgotten." This house, now known as the Old Stone House, is still standing and serves as an office for the Dingmans Ferry Bridge Company.

PUBLISHED BY GEO. V. MILLAR & CO., SCRANTON, PA.   OLD STONE HOUSE, AT DINGMAN'S FERRY, PA.

Old Stone House, Built 1808, DINGMANS FERRY, Pa.

OLD STONE HOUSE, CIRCA 1917

According to an article in the Tri-States Gazette published in 1998 regarding Judge Dingman: "His professional life aside, his personal conduct reflected very much that of a man who had been raised on the edge of the wilderness. Described as peculiar and eccentric, but possessing a 'large native intellect,' Dingman held court barefoot and had a habit of addressing his associate Coolbaugh as 'Bub.' In 1804 he built the stone ferry house in Dingmans Ferry and it was often the scene of political rallies. In 1818, he hosted a celebration picnic to praise the election of 'Old Hickory,' Andrew Jackson. The celebration was enlivened by the hoisting of a new flag on a hickory pole. The pole was later shipped by raft to Easton and made into canes, one of which was presented to General Jackson and one to Judge Dingman. Solomon Dingman, his grandson, presented the cane to the Pike County Historical Society."

MAIN STREET LOOKING NORTH, CIRCA 1906

MAIN STREET, DINGMAN'S FERRY, PA.

1906

The house pictured on the left with the picket fence was the home of Harry Briscoe. It was adjacent to the south side of the Delaware House. At one time it had housed the post office and later was enlarged to a boarding house. Harry lead a very active life. He was a mason, the owner of the Indian Ladder Farm, a justice of the peace, a member of the school board and a county superintendent of highways. Marie Hoffman tells us at one time Harry rented the whole house to the Theurich family for twenty-five dollars a month. In the 1940s Marie's father, Karl Froese, purchased the property. Later the house was converted to two three-bedroom apartments.

BICYCLE SHOP

Mr. Henn tells us the blacksmith shop, owned by Browne and VanAuken, was later converted to a bicycle shop owned by Browne. He says the Pike County Press reported in 1904 that the first brake for a bicycle was made in A.D. Browne's shop. The brake was invented by a boarder who sold the patent for twenty-five thousand dollars. Photo courtesy of Sandy Leiser.

THE SHOEMAKER FAMILY

The Shoemaker family operated a summer boarding house called "Bald Hill." Their son, Byron, converted the Shoemaker farm into a golf course and the homestead into a club house. He called his establishment the Pine Hill Golf Club. During World War II the golf course was turned into farm land. In 1948 Carl Schneider bought and farmed the property.

QUAINT HAMLET

The back of this card proclaims this picture to be that of "a quaint hamlet, nestling at the foot of the Pennsylvania Hills." We're certain the reader will agree the village of Dingmans Ferry as shown in these postcards and explained in the text was a quaint hamlet. Today the few buildings that remain in the village include the school and firehouse which are both used by the National Park Service. The scattering of houses remaining are leased by the Park Service to individuals and are used in various ways. The Tocks Island project caused the buildings of the town to be destroyed but the resilient inhabitants were not destroyed. Many resettled in the hills of Delaware Township in newly formed residential communities such as Birchwood Lakes, Marcel Lake and Wild Acres. New buildings to house schools, churches, firehouses and businesses were erected on Route 739, Silver Lake Road, Route 2001 and Myck Road. And books such as this one have been written that will forever keep the spirit of the quaint hamlet of Dingmans Ferry alive.

BIBLIOGRAPHY

Beers, J.H., Commemorative Biographical Record of Northeastern Pennsylvania, Illinois, J.H. Beers & Co., 1900

Bertland, Dennis N., Patricia M. Valence, Russell J. Woodling, The Minisink, Monroe County, 1975

Best,G.M. "The Milford, Matamoras & New York Railroad"

Bournique, Paul, "Bluff House," proprietor, Milford, PA

Commemorative Booklet, "One Hundred and Fiftieth Anniversary of the First Presbyterian Church of Milford," Milford, PA, 1975

Crerand, Teresa, "First Beer Bottled in Pike County," Pike County Dispatch, Milford, PA, August 23, 2001

______ "A Place in History," New Jersey Herald, April 2, 2000

______ "Marie Zimmermann," information obtained from the Delaware Township/Dingmans Ferry Historical Society and National Park Service

Dale, Frank, Delaware Diary Episodes in the Life of a River, New Brunswick, New Jersey, Rutgers University Press, 1996

Dean, Howard J., Where We Came From, Orange, Putnam, and Steuben Counties, NY, 1991

Durham, Andrew E., Epistles from Pap, Indiana, Guild Press, 1997

Fitzpatrick, Jim, "Julio Santos: Pike County Farmer," Pike County Dispatch, Milford, PA, 1990

Fluhr, George J., "Pike County Notebook," Pennsylvania, Pike County, 1999

______ "Historic Site and Scenic Area Survey, Volume IV, Shohola Township," Milford, PA

Friends of Marie Zimmermann, Bill Kiger, "Marie Zimmermann in Pike County"

Grey Towers National Historic Site Historical Information, James Wallace Pinchot, 1/12/05

Gifford Pinchot

______ Governor Pinchot

______ Amos Richards Eno Pinchot

______ Conservation

______ Cornelia Bryce Pinchot

______ Grey Towers Virtual Tour

______ Theodore Roosevelt

______ About Us

______ Gifford Bryce Pinchot

______ Yale Summer School of Forestry

Hankins, Frances I., "Stories and Tales of Pike County Pennsylvania"

Hartz, Dorothy, "Matters of Taste," The River Reporter online, New Lobster Newberg (Newburg)

Hay, Doug, "An Illustrated Historic Survey of Westfall," Milford, PA

Henn, William F., The Story of the River Road, Pike County Dispatch, Milford, PA, 1975

______ Westfall Township, Gateway to the West, Pike County Dispatch, Milford, PA, 1978

______ The Mills of Milford, Pike County Historical Society, Milford, PA, 1968

Huff, Tom, Video: "A Twin Lakes Scrapbook," narrated by Tom Huff, Twin Lakes Property Owners Association, 1987

Hulse, David, Upper Delaware.com. "Grey Towers: Restored and even better, " news and columns provided by "The River Reporter," web site information, February 6, 2006

Kinsey, Fred W.,III, <u>Archeology in the Upper Delaware Valley</u>, Harrisburg, Pennsylvania Historical and Museum Commission, 1972

Kleinstuber, Ross, "An Illustrated Historic Survey of Dingman," Milford, PA

Kraft, Herbert C., John T. Kraft, <u>The Indians of Lenapehoking</u>, New Jersey, Lenape Books, 1999

Leek, Tom, "For Whom the Bell Tolls," Tri-States Gazette, Port Jervis, NY

_____ "Milford Bell Has a Home in Nation's Capital," Tri-States Gazette, Port Jervis, NY

Lehde, Norman, <u>Heritage: 250</u>, State College, Pennsylvania, Josten, 1983

_____ <u>Pike County Pennsylvania</u>, State College, Pennsylvania, Josten, 1989

_____ George W. Turner, <u>A History of Milford High School</u>, Milford, PA, 1952

Leiser, Sandy, "Squire Brink," Milford Magazine, volume 1, number 1, Port Jervis, NY, July 4, 2001

_____ "Judge Dingman," Tri-States Gazette, Port Jervis, NY, 1998

Leslie, Vernon, <u>Faces in Clay</u>, New York, T. Emmett Henderson, 1973

Mathews, Alfred, <u>History of Wayne, Pike, and Monroe Counties, Pennsylvania</u>, Philadelphia, PA, Peck, 1886

McCaslin, Forrist, "An Illustrated Historic Survey of Matamoras Borough," Milford, PA

Methodist Episcopal Church, 100th Anniversary, Directory and Program, Milford, PA, October 31, 1926

Mickley, Susan Titus, <u>Milford to the Minisink Valley</u>, South Carolina, Arcadia, 2005

"Milford, Pike County, Pennsylvania," The Milford Chamber of Commerce, Milford, PA, 1923

_____ "Community House, Broad & Harford Streets," Milford, PA, 1923-1953

Milford United Methodist Church, 175th Anniversary, Milford, Pennsylvania, 2001

Nestor, Marilyn, "Down on the farm:Julio Santos still making hay," Tri-States Gazette, Port Jervis, NY, July 12, 1996

Newark Star Ledger, "A Bridge so Dear - Old Span Greets New Century," Newark, NJ, November 21, 2000

"1941 Northeastern Pennsylvania Pocono Mountains and Delaware River Valley Vacationland" pamphlet

Osterberg, Matthew M., <u>Matamoras to Shohola</u>, South Carolina, Arcadia, 1998

_____ <u>Dingmans Ferry</u>, South Carolina, Arcadia, 2005

PBS, "New Perspectives on the West," Theodore Roosevelt, web site information, February 9, 2006

Pennsylvania Historical and Museum Commission, "Pennsylvania Governors Past to Present," Governor Gifford Pinchot web site information, February 6, 2006

Pennsylvania Historical and Museum Commission, Bureau for Historic Preservation, "Milford Community House"

Perper, Roy, "A Brief History of Twin Lakes Preserve and Its Ancestors," Twin Sails

United Methodist Church, 150th Anniversary, Milford, PA, October 10, 1976

Reber, Bill, "Man Believed Killed as Rig Rams Home on 209," Pocono Record, Stroudsburg, PA, January 3, 1979

Squeri, Lawrence, Better in the Poconos, The Pennsylvania State University Press, University Park, PA, 2002

The Passenger Department Lackawanna Railroad, "Mountain and Lake Resorts on the Lackawanna Railroad," 1908

Times Herald Record, Obituaries, Middletown, NY, November 19, 2004

United States Forest History Society, "Gifford Pinchot, 1st Chief of Forest Service," October 13, 2005

Van Lierde, Cynthia and George Fluhr, "Historic Sites in Milford, Pennsylvania," Milford Architectural Study Group, Milford, PA, Pike County Dispatch, 1980

_____ Crossroads, Milford, PA, 1980

Van Demark, John W., Walter B. Van Demark, Kate Koon Bovey, Loretta M. Hauser, Clarence E. Hauser, "Van De Mark or Van Der Mark Ancestry," Minneapolis, Kate Koon Bovey, 1942

Web site: Hotel Jobs Employer Profile: Hotel Fauchere

Web site: "What's Cooking America, History of Lobster Newberg"

Wood, Leslie C., "Rafting on the Delaware," Livingston Manor Times, Livingston, New York, 1934

Copyright 2007 by Randolph A. Gregory
First published 2007

ISBN 09793493-0-3

Published by:
Randolph A. Gregory
PO Box 308
Milford, Pa. 18337-0308

Printed by:
Jostens Commercial Publications
401 Science Park Road
State College, PA 16803

Printed in the United States of America

Library of Congress Control Number: 2007901773

For all general information, contact Randolph A. Gregory
Telephone: 570-296-5859
Fax: 570-296-6674

INDEX